THE AMRITSAR MASSACRE

Twilight of the Raj

Alfred Draper

BUCHAN & ENRIGHT, PUBLISHERS
London

First published as *Amritsar: The Massacre that ended the Raj*
in 1981 by Cassell Ltd

This edition first published in 1985 by
Buchan & Enright, Publishers, Limited
53 Fleet Street, London EC4Y 1BE

British Library Cataloguing in Publication Data
Draper, Alfred
    (Amritsar) The Amritsar massacre: twilight of the
Raj. — (Echoes of war)
    1. Amritsar (India) — Massacre, 1919
    I. Title   II. Series   III. The Amritsar massacre:
twilight of the Raj
    954.03'57   DS480.5

ISBN 0–907675–39–5

Printed in Great Britain by
Redwood Burn Limited, Trowbridge, Wiltshire
and bound by Pegasus Bookbinding, Melksham, Wiltshire

CONTENTS

To Juliana

ILLUSTRATIONS

ACKNOWLEDGEMENTS

Long Ashton, on the outskirts of Bristol, is what the brochures delight in describing as a 'picture postcard' village. It was there I met a charming lady in her nineties who recalled meeting, more than fifty years back, a frail and prematurely old man who told her, 'If I had my life over again, I would do exactly the same'. Soon afterwards he died. He was Brigadier-General Dyer.

He was referring to the shooting in the Jallianwala Bagh in April 1919, which led to him being hailed as 'The Saviour of India' by some, and branded as an inhuman monster by others.

In this book I have presented the evidence of both sides, not with a view to reopening an old controversy, but to put his action in perspective. Amritsar was just the tip of a political iceberg. Far more was at stake than the reputation and honour of a soldier who committed an error of judgement.

During the long and intensive research for the material in this book, I have been privileged to see many hitherto unpublished documents — many of them closed till 1971 — which have enabled me to make a completely fresh appraisal of the tragic events which divided India at the end of the First World War.

I am particularly indebted to the staff of the Public Record Office for their unfailing help and assistance; in particular to Mr R. R. Mellor of the Search Department at Kew.

My sincere gratitude is also extended to the staff at the India Office Library and Records, and to Mr Philip Dymond for tracing the documents relating to the trials and appeals of Doctors Kitchlew and Satyapal.

My sincere thanks to:

Lieutenant-Colonel M. P. Dowling of the Gurkha Museum for the article written by Frank McCallum on the role of the 1/9 Gurkha Rifles; Mr Ulric Nisbet for permission to quote from his diaries in the Imperial War Museum, and to the Museum for the eye-witness account of Lieutenant-Colonel M. H. Morgan, who was at Jallianwala Bagh; The British Museum Library, and the Newspaper Library at Colindale; Mr David English, Mr William Rees-Mogg and Mr Derek Jameson, Editors of the *Daily Mail, The Times* and *Daily Express*; Mr George Rainey of the *Daily Telegraph*.

Much of the information relating to the trial of Udham Singh was obtained through the courtesy of Mr Richard Grobler, the former Courts Administrator at the Central Criminal Court, and Mr Gurbachan Singh who gave me a vivid account of his friendship in London with Udham Singh.

The description of the conditions in the Amritsar Fort are drawn from an article which appeared in *Blackwood's* in April, 1920. I am also indebted to William Blackwood & Son for permission to quote from Ian Colvin's *Life of General Dyer*. The extracts from Edwin Montagu's *An Indian Diary* (edited by Venetia Montagu) are reproduced by kind permission of William Heinemann. I have also drawn from Sir Michael O'Dwyer's *India as I knew it* published by Constable and Company. Ernest Benn Ltd have kindly allowed me to use material from *Our Duty to Amritsar* by B. G. Horniman.

My personal thanks to Mr Rupert Furneaux, author of *Massacre at Amritsar*, for passing on some valuable unused material.

I owe much to Mr Donald Anderson and his mother who not only provided the photograph of the late Sergeant William Anderson but recalled all he told them of his service in Amritsar. And to Mrs J. Benson whose late husband's book *Six Minutes to Sunset* by Arthur Swinson was so helpful.

There are many others who wish to remain anonymous. I express my thanks and honour their request.

Lastly, I wish to express my gratitude to Air India for providing air passage to Delhi.

In India I am grateful to:

Mr G. R. Sethi, the distinguished journalist, for his recollections of Amritsar at the height of the troubles; Professor Parkash Singh, head of the Sikh History Department at Khalsa

College; Professor J. S. Grewal, Head of the Department of History at the Guru Nanak University, and Mr H. K. Puri, of the Department of Political Science, for making available their edited collection of Udham Singh's letters; Mr U. N. Mukerji, Secretary of the Jallianwala Bagh Trust, Atma Singh Sadhu and Daulat Ram Bhatia who survived the shooting and recalled it for my benefit; the Custodians of the Golden Temple and Museum; those residents of the Kucha Tawarian who lived again through the 'Crawling Order'; Mr B. S. Maighowalia, Advocate of the Punjab High Court, for allowing me to use material from his pamphlet *Udham Singh. The Avenger of the Massacre of the Jallianwala Bagh*.

In Delhi to: Mr K. G. Pant, General Secretary of the All India Congress Committee, for permission to quote from the Indian report into the disturbances; Mr B. R. Nanda and the staff at the Nehru Memorial Museum and Library; Toufique 'Toffee' Kitchlew for details about his father; and Mrs Indira Gandhi for providing information about her father; Prakash Chandra, the Delhi correspondent of the *Daily Express*.

Lastly I would like to thank my wife Barbara without whom the book would not have been possible.

Foreword

*'Plassey laid the foundation of the British Empire,
Amritsar has shaken it.'* — Gandhi.

It was a few minutes short of five o'clock in the morning when
the first fitful fingers of daylight began probing through the
canopy of pewter-greyness which invariably seemed to cover
that area of London a few hundred yards north of King's Cross
and St Pancras. The date was 11 July. The year 1974. Silhouet-
ted around a small grass patch no bigger than a weekend
allotment stood a group of men, talking in whispers, as if afraid
their voices might carry to the darkened cell blocks of Pentonville prison behind them. But there was no real need for silence.
It would be two hours before the prisoners were awakened to
'slop out', that primitive ritual of emptying chamber pots.

The group assembled beside the small grass patch below the
outer wall consisted of the prison's Senior Works Officer, a
working party of prison officers under the Trades Officer, a
pathologist, an undertaker with a new coffin, and, somewhat
incongruously, the Senior Medical Officer. The latter had no
useful role to fill for the object of the dawn gathering was long
past any aid that even the modern world of surgical miracles
could perform. But protocol had to be observed. There was,
however, some purpose in the pathologist's presence: he was
concerned with death and its cause, although in this case there
could be no question of doubt as to the cause of death of the
fleshless remains he was interested in. His attendance was
deemed necessary as the event had political implications and it
was vital that the right remains were dug up. The assassin of a
public figure was about to be exhumed. His name: Udham
Singh.

One of the prison officers stared at a crude map. On it were marked the numbered graves of the nameless persons buried there. They were not instantly identifiable for there were no mounds and the restricted space meant that there were several layers of bodies. When he was satisfied that he had pinpointed the right grave he ordered the working party to start digging. Secret exhumations were rare but not unknown at Pentonville: in February, 1965, a similar event had taken place at dawn when the remains of Sir Roger Casement, hanged for treason in the First World War, had been dug up and returned to Dublin for a martyr's reception. The columns of the London newspapers had been filled with the news of Prime Minister Harold Wilson's magnanimous gesture towards a better understanding between the two nations, and a grateful Eire Government had even presented the working party with gifts of Waterford glass. But the publicity had had its drawbacks; it resulted in rather tasteless speculation as to whether the right remains had been returned to Ireland.

That error would not be repeated. There would be no fanfare of publicity for Udham Singh. His denunciation of the British rule in India, made from the dock of the Old Bailey's Number One Court when he was sentenced to death, had been ruthlessly suppressed and there was no intention on the part of the authorities for that long forgotten incident, and what led up to it, to be revived.

When the crude coffin containing the remains of Udham Singh was finally uncovered, the bones were transferred to a new coffin and placed in an undertaker's van which drove through the still deserted streets to Heathrow Airport.

Fortunately, there had been no 'leak' to the press. Not that it would have created much of an impact. It might have struck a distant chord in the memories of a few Britons, but to the majority the crime of Udham Singh would not have meant a thing.

As people read their morning papers, an Air India jet was on its way to Delhi with the bones of Udham Singh aboard. Only the Prime Minister, the Home Secretary and a handful of top Home Office officials were party to the secret negotiations which had made it possible. They were delighted it had been accomplished without a hitch. Relations with India were stable and friendly and the gesture could only serve to enhance them.

The request for the return of his remains might suggest that India had not forgotten the events of 1919, but there was no reason why the British should recall them. With the exhumation of Udham Singh it was devoutly hoped that any lingering bitterness would be forgotten. No useful purpose would be served by recalling a massacre at the end of the First War finally avenged by an obscure Sikh from Amritsar when he shot Sir Michael O'Dwyer at Caxton Hall on 13 March 1940. Only those whose memory stretched back to the First World War would have recalled that O'Dwyer was Lieutenant-Governor of the Punjab at the time of the Jallianwala Bagh massacre on 13 April 1919, when Brigadier-General Dyer had ordered a small force of Indian soldiers to open fire on a crowd of 20,000 people.

Three days previously a mob of several thousand had run riot in Amritsar looting European property, in the process of which they had burned down banks, attacked two white women, and murdered several Britons in horrifying circumstances, and but for Dyer's bold and effective counteraction the whole of the Punjab might have risen in open revolt against the British and set an example for the rest of India to follow. Not only had he taught the people who attended the seditious meeting a lesson they would not forget, he had averted a second Mutiny.

Sir Michael O'Dwyer approved his action, as did his military superior, and to the vast majority of Anglo-Indians Dyer was a hero. He was hailed as 'The Saviour of the Punjab'. There, said those whites who had lived through the terror, the matter should have been allowed to rest. A few hundred people had been killed to prevent India plunging headlong into a blood-bath — a small price to pay in a land where millions died unmourned and unnoticed, the victims of disease, disaster and famine. It was described as a massacre, but many objected to the use of that emotive word for what was a purely disciplinary action. It was not a view the Indians shared. For millions of them the two men became objects of hatred, symbolizing the belief that Britain was indifferent to their political aspirations and determined to hold India by the sword.

Dyer was 'sacked' from the Army and a controversy developed that divided both England and India. His supporters claimed that he was a victim of the political expediency of

14

Edwin Montagu, Secretary of State for India, who was more concerned with appeasing extremist Indian opinion than heeding the warning voice of the men who knew and ruled the country.

Millions of words were spoken and written about the Punjab riots and always the emphasis was on the action of General Dyer; a total preoccupation with the incident in the Jallianwala Bagh blurred the overall picture. But Dyer was just one piece in what could be likened to a jig-saw picture of the whole of the Province. His action *was* important, but only when viewed in relation to all the events of 1919. The tendency was to cast him as the sole actor in a disastrous tragedy: the simple soldier motivated by a deep sense of duty and thrown to the wolves because of it.

No one did more to perpetuate that image than Sir Michael O'Dwyer who devoted his immense talents and energy to clearing Dyer's name, thus diverting attention from what Indians considered the crux of the matter: namely the way the Punjab was administered and the way in which the Anglo-Indians were determined to rule the sub-continent.

The bulk of Indian opinion believed that what happened in the oven-heat of the Punjab at the end of the war was a deliberate and calculated campaign to impose a method of government that was no longer acceptable. And in their eyes the personification of that attitude was O'Dwyer who could not and would not evisage an India governed on an equal partnership basis.

Udham Singh also saw him as the real culprit for the Jallianwala Bagh massacre. Having survived the shooting, Udham Singh had gone to the Golden Temple and immersed himself in the holy 'pool of nectar' and sworn a solemn oath to avenge it with the blood of O'Dwyer.

The view that O'Dwyer was equally responsible for the events in the Punjab was, in fact, shared by Edwin Montagu and other members of the Cabinet Committee set up to consider the findings of the Hunter Commission which was appointed to investigate the disturbances. Unfortunately their forceful criticisms were watered down, and it was only when the Cabinet Papers and other official documents relating to the period were made public under the Fifty Year Rule that the

15

truth was at last available.

They shed a completely new light on the events that tore India asunder at the end of the First War. What emerges is a story of deception and moral cowardice on the part of Edwin Montagu, and a clear picture that what occurred was part of the concerted policy of O'Dwyer and his supporters to convince the Indians that the British were there to stay — by military might, by the negation of democracy and by the suspension of the inalienable right of all the King's subjects to a free and fair trial.

Edwin Montagu believed that to be the case and said so — unfortunately in confidential papers. For the sake of political harmony between Westminster and Delhi he permitted himself to be gagged and a party to what was little less than a sordid and distasteful cover-up.

A form of cover-up still exists today. The Home Office politely but firmly refuses access to important papers relating to Udham Singh. Through an Order made by the Lord Chancellor they will remain closed for a hundred years.

In Britain, even when it no longer matters, there is still a marked reluctance to accept that O'Dwyer was responsible for a turning-point in British-Indian relations. By some contrary form of logic many believe that a little more O'Dwyerism and Dyerism would have ensured the continuance of the Raj for another hundred years or more. O'Dwyer's rule shocked and appalled Montagu who misguidedly believed it was unwise to say in public what he said in private. So desperately anxious was he to close the rift between Indians and English that he only succeeded in widening it.

The Indians were not to know that he had been determined that there should not be a 'whitewash' when the Hunter Committee was appointed, but under pressure from the Viceroy and Government of India he had watered down his criticisms of O'Dwyer when the Report was published. If he had not lacked the courage of his convictions and spoken his mind Udham Singh might well have been deterred from pursuing his vendetta, but, even more important, the transition to full Independence would not have been so bitter and acrimonious.

In his censure of Sir Michael O'Dwyer and his attitude to reforms, Montagu used the words, 'History alone can pronounce on those views'. He made the observation in a secret document dated 6 May 1920. Sixty-two years after the Jallianwala Bagh massacre seems an appropriate time to put his words to the test.

Alfred Draper
1981

PREFACE TO
THE SECOND EDITION

Since this book was first published, Amritsar and the Golden Temple have again figured prominently in the news, and several people in letters to the newspapers have seen the present crisis in the Punjab as a justification for the action taken by General Dyer in the Jallianwala Bagh in 1919.

Now, as then, the trouble started with a peaceful protest; in 1984 that trouble also ended in a bloodbath when Mrs Indira Gandhi ordered troops to storm the Golden Temple. Hundreds died and the Indian Government imposed a news blackout and a curfew, and sealed off the Punjab. Mrs Gandhi — like Sir Michael O'Dwyer, the Lieutenant-Governor of the Punjab in 1919 — was also to become the victim of a revenge killing by a Sikh.

All of which is reminiscent of General Dyer. Tragically, the lesson has still to be learned that freedom and genuine political aspirations cannot be stifled through the muzzle of a gun. There is, however, a crucial difference between the two Amritsar massacres: the rebels in the Golden Temple were armed to the teeth; the crowd on which Dyer fired held only defenceless men, women and children. It seems incredible, therefore, that after such a long passage of time there are still those who seek to justify the actions of General Dyer, and to cast him in the role of the martyred scapegoat.

There are others, however, who, since reading this book, have modified their views. Among the many letters I have received was one from Mrs Doris Price Jones whose father, Alfred Brasher, a Sessions Judge in Amritsar, tried the doctors Kitchlew and Satyapal. General Dyer stayed at her parents' home at the time of the massacre; she wrote to me: 'I feel I must tell you how horrified I was at the atrocities committed by General Dyer — I relived the Rebellion and realised how my parents had sheltered us from its horrors. It must have been "panic stations" that caused it, as we were so hopelessly outnumbered by the Indians and the ever present fear of a repeat of the Mutiny.'

She added, in a personal account of her experiences in Amritsar at the time: 'I did not know much of the Jallianwala Bagh except that there was an unlawful gathering of Indians compelling the troops to fire and about 300 had been killed. Father was very terse about it and hated the crawling order and we were not allowed to go out while it was in force. He said it was very undignified and would not allow Indians to do it, so we stayed in.'

She also recalled the man behind these events: 'I well remember General Dyer walking up and down most of the night in an agitated manner, muttering, "I had to do it", and obviously going over the same ground. I did not know to what he was referring.'

This book has attempted to be an impartial account of the tragic events in Amritsar in 1919, and Mrs Price Jones's letter is a comforting reminder that it has to some extent succeeded in chronicling the events which had such a devastating after-math, and which she found 'so unbiased'.

It is up to the reader, however, to decide whether Brigadier-General Reginald Dyer was right in his assertion that he had no alternative but to open fire.

Alfred Draper
1985

1. Uneasy Peace

'A democracy in India could be nothing but a sham, a façade.' Sir Michael O'Dwyer.

The men of the 25th (Cyclist) Battalion, The London Regiment, cut a most unmilitary figure as they boozily wended their way to the railway station at Simla and the train that would return them to their garrison headquarters at Jullundur. The four-abreast column of heavy-legged soldiers led by their Colonel, erect and apart in his sobriety, and followed by the C.S.M. leading the 1st Company, straggled like a crippled centipede for almost a mile behind.

This drunken conduct, which normally would have resulted in the men being severely punished, was condoned because the circumstances were exceptional. It was 12 November 1918, and that morning the men of the 25th had been given the honour of furnishing the Guard of Honour for Lord Chelmsford, the Viceroy, while he publicly read out the terms of the Armistice that was formally to end the World War. Afterwards the officers of the Headquarters Staff had invited the rankers to partake of unlimited drinks — a most unusual occurrence and a rare departure from the strict protocol that governed everything in India.

The men, to use their own barrack-room jargon, 'didn't give a sod' if one or two people frowned disapprovingly at them for making fools of themselves and committing the unforgivable sin of providing an object of mirth for the watching Indians. They had done their duty. The war was over and they had played their part in saving the Empire, and for a brief time the drawbridge had been lowered over that normally unbridgeable moat of social aloofness. The soldiers themselves couldn't get out of India quickly enough; their horizon was bounded by thoughts of the troopship that would take them back to Blighty.

Since mobilization they had spent five Christmases abroad, much of the time in the Punjab garrison at Jullundur where sheer unmitigated boredom was their lot for most of the year. In the hot months when the temperature was so high it almost blew the top off the thermometer there was so little for them to do when their day ended around 9 a.m. that they spent seemingly endless hours 'charpoy bashing' under a mosquito net.

The Armistice ceremony had taken place at the end of the season, when the Viceroy moved to his summer residence in Simla along with the staff of the Supreme Government to escape the hot weather in Delhi. There was also an exodus of white women and their children. Simla, perched 7000 feet high at the foot of the Himalayas, was a place of breathtaking beauty and the nearest thing in India to 'Home'. The tiered slopes were dotted with attractive bungalows with manicured lawns and carefully cultivated English flower-beds. The social life during the season had to be experienced to be believed. It was an endless whirl of luncheon parties, dinner parties, balls, tennis, golf and polo, with picnics at haunts with delightful names like Wildflower Hall. It was as if life had been frozen in Victorian times, for little had changed since Kipling worked there as a young reporter for the *Civil & Military Gazette*.

The Indian community also shared in the Victory jubilations, for they had made a generous contribution in men, money and materials towards the defeat of the common enemy and were looking forward to the long-promised reforms which would give them a greater share in the running of their own country. Both were soon to be bitterly disappointed. The men of the London Cyclist Battalion were among many B.O.Rs soon to be asked to 'volunteer' to remain in India and help defend the Raj against the mounting discontent of the Indians who felt they had been betrayed by unfulfilled promises of political advancement.

None of that was known to the entraining Londoners, and when they returned to Jullundur they good-humouredly accepted the, to them, pointless field training, in the knowledge that it would all soon come to an end. The weather was still cool and the soldiers played a lot of sports, created their own evening entertainment and ticked off the days on the calendar.

Commanding the Brigade of British and Indian troops was a tough, rather grizzled soldier, Brigadier-General Reginald Dyer, a veteran of Frontier warfare and cast in the same mould as those heroes who figured in the adventure books for boys so popular in England. The young British soldiers listened entranced when he recounted his adventures in the Sarhad. The Indian troops were also devoted to him for he spoke their language, respected their customs and looked after their interests with a paternal affection.

Dyer was 55 and, although still remarkably handsome, looked much older than his years. His close-cropped hair was greying and his eyes had the heavy-lidded appearance of a man who had spent too much time squinting into brilliant sunlight. He was a chain-smoker with the untidy habit of stuffing cigarettes into nearly every pocket of his uniform; some were loose and crumpled, others were tucked away in envelopes.

The incredible contrasts of India which so fascinated and often appalled the visitor were unnoticed by Dyer, for he had known little else. He came from a family with long associations with India on both sides, and it never entered his mind to question the British way of life there, nor the manner in which the country was administered. He was born in Murree on 9 October 1864, where his father was establishing a reputation as a brewer. At the age of two Reginald, or Rex as he was known to the family, moved to Simla so that his father could be near a new brewery he had opened in the area. There the Dyers and their eight children lived in a beautiful English-style house called Ladyhill. Rex and his brothers rode, hunted, fished and explored the countryside.

Rex attended the famous Bishop Cotton's School in Simla where young and impressionable boys were encouraged to believe that the whites were a race apart, and women objects to be preciously defended and looked upon as something sacred. At home he listened to the dinner-table conversations of army officers, policemen, magistrates and Punjab administrators, and never questioned their belief in a divine right to rule. It was only natural that with the family's background the talk should often dwell on The Mutiny which was still fresh in the eyes and memories of the older people. The memory hung over them like the sword of Damocles and the fear of a fresh uprising was never far from their thoughts. Constant vigilance for the slightest sign or hint of a Second Mutiny became a part of everyday life. The least breeze heralded the hurricane; shadows became tangible forms. And so the young boy was conditioned to believe that he was sitting on a powder keg. The safety and protection of the women in the event of an explosion was drummed into him so well that it almost became an obsession.

Paradoxically the women often dominated their menfolk and Mrs Dyer was no exception. She was a strong-willed, forceful woman, and although her husband was an extremely astute businessman he was very much under her thumb. She also had very rigid views about mixing with Indians other than servants. When her husband humorously recounted that he had once taken a light for his cigarette from a Burmese girl's cheroot she rounded on him and snapped angrily, 'That sort of looseness is what has peopled Simla with thirty thousand Eurasians'. Her aggressiveness may in part have been due to the fact that she had a pronounced stammer which she struggled hard to control. It was an impediment that young Rex inherited and the teasing he got from his classmates made him sensitive, quick-tempered and aggressive. He became a very good boxer and his classmates soon discovered that pulling his leg over his stutter could be a very painful business. If he suffered the same impediment as his mother he also inherited some of her strong personality. He overcame his stammer by going off on his own to some solitary spot where he forced himself to control it.

When Rex was eleven he was sent with his older brother Walter, aged thirteen, to Middleton College, County Cork. Eccentricity was commonplace in India and not unusual in Ireland, but it was difficult to appreciate why the two boys arrived wearing solar topis with Gurkha kukris tucked into their cummerbunds, a cheque book each and a bank account. Their appearance led to a lot of good-natured ribbing and they were dubbed 'the wild Indians'.

It was the family's intention that both boys should study medicine, but when they went to the College of Surgeons in Dublin Rex was sickened by the atmosphere of the dissecting room. He decided instead to enter the army and went to London to cram for Sandhurst.

Rex passed out from Sandhurst in 1885 and was gazetted to the Second Battalion the Queen's Royal West Surrey Regiment. After service in Ireland, keeping the peace between the Orangmen and the Republicans, he saw action in Burma where he was awarded a medal and two clasps. But his early career was twice jeopardized by his fiery temper and an inclination to sort things out with his fists. In 1887 he was travelling down-river to Rangoon en route for leave in India when his bearer was attacked by some members of the ship's crew. Dyer promptly waded in and routed the sailors in a hectic punch-up. The master and crew instituted a civil action against him and the matter was referred to the Army Council. Dyer's report on the incident was submitted to the Commander-in-Chief, Sir Frederick Roberts, but fortunately he heard no more about it.

He was again in trouble some time later when the gharry he had hired to carry his luggage was commandeered by a Tehsildar, a village headman. Dyer took his horse from its box and galloped after him. A blazing row developed and several natives went to the aid of their local dignitary. Dyer, his back to the wall, knocked several of them to the ground, then grabbed the Tehsildar by the scruff of the neck and put him in a painful headlock which he refused to ease until the natives withdraw. They refused and began to beat him over the head with sticks. It was only the timely arrival of some of his Sikh soldiers that saved him from serious injury. The Tehsildar brought a civil action against him but the case was dismissed. Again the un-officer-like conduct was overlooked.

At that stage Dyer had transferred to the Indian Army and his swashbuckling handling of the Sarhad campaign was to make him a household word in India. He was made a Companion of the Bath. He was a Lieutenant-Colonel at the time, but, as he enjoyed recalling when he related his adventure to his men, 'I proclaimed myself a General and advised Simla that the rank was necessary for my purpose. The reply came back, "You are a General".' During the Sarhad campaign in Persia some tribesmen had been captured and imprisoned. One evening whilst doing his rounds Dyer saw the guards relieving the prisoners of their personal possessions. An officer recalled, 'Dyer went off the deep end . . . he fell on them with his stick and belaboured anyone within reach.'

Everything about him was just a little bit larger than life.

23

Even his courtship of Anne Ommanney, daughter of his Colonel, had to be romantically unconventional. In those days the officers' ladies and their families followed the regiment and Rex's favourite courting spot was literally marked on the map by 'Dyer's Hill'. The strength of his attachment can be measured by the fact that he ignored his mother's objection to the marriage, and with typical bravado bought a lump of gold from a bazaar and hammered it into a crude wedding ring.

Only Dyer's wife and his Brigade Major, Captain F. C. 'Tommy' Briggs, knew that he was an extremely sick man. Much of the time he was in acute pain, and it was only through superhuman self-control that he was able to hide his condition from his men.

Although immensely strong physically, his life had been dogged by ill health and injury. At the beginning of his army career he had been seriously ill with pleurisy, his palate had been smashed by a blow from a hockey stick, and he had been injured in the first of two riding accidents. He had watched a young subaltern kill himself trying to jump a wide ditch. Dyer foolhardily set his horse at the same target and was also thrown, striking his head on the same obstacle. He suffered from severe concussion. The Persian campaign further undermined his health for he suffered from heat stroke, fevers and malaria, and he was ordered back to India for a complete rest. In 1917 he was gravely injured in another riding accident when his horse fell on him as he was trying to jump a ditch. By sheer physical strength he supported the weight of the animal and although still very badly injured he saved his own life.

As a result of his appalling injuries he was sent to England — 'the wreck of a man' — to recuperate. In constant pain and only able to struggle a few steps at a time with the aid of two sticks, he willed himself to walk naturally. Although he could hardly open his legs, he forced himself to ride again. Before he was allowed to return to India he had to undergo a strict medical check-up and somehow or other he carried out the stringent tests and managed to fool the doctors. When he returned to Jullundur he had recovered to some extent but 'injuries, deep and permanent, remained to torture him with frequent and intolerable pain'. On top of all that he was suffering from arteriosclerosis, a degenerative and incurable disease. He was hardly the ideal person to command an area that was seething

24

with discontent. With his violent temperament aggravated by physical pain, he was liable to overreact in an emergency. And the storm clouds were approaching in Amritsar which was in his command area.

✻   ✻   ✻

India is a land of atmosphere and premonitions, and there was an indefinable air of tension abroad. It was felt if not understood. The officers in Dyer's headquarters in Jullundur slept with revolvers under their pillows, although the relaxed social life they were leading indicated that such precautions were quite unnecessary. One young officer was Ulric Nisbet, attached to the 3/23rd Sikh Battalion, who had spent most of the war on the Western Front and, like the men of the 25th, was just passing away time until he returned to England. During his comparatively short stay he kept a diary in which he jotted down the day-to-day life of the garrison and which provides an interesting account of army life but sheds no light on the need for the concealed revolvers.

On 29 November he recorded that the Indian Army was in the midst of a ten-day holiday to celebrate peace and there was a welcome respite from parades. The next day passed idly with a cricket match between the 25th London and the Station, followed in the evening by a *Café Chantant* at which the Londons provided the music.

Day followed day with the same unvarying routine. At the bar he ate prawns and oysters transported from Karachi. He watched polo, played more cricket, went on night hunts for pi-dogs armed with a .22 or a lance, took language lessons from a munshi, danced the nights away, and went buck hunting. He was invited to the Dyers' house for 'good hard sets of tennis' with the ladies. There was tiffin and tea and shopping in the bazaars for ivory and brassware. When Christmas arrived they put on dinner jackets and the New Year was celebrated with a fancy dress ball.

The social conventions had to be strictly observed:

> Much calling and leaving two cards in the small box by the gate was absolutely obligatory. I have not mentioned all the calls I made. Great offence was given, if one omitted calling

on certain people — for whatever reason.

But he did not elaborate on the terse entry, 'There are hints that there will be a sudden *alarm* soon'.

Ulric Nisbet was fortunate. At the beginning of April he received orders to proceed to Bombay and join a homeward-bound trooper. A few days later General Dyer was ordered to Amritsar to quell a bloody riot that threatened to erupt into a second Mutiny.

Tragically it happened at a time when Lloyd George's Government was anticipating the dawn of a new and more enlightened era in the sub-continent when Indians would be granted a bigger role in the government of their country.

The architect of the reforms was Edwin Montagu, the Secretary of State for India, a tall, balding, scholarly-looking man who saw himself as a man of destiny as far as the future of India was concerned. Indeed he had only agreed to join Lloyd George's Government in July 1917 on condition that he should go to the India Office. Montagu was idealistic, very introspective and tortured by self-doubts, not ideal qualities for the ruthless arena of party politics.

On 20 August 1917 he had told a crowded House of Commons, 'The policy of His Majesty's Government, with which the Government of India are in complete accord, is that of the increasing association of Indians in every branch of the administration and the gradual development of self-governing institutions with a view to the progressive realization of responsible government as an integral part of the British Empire.'

There were provisos, of course: progress would be in stages and the British and Indian Governments would be responsible for the timing of each step. It was greeted as a momentous pronouncement and a milestone in Indian history by the majority of educated Indians and politicians who for years had been seeking a greater role in the running of their own nation. It seemed to offer all that they had asked for. They did not envisage or, for that matter, aspire to, anything beyond self-government within the Commonwealth, with dominion status like Canada and Australia. They had contributed 1,300,000 men who had fought in nearly every theatre of war and they believed their loyalty was at last to be rewarded.

The enthusiasm was not so marked among the British in

India. A great many were violently opposed to change and thought it would herald the introduction of widespread corruption; furthermore, they genuinely believed that the religious differences and the rigid caste system would prove an insurmountable barrier to self-government. On the whole, the administrators and British members of the Government of India accepted that there had to be some reforms, but they would have to be introduced extremely slowly: India would not be ready for self-government for a hundred years or more.

On 18 October 1917 Edwin Montagu and a ten-man delegation left London and travelled overland to Taranto, boarded HMS *Bristol* and sailed for Port Said where they transferred to the P. & O. liner *Kaiser-i-Hind* and headed for India.

At the start of his personal odyssey, Edwin Montagu began to keep a detailed diary of events and to chronicle his personal opinions. He dictated thousands of words to his shorthand writer at all times of the day and night. His idea was to send off to Lloyd George, by every available mail, batches of his diary which would serve as 'progress reports'. As he had no intention of publishing them he was extremely frank, often indiscreet, impulsive, humble, frequently pompous, and sweeping and hasty in his judgements. He was sometimes depressed, occasionally elated, but never uncertain of the importance of his mission:

> My visit to India means that we are going to do something, and something big. I cannot go home and produce a little thing or nothing; it must be epoch-making, or it is a failure; it must be the keystone of the future history of India. Why do I say this? Well, because it has shaken and disturbed to its roots a country which was rolling, as I believe, to certain destruction.

It was, as he was soon to realize, an overhasty assessment. There were few British in India, least of all among the politicians and members of that 'heaven-born' élite, the Indian Civil Service, who shared his fears or beliefs. Many of them had arrived with grandiose ideas of how they would change things. In time they learned to conform.

Montagu was soon to discover that it was one thing to dictate his intentions to a shorthand writer and quite another to implement them. Within a very short space of time he realized

that India, with its pomp, its pageantry, its clearly defined
social strata and blatant racial discrimination, was a million
light years away from England where political and social
revolution was in the offing. It appalled his liberal beliefs.
Every official function was like a scene from a Ruritanian
musical: magnificent uniforms, glinting swords, guards of honour and literally the red-carpet treatment. He thought it was
all very much overdone. In Delhi a huge tented camp was set
up in the grounds of the Viceregal Lodge to accommodate his
delegation and a number of VIPs who had been invited to meet
him. 'Tent' is a misleading description, for Montagu found
himself living in great comfort, waited on hand and foot by an
army of servants. The tent was more of an opulent canvas
apartment. It was well furnished with two sofas, two writing
desks, an abundance of armchairs, windows, a fireplace and a
passage that led to a dressing room and bathroom. But the tents
were all pitched in strict order of precedence and the size varied
according to the status of the occupant. 'You could not want a
better illustration of the way things are done in India,' he
commented sourly in his diary, for Montagu fervently believed
that 'the social side of the question is at the bottom of the
political mess in which we have landed ourselves'. His views
were secretly shared by some Anglo-Indians, but they were
seldom voiced. To survive in India one had to conform and
sooner or later that message got home to potential rebels;
otherwise they were ostracized.

Ironically, it was the opening of the Suez Canal which, by
shortening the passage to India, widened the gulf between the
white and black population and was largely responsible for the
creation of the strict social code and conventions. The short-
ened voyage resulted in more and more English women going
to India. Before that the Englishman had mixed quite freely
with the native population and often married an Indian woman.
That ended when the memsahibs arrived in force and exercised
an influence which amounted to petticoat rule. Socializing
with the Indians virtually halted. And for the white women
with little to do and too much time in which to do it, status and
precedence assumed an almost ludicrous importance.

The British in India established an aristrocracy every bit as
exclusive as that in England. Some families had served India for
generations and it was not just a question of thinking they were

superior; they *were*. And there were classes within classes. The élite was the small but immensely powerful Indian Civil Service. Entry into the I.C.S. was not, however, a pushover depending on family connections; standards were extremely high and competition very keen, so the service was able to pick from the cream of the applicants. Dedication was a word that was frequently used, and deservedly so, but the rewards were high and if you lived to get it there was a fat pension at the end. The churchyards of India contained abundant proof that many did not.

The Indian Political Service also wielded vast influence and like the I.C.S. its servants were graded according to rank and seniority. They looked down on the army and the army did likewise among its own fraternity. The British Army felt itself a cut above the Indian Army, which in turn felt superior because they spoke Indian to their servants. The cavalry looked down on the infantry, and the snobbery continued until you reached the Ordnance Corps. The police were somewhere in between, as were the boxwallahs or businessmen.

Life was cheap in India and the threat of sudden death never far away. In the evening you could be fit and well and dead next morning. So one didn't keep glancing over one's shoulder for a glimpse of the ever-present spectre but accepted it with stoicism. Just before the Armistice a 'flu epidemic had swept the world: in India alone 12,000,000 died, far more than had perished on the battlefields. In Simla women had travelled to social functions during the epidemic without giving a second glance at the piles of unburied dead by the roadside.

The whites nearly all operated a strict colour bar. While they would work with Indians they would not relax with them, although they might have been to the same public school and university. Some clubs—but they were few and far between—did admit Indian members but often the criterion was whether they came from families which had remained loyal during the Mutiny. It was a constant source of friction, for many Indians objected to this race distinction, but many British insisted it had a practical application. The club was the one place where he could let his hair down and he could not do that if there were Indians present.

The memsahib adopted no such subterfuge. She wanted the Indian kept at arm's length and, although many of them did excellent charity work in clinics and hospitals, a line was drawn beyond which they would not step. As Montagu lamented in one of his mailed comments to the Prime Minister:

> Again I say that the social question, the fact that the civil servant is willing to work with the Indians but not to play with them, the fact that the Boxwallah will have nothing to do with them, has brought the present political situation upon us.

To his dismay he discovered that Indian children were not admitted to the Boy Scouts; it angered him so much that, busy as he was, he raised the matter with the Viceroy and London.

He seemed incapable of grasping the simple fact, readily accepted by most Europeans, that the insistence on racial superiority was essential if the British were to continue to rule. The British did possess qualities that the natives lacked. The highest praise that could be paid to an Indian was to credit him with those virtues. As Kipling put it:

> An' for all 'is dirty 'ide
> 'E was white, clear white, inside.

The British may have originally gone to India in search of prosperous trade, but exploitation was no longer the reason for their continued presence. Those appointed to govern, administer and enforce law and order believed it was their duty — a God-appointed task and the white man's burden. It was an attitude that confused the Indians, for it was a burden they stubbornly refused to lay down even when the Indians offered to relieve them of the weight.

That was the India Montagu encountered when he arrived to fulfil his self-appointed mission in life. And to his chagrin he found that the man he had to work with so closely and intimately, the Viceroy, was the hub around which the social circle revolved:

> The thing that alarms me in all Chelmsford's talks seems to me to be that so little has reform sunk into his mind that he seems to think everything will go on as it is.

The Indians were not particularly impressed with Chelmsford, whom they thought knew little about India and was ill-equipped for his high office, having only been appointed by Asquith because of his marital connections with a prominent Liberal family. From their first meeting it was clear to him that a rough and stormy passage lay ahead.

Physically he found Chelmsford impressive: 'Quite good to look at, with a fine, athletic figure, square shoulders, small hips, well-shaped head, and a graceful forward inclination of the body'. But in the area where things really mattered he was less impressed. Although Chelmsford was 'a really good fellow', he was cold, aloof, reserved and very prejudiced in his views — except that they did not appear to be *his* views, but those imposed on him by others.

Soon after he arrived, Montagu began to come to the view that the Viceroy could not be the ceremonial head of India as well as its political leader. The two roles were incompatible:

> I am not at all sure that my mind is not now moving to a Royal Viceroy, with a Prime Minister appointed from home for all work except that of a functionary.

Montagu found the Viceroy and his Government obsessed with files and regulations, far too rigid, lacking in appreciation of Indian political aspirations, and everything dominated by 'precedence, precedence, precedence'.

He wrote despairingly of Chelmsford:

> He never moves an inch without consulting his Council. He never expresses an opinion without consulting his Council. The whole time, charming man though he is, every document I show him he has to consult somebody before he expresses an opinion.

The Army in India also occupied a unique position and anyone who wished to introduce reforms of any kind had to have the support and trust of the military, and that Montagu certainly did not have. General Sir Charles Monro, the Commander-in-Chief, was outspokenly hostile:

> When I am with Mr Montagu I feel that I am walking with a man who is steadily edging me towards a precipice and when he gets me near enough will push me over.

It was understandable that Montagu often reached the depths of despair and wondered whether England had any idea of how the Government of India operated. Meeting Indian leaders informally proved even harder — obstacles were deliberately put in his way. But he was persistent. He met Mohamed Ali Jinnah, the Muslim lawyer-politician, and thought it was an outrage that a man of his intelligence should have no hand in the running of his own country. He was equally impressed with Gandhi:

> He wants millions of Indians to leap to the assistance of the British throne. In fact, I may say here, that revolutionary or not, loathing or not as they do the Indian Civil Service, none of these Indians show any sign of wanting to be removed from connection with the British throne.

The man he had singled out for such high praise was soon to alter his views and become an implacable opponent of the British Raj, but there was no inkling of this as Montagu worked tirelessly in pursuit of the reforms so dear to his heart.

He toured India meeting people, putting out feelers and taking soundings of their opinions. Among those he met was Sir Michael O'Dwyer, who was to become his personal albatross. From the outset the pugnacious, outspoken Irishman made it clear that he did not think much of Montagu or his reforms. Both men loved India passionately, but their views on the future of the country were diametrically opposed. Montagu looked upon the educated Indians as an integral part of his reforms; O'Dwyer detested them, mistrusted them, and often expressed his views with a vigour and frankness that bordered on the downright rude. Such antipathy did not make for harmonious relations, and they came to dislike each other with equal fervour.

O'Dwyer, one of fourteen children of an Irish landowner, was born in 1864 a few miles from Tipperary. He was educated at a Jesuit College, applied to join the Indian Civil Service and in 1882 entered Balliol as a probationer. He was not only brilliant academically, but a first-class sportsman: He went to India, like so many men that Oxford had produced for the I.C.S., full of confidence and imbued with the firm conviction that they had a divine right to rule.

In 1913, at the age of fifty-four, he became Lieutenant-Governor of the Punjab and from the outset made it clear he considered the peasant behind the plough to be the backbone of India. He had a deep affection for them and looked upon them as his children. Their welfare was dearest to his heart and, as head of the Province, *he* would administer it with their wellbeing foremost in his thoughts and brook no interference from the educated classes. He made this apparent very early on when replying to an address of welcome at which some suggestions were put forward for reforms in the Government of the Punjab. He dismissed them with a brusqueness that deeply offended his audience. He underlined his views by quoting Alexander Pope to those who felt there was room for reforms:

> For forms of government let fools contest;
> Whate'er is best administered is best:
> For modes of faith let graceless zealots fight;
> His can't be wrong whose life is in the right.

O'Dwyer was fond of quoting other men's words to reflect his own views, and he further alientated the educated classes when he insisted that the interests of the silent masses should be given priority over the 'clamour of the politicians', adding:

> 'Because half a dozen grasshoppers under a fern make a field ring with their importunate cries, while thousands of great cattle, repose beneath the shadow of the British oak, chew the cud and are silent, pray do not imagine that those who make the noise are the only inhabitants of the field.'

In one of his despatches to Lloyd George Montagu commented ruefully that O'Dwyer 'is still opposed to everything . . . he is determined to maintain his position as the idol of the reactionary forces, and to try and govern by the iron hand'.

Without a doubt the fiery Irishman was a force to be recognized; his views carried a lot of weight. To the majority of Anglo-Indians he was the epitome of the British Raj, the kind of man who would not stand idly by and see the simple peasant become a pawn in the power game being played with such unscrupulousness by the educated Indians. Furthermore, there would be no insidious undermining of the way of life the British enjoyed so long as men like O'Dwyer had any say in things. He worked hard and he played hard. But the problems of high office and the enormous responsibilities he carried never caused him a sleepless night nor upset his routine. On his own admission he rarely missed his morning ride and aftecoon game of golf or tennis. When the welcome cold weather arrived in Lahore he rode to hounds twice a week, and the pressures of work were further lightened by duck shoots in Bahawalpur, pig-sticking in Patialia, and stag hunting in Kashmir. 'It may be put down either to a good conscience or a callous one, but it is a fact that public cares never lost me half an hour's sleep,' he boasted.

It was with the vacillating Chelmsford—'I am so afraid of putting my signature to something which will be criticized and held up to scorn'—and the forceful O'Dwyer, who was never tormented by misgivings or indecision, that Montagu beavered away at his reforms. But, eventually, after a lot of heart-searching on both sides the Montagu-Chelmsford reforms were drafted.

When Montagu finally sailed for home aboard H.M.S. *Dufferin* on 24 April 1918, he felt that, if all the high hopes with which he had set out had not been accomplished, progress had certainly been made. He was as yet unaware that the Indian politicians would be hostile to his proposed reforms on the grounds that they left them in a position no better than that of an articled clerk when it came to the actual running of their own affairs.

Also on board was Mr Justice Rowlatt whose name would soon sweep across India like a fire in a field of stubble. When the decision was taken to replace the Defence of India Act, which gave the Government powers to curb any movements which might have hampered the war effort, a committee under Sir Sydney Rowlatt of the King's Bench Division sat in camera to draw up legislation which gave the Government special powers to suppress sedition. The result was two Bills, although only the first, the 'Anarchical and Revolutionary Crimes Act, 1919', became law.

When the details of the legislation became known there was a violent and widespread reaction to what were considered repressive measures and a total denial of freedom. It became known as 'The Black Act'.

The Indian politicians regarded it as a typical example of British hypocrisy. With one hand they were being offered advancement, with the other they were being threatened.

When the first Rowlatt Bill came to be debated in the Imperial Legislative Council, the Indian members were unanimous in their condemnation. On 6 February 1919 Jinnah stood up and proclaimed that he considered it was his duty to warn:

> If these measures are passed, you will create in the country from one end to the other a discontent and agitation the like of which you have not witnessed, and it will have, believe me, a most disastrous effect on the good relations that have existed between the Government and the people.

His prophetic words went unheeded by the British. All but one of the Indian members voted for it to be deferred for six months while the British members pressed for it to become law. It resulted in the resignation of Jinnah, Pandit Mandan Mohan Malaviya and Mr Mazharul Hacque. Within a month widespread disturbances were to break out in the Punjab.

2. Satyagraha and Rowlatt

'Even in its purest form the Passive Resistance Movement, which preaches disobedience to certain laws as a means of procuring repeal of a particular law is, in my opinion, a conspiracy to do a legal act by illegal means.' — Legal Remembrancer to the Punjab Government.

Outwardly Amritsar seemed as placid as the blue waters of the man-made 'Pool of Tranquillity' where pilgrims bathed and from which the sacred city of the Sikhs took its name. In the centre of the lagoon, at the end of a long pier-like walk, was the Golden Temple. Day and night the sound of non-stop hymns echoed across the water as worshippers removed their shoes and walked through shallow troughs of cleansing water before entering the holy precincts. People slept in the shade of the arched cloisters that skirted the lagoon, the cool white marble providing a welcome protection from the pitiless sun overhead. The cold weather had gone and the summer was approaching its zenith.

Apart from being a centre of pilgrimage the walled city, with its massive arched gates, was a prosperous trading centre and a bustling anthill of human activity. Within a stone's throw of the temple stretched a labyrinth of dark, narrow streets lined with squalid ill-lit houses. The bazaars, with shops little bigger than booths, teemed with people gesticulating feverishly as they bartered for the vast assortment of goods on sale. Gleaming copper pots bubbled over braziers at the eating houses. The air was filled with the smell of rich spices. Money-lenders touted loans which would place the borrower in lifelong bondage. Sacred cows walked unmolested. Rickshaws jostled for position and women with long, hooked noses and plaited hair as black as raven's wings, wearing silk pantaloons walked alongside women in gaily coloured saris. A fine dust filled the air; the potholes in the streets, which in the wet weather were muddy quagmires, were now dustbowls. Overhead kite-hawks—'shite hawks' to the soldiers—wheeled with effortless ease. Vultures perched patiently on vantage points waiting for carrion — animal or human.

The city also contained a British community — small in number but big in influence. They had established spacious banks in the commercial area, opened schools, missions, hospitals, post offices, a telegraph office, a court, an electricity generating plant, a waterworks and a cinema. An imposing statue of Queen Victoria served as a silent symbol of their permanence.

They worked in the city but lived outside its walls in the Civil Lines, which were literally on the other side of the tracks, for the railway bisected the city and provided a clear demarcation line. As in most Indian towns and cities where the British had entrenched themselves there was a Mall — a wide tree-lined street, clean and free of refuse with white-walled bungalows set back on well-watered lawns.

This, then, was Amritsar in the early months of 1919 — on the surface relatively cool, but deeper down a feeling of discontent. The Rowlatt Acts provoked indignation through the length and breadth of India, but nowhere was it more acute than in Amritsar. Apart from sharing the general feeling of war-weariness, the city felt it had suffered more than most other places. The trade in hides and skins had been particularly hard hit as it was mainly in the hands of Germans. It was also the distributing centre for piece goods and that had also suffered badly through the war. In addition, it was the centre for a great deal of speculative trading in grain, and the export of much-needed food to Europe had sent prices rocketing. The growers and merchants had made handsome profits; the poor could barely afford to eat. High taxation and contributions to War Loans had further aggravated a sense of grievance.

The Punjab was also the 'buckler of India', providing the bulk of the army from its warrior classes. The people had responded magnificently to the ever-increasing demand for men, but there was a deep-rooted resentment at the methods of recruitment which smacked of the old naval 'press gang'. They claimed that, although Sir Michael O'Dwyer publicly disapproved of such illegal measures, in practice he turned a blind eye to them.

A further cause of discontent came from the large number of Kashmiri Muhammadans who resided in and outside the city. The Sultan of Turkey was the Caliph or Supreme Head of the Muslims, and with the end of hostilities they feared for the future of Turkey. Rumours were rife that the Turkish Empire was to be dismembered and the Caliphate abolished.

The Rowlatt Acts seemed the final straw to all sections of the native population. Instead of being rewarded for their war efforts they were to be punished with repressive measures.

In Amritsar two undisputed champions of the people emerged. They were a Hindu and a Muslim, a combination which surprised the British, who firmly believed they would always be at loggerheads. The enmity which existed between the two had always been a main plank in the British argument as to why Indians could never govern themselves. The two men dismissed this as part of the 'divide and rule' policy of the Raj.

The first was Doctor Saif-ud-Din Kitchlew, a Kashmiri Muhammadan who had been at Cambridge with Nehru. According to his son, 'He was a keen sportsman who got a blue for something or other', and was 'a bit of a lady killer'. He read for the Bar and was a member of Lincoln's Inn. Before the war he had obtained his PhD at Munster University, which led to his being branded as pro-German. He was an eloquent public speaker — an art which he had learned at the Cambridge Debating Society. He was a staunch supporter of Home Rule, although he claimed that he did not envisage an India outside the Empire. At Cambridge he had become an admirer of Keir Hardie, which to most Anglo-Indians made him a Bolshevik. In Amritsar he had a flourishing legal practice which enabled him to support his wife and two children in comparative comfort.

The other, Doctor Satyapal, came from a middle-class Khastri family. He had graduated from the Forman Christian College and gone to the Medical College, Lahore, where he was an outstanding student. He was a reserved man, married, with two daughters, simple and temperate in his habits. He too was a forceful orator and a progressive Nationalist who believed in peaceful and constitutional methods to obtain political freedom. During the war he had served as a doctor with the Indian Medical Service.

Both were thirty-five years old.

They had first come to prominence when they led a local protest over the decision of the railway authorities to stop issuing platform tickets to Indians. They protested that it was racial discrimination, although the authorities argued that it was purely a move to stop over-congestion.

They again joined forces over the Rowlatt Acts and demanded their repeal. As a result they came under the constant surveillance of the C.I.D. who diligently reported their speeches and movements to headquarters. Officers in disguise took notes of their speeches and the personal dossiers on the two men got fatter and fatter. The British openly admitted the corruption that existed among Indian members of the Force, who were often susceptible to bribes, prone to blackmail, and reported not what they had heard but what they believed their superiors wanted to hear. The informer, in his desire to ingratiate himself, was even more unscrupulous: he thought nothing of fabricating evidence against somebody if he thought it would stand him in good stead.

The Rowlatt Acts had no fiercer opponent than Gandhi, and almost overnight he was elevated from an obscure politician to a national leader. Before that the British had had very good reason to be grateful to Gandhi; in the First Boer War he had served as a stretcher bearer and been awarded the Zulu War Medal and the Kaiser-i-Hind Medal. And during the war which had just ended he had encouraged recruiting and wholeheartedly supported the Allied cause.

On the political front he was an enigma not to be taken too seriously. The British regarded him as an unworldly crank, totally divorced from the realities of life. The word 'phoney' was in their minds if not on their lips. Sir Michael O'Dwyer, however, considered him an arch-criminal: 'An unctuous hypocrite with his ascetic pose'.

As the agitation against the Acts increased, the cry 'No *vakil* (lawyer), no *daleel* (argument), no appeal' echoed throughout the sub-continent. It summed up the general feeling towards the emergency measures which empowered the Executive to arrest and search people and property without warrant, detain suspects without trial, and try people before special courts where there were no juries and no right of appeal. The agitation was further inflamed by a crop of wild and completely untrue rumours about the Acts.

Nevertheless, a great many of the uneducated masses believed the rumours. In the crowded bazaars they whispered that a policeman who coveted another man's wife could get the husband out of the way through the Acts. Every bride and bridegroom would be inspected by a British doctor before the ceremony was permitted to take place. Parents of the newly-weds would also have to give the Government a sum of money equal to that spent on the wedding. Not more than four persons would be allowed to follow a funeral procession. A tax was to be imposed on the birth of every child. Not more than four people were allowed to sit together at any time or place. The Government of India distributed 75 million leaflets explaining the Acts, but the rumours persisted.

Gandhi decided that the best way to force the Government's hand was through Satyagraha or 'soul force', which was simply an extension of the 'passive resistance' he had first envisaged as a political weapon in South Africa. Vast numbers of people took the Satyagraha oath:

> I will never forsake truth in all matters in which I can promote Satyagraha. I will never support 'untruth' and will never injure any person or any property and shall never try either directly or indirectly to do such things. I also swear to make others believe and act upon those principles. I will also inform men all over the land that truth should be observed in everything and violence should not be shown towards brothers.

Gandhi's problem was how best to make its impact felt and bring it into practical effect. He hit upon the idea of a 'hartal':

> The idea came to me last night in a dream that we should call upon the country to observe a general hartal. Satyagraha is a process of self-purification, and ours is a sacred fight, and it seems to me to be in the fitness of things that it should commence with an act of self-purification. Let all the people of India, therefore, suspend their business on that day and observe the day as one of feasting and prayer.

It was in effect a call for a 24-hour national strike that would virtually paralyse the country through a campaign of civil disobedience. The date was initially fixed for 30 March, but it was subsequently changed to 6 April as it was considered that not enough notice had been given. But news of the cancellation came too late in some areas, and a hartal was held.

Sir Michael O'Dwyer, who was watching events very closely, sniffed the scent of rebellion in the air and was determined to snuff it out before it got out of control. Gandhi's 'soul force', he said contemptuously, would be met with 'fist force'. And again he resorted to the words of someone else to justify the strong action he contemplated. Sadi's couplet came easily to his lips:

A stream can be stopped at its source by a twig;
Let it flow, and it will drown even an elephant.

Sir Michael had proved the effectiveness of this when he crushed the Ghadr movement early in the war. At the turn of the century thousands of Indians, many from the Punjab, had emigrated to Canada and the Pacific coast of America in search of a new and better life, but their hopes of improved pay and conditions were short-lived; they found that colour prejudice in the New World was just as prevalent as in their homeland and their efforts to settle were further hampered by the strict Canadian immigration laws. In the hope of speaking with one voice they formed The Hindustani Workers of the Pacific Coast, which soon developed into a militant revolutionary movement. One of the key figures was a brilliant Indian student, Lala Hardyal, who had won a scholarship to St John's College, Oxford. There he became actively engaged in politics and developed a bitter hatred for the British Raj. In 1911 he sailed for America where he identified himself with the discontented immigrants. In San Francisco in the summer of 1913 he helped to found and personally edited a fiery newspaper, *Ghadr*, which literally meant revolution. Sensing that war was imminent, he enlisted the all-too-willing assistance of Germany which for purely selfish reasons was keen to foment revolution in India.

Copies of the newspaper were widely circulated in America and large numbers were smuggled into India. The Americans, although no great admirers of British imperialism, found Hardyal's activities an embarrassment and he was arrested as an

41

undesirable alien, but he jumped bail before he could be deported. He fled to Germany where he set up a bureau which worked closely with the German Foreign Office. His plan of action was to convince Indians that their homeland was now ripe for revolution.

The idea was given added impetus by the S.S. *Kamagata Maru* incident. This Japanese ship had been chartered in 1914 by a wealthy Amritsar Sikh, Gurdit Singh, who had settled in Singapore, with the original intention of forcing a showdown with the Canadians over their immigration laws. He had filled it with Indians and sailed for Vancouver, where it was 'blacked', and only those with valid papers were allowed to disembark. It was too good an opportunity for the Ghadrites to miss and the case was taken to court. But the court ruled that it could not interfere with the immigration laws. The passengers promptly seized the vessel and only the intervention of a Canadian cruiser which threatened to open fire forced the ship to leave Canadian territorial waters. The *Kamagata Maru* turned round and headed for India. Hidden among copies of the *Granth Sahib*, the Sikh holy book, were a number of rifles and a quantity of ammunition.

War had meantime broken out, and when the ship docked at Calcutta the authorities, primed as to the intentions of the revolutionaries aboard, ordered them to board a train and go to the Punjab, where a strict watch could be kept on them. Gurdit Singh and his followers refused, and in an armed clash with police eighteen people were killed and twenty-five wounded. Many were interned and the remainder sent to the Punjab.

The wisdom of the move was debatable for it meant that the Punjab now contained a hard core of dedicated revolutionaries.

Meanwhile, Hardyal's 'Berlin Group' was keeping the pot of rebellion boiling with German money. A carefully planned operation was mounted to incite further trouble in Kashmir with liberation held out as the final goal. The Punjab, North-West Frontier Province and the United Provinces were also singled out as special targets for widespread disorders which would eventually spread to the whole of India. Bomb factories were set up in the Punjab and envoys sent to nearly all military centres to seduce the Indian troops from their allegiance to the Crown. A combined action by the Germans and Turks would cut off the vital lifeline of the Suez Canal and isolate the sub-continent.

Money was also raised in the States to buy arms and ammunition, much the same as it is today by the I.R.A. An American ship sailed with 5,000 smuggled revolvers aboard, but fortunately it was intercepted by the Royal Navy. A further attempt was made soon afterwards when the *Annie Larsen* with a huge consignment of arms aboard set course for India. Following in its wake was the tanker *Maverick* with five Ghadrites aboard disguised as waiters. The carefully devised plan was for the two ships to rendezvous at sea where the five rebels would take over the ship, transfer the arms from the *Annie Larsen* and conceal them in the *Maverick*'s oil tanks. This time United States warships intervened and impounded the *Annie Larsen* for carrying contraband.

Despite the setbacks, a campaign of terrorism was launched in India, marked by a series of bomb outrages, shootings and numerous acts of arson, sabotage and dacoitry. But the majority of Indians remained loyal and O'Dwyer crushed the attempted revolution. Many went to the gallows and even more were transported to penal settlements in the Andaman Islands.

O'Dwyer was never allowed to relax. Religious affinity with Turkey brought a fresh danger in the form of the Pan-Islamic Movement, which was only thwarted by the exposure of the 'Silk Letter Conspiracy' which aspired to unite the Turks and Muhammadans of India in a concerted effort to overthrow the British. A special envoy was captured and found embroidered into his clothing were messages in Persian skilfully written in lengths of yellow silk. When they were deciphered the plot was revealed. Again O'Dwyer acted firmly and vigorously.

But the Germans persisted in their efforts to divide India. With the co-operation of the 'Berlin Group', an even bigger operation was planned. Three German troopships loaded with arms were to sail for India; one with 500 officers aboard would stop at the Andamans and release the convicts, many of whom had been jailed for their political activities; the second was to head for a Bengal port, the third for the west coast.

In Kabul a German mission was busy plotting to enlist the support of the Amir of Afghanistan, who had assured them he would enter the war when a joint Turkish-German force arrived in his country. The British managed to buy him off with a hefty increase in his subsidy.

A breakthrough in Burma was to have been the signal for a general rising in India, but the whole thing collapsed in a shambles.

It is doubtful whether the Germans ever believed that such a sweeping operation would succeed but the internal dissension that was created made the efforts well worth while, and anything that helped stifle the flow of recruits in the Punjab created manpower problems for the British. The fact that the mercurial Hardyal, who had bitten the hand that educated him, became disillusioned with the Germans and returned to lick it, was no consolation to O'Dwyer. The conversion from extreme violence to an almost sycophantic respect for the British simply confirmed O'Dwyer's low opinion of the educated Indian.*

The Bolsheviks also stuck their finger in the pie and their agents established contact with dissident groups and promised support in cash and arms.

Having scotched all these plots and seen the Empire emerge victorious, it was pefectly understandable that Sir Michael O'Dwyer should have developed a suspicious nature. He observed Gandhi's growing influence and the increasing support for his campaign with mounting apprehension. It also provided him with another stick with which to beat Montagu; he attributed Gandhi's success to the Secretary of State's praise of the Indian politician, which further convinced him of Montagu's unsuitability for high office. The country would be aflame if such men were to have an unfettered say in the affairs of India. He for one would not sit idly by until events got out of hand, and he quoted Sir Henry Main, Legal Member of the Supreme Council in India 1862-69:

> The Governor who waits to recognize a rebellion till it looks like a war will probably find he has waited too long.

On 29 March his Government passed an Order forbidding Dr

---

*Hardyal returned to America where he affected to look down on everything Indian and admire everything Western. He became a professor of Sanscrit and philosophy at Berkeley University, California, and later moved to Stanford University. His last years are shrouded in mystery and he died, some claim was murdered, in 1939.

Satyapal to speak in public and confining him to the Amritsar area. The Lieutenant-Governor had already taken firm steps to curb the activities of the more outspoken elements of the Punjab press and several papers had been forced to cease publication. Rather than defusing the tension, this merely aggravated it and brought about bitter allegations of censorship aimed at stifling the legitimate political aspirations of the people.

A hartal took place in many towns on 30 March. In Delhi it resulted in the police opening fire and several people and policemen being killed. It was also observed in Amritsar; all the shops closed and business ceased, and at a meeting in the Jallianwala Bagh attended by 45,000 people and presided over by Doctor Kitchlew, resolutions were passed calling for the repeal of the Rowlatt Acts. It was agreed that copies of the resolutions should be sent to Gandhi. Kitchlew's closing words counselled caution:

> We will ever be prepared to sacrifice personal over national interests. The message of Mahatma Gandhi has been read to you. All countrymen should become prepared for resistance. This does not mean that this sacred town or country should be flooded with blood. The resistance should be a passive one.

The meeting was observed by Sir Miles Irving, the Deputy Commissioner of Amritsar, who was relieved that there were no incidents. The hartal had been a complete success.

Miles Irving had spent eighteen years in the Punjab but was new to his post in Amritsar. Although a well-meaning and well-intentioned man, he did not command a great deal of respect among the British who thought he would allow the snowball to develop into an avalanche before he took decisive and firm action. True, he had summoned Kitchlew to his bungalow and warned him that 'loyalists' had reported unfavourably on his activities. Kitchlew had been incensed and insisted that nothing he had said was unconstitutional or illegal, and he asked for the courtesy of being informed when fresh allegations were made against him so that he could confront those making them. Irving appeared to have been placated. A section of the British community believed he was easily duped. They thought more along the lines of Sir Michael

O'Dwyer, and they soon got in contact with him and informed him of what they believed was the true position in Amritsar.

On the other hand Irving had very little concrete evidence to suggest that Kitchlew was advocating violence; on the contrary, he repeatedly condemned it.

Another meeting was held in the Jallianwala Bagh on 2 April at which a visiting holy man spoke about 'soul force'. The next day Sir Michael O'Dwyer passed an Order banning Kitchlew from speaking in public or communicating with the press, and confining him to Amritsar. It was personally served on him by Miles Irving.

Although the hartal of 30 March had been a complete success, it was still felt that another should be held on 6 April as had previously been announced. Miles Irving was becoming increasingly agitated and the strain was beginning to show. On 5 April he held a meeting at his bungalow to which he invited local magistrates and other leading citizens and asked them to use their influence to get it cancelled. They agreed, and their view was endorsed by the Congress Reception Committee which was in the city making arrangements for the next annual session of the All India Congress Committee, which was to be held in Amritsar. Kitchlew and Satyapal may have been silenced, but they still had influence and they firmly opposed any cancellation.

At nine o'clock that evening a crowd of about two hundred people went through the streets of the city proclaiming that the hartal would be held. In the morning Amritsar was virtually at a standstill. Shops and businesses were again closed, and tongas and rickshaws were stopped and their passengers persuaded to dismount and walk. It was not all gentle persuasion — a great deal of intimidation was used against those who had misgivings.

At Aitchison Park the final game in a cricket tournament was being played between the Mamdot Club and the Hindu Sports Club. Among the spectators was Mr R. Plomer, the Deputy Superintendent of Police. Suddenly the ground was invaded by a large crowd, many of whom were small boys clearly intent on mischief, and the matting pitch was ripped up and the stumps withdrawn. Prominent in the disruption was a young man called Hans Raj who helped to tear up the matting and was as loud as anyone in the denouncements. A magistrate intervened and play was resumed, but the crowd regathered and the match was cancelled.

Later in the day a meeting was held in the Jallianwala Bagh attended by 50,000 people, and resolutions were passed urging the King Emperor to withhold his Royal Assent to the Rowlatt Acts. Protests were also made against the gagging of the two doctors and resolutions were passed demanding the Orders to be rescinded. Emphasis was again placed on the need for 'passive resistance', and the meeting ended without any violent incidents. But a mysterious handbill appeared on the clock tower: 'Prepare yourselves to die and kill others'.

Miles Irving, in a report to Mr A. J. W. Kitchin, the Commissioner for the Lahore Division, described it as 'a day which a London policeman would have described as a picnic', but added ominously, 'unfortunately we are not in London and I regard the situation with very grave concern'.

The day after the hartal, Sir Michael O'Dwyer, who was soon to retire, presided over his final meeting of the Legislative Council at Lahore. It was, therefore, something of a formal occasion at which there was no shortage of empty platitudes and insincere tributes from some Indian members to Sir Michael's six years of office. Sir Michael himself, however, was not a man who was capable of saying one thing while believing another. Having praised the loyalty of the martial classes he proceeded to deliver a scathing attack on those who opposed the Rowlatt Acts:

> The Government of this Province is and will remain determined that public order, which was maintained so successfully during the time of war, shall not be disturbed in the time of peace. Action has, therefore, already been taken under the Defence of India Act against certain individuals at Lahore and Amritsar, who, whatever their motives, were openly endeavouring to rouse public feeling against the Government. The British Government, which has crushed foreign foes and quelled internal rebellion, could afford to despise these agitators, but it has a duty of protection to the young and the ignorant, whom they may incite to mischief and crime, while themselves standing aside. I, therefore, take this opportunity of warning all who are connected with political movements in the province that they will be held

responsible for the proper conduct of meetings which they organize, for the language used at and the consequences that follow such meetings.

He then went on to criticize Indian members for not exercising a more restraining influence on the vociferous agitators. They shrank from attending meetings because they were more concerned with their *Izzat* (prestige).

Restraining influences are, therefore, either absent or not exercised. Hence the necessity for my warning, which is addressed to the press as well as to the platform.

And just in case the point had not got home he quoted Aesop's story of the enemy trumpeter who begged a soldier from the victorious army to spare his life as he was a non-combatant:

The soldier quite rightly refused, pointing out that without the trumpeter's call the enemies' soldiers would not have advanced to the fight.

The Indian members were incensed at this attack and even more annoyed at the manner in which O'Dwyer spoke of the inoffensive nature of the Rowlatt Acts. Insensitive to the indignation his words had aroused, he said:

The recent puerile demonstrations against the Rowlatt Acts in both Lahore and Amritsar would be ludicrous if they did not indicate how easily the ignorant and credulous people, not one in a thousand of whom knows anything of the measure, can be misled. Those who want only to mislead them incur a serious responsibility . . . Those who appeal to ignorance rather than to reason have a day of reckoning in store for them.

The final words struck a chill of fear in some of the audience. Sir Michael's speech was not favourably received by the Indian press. They considered his remarks insulting and inflammatory. He was back on his favourite hobby-horse — denigrating the educated Indian. *The Tribune* of Lahore described his speech as 'a blazing indiscretion'.

O'Dwyer was not, however, a man who indulged in empty threats. He was prepared to back his words with deeds. The Legal Remembrancer to the Punjab Government. Mr J. P.

Ellis, was asked to give an opinion on Satyagraha and his words justified the firm action threatened by Sir Michael:

> Even in its purest form the Passive Resistance Movement, which preaches disobedience to certain laws as a means of procuring repeal of a particular law is, in my opinion, a conspiracy to do a legal act by illegal means: much more it is a conspiracy where, in pursuit of the object and in order to achieve that object, acts of misrepresentation intended or likely to excite hostility to Government or acts of intimidation directed against particular individuals are committed.

In short, under the Indian Penal Code anyone who took the vow or participated in a hartal was taking part in a criminal conspiracy.

As the meetings in Amritsar had all passed off peacefully, the Indian politicians who had been harangued by the Lieutenant-Governor were bemused by his belligerence. Even the interrupted cricket final had resumed the next morning. Sir Michael's intemperate address was hardly likely to encourage the co-operation he asked for.

Miles Irving, however, was still hopeful that those responsible for the agitation would avoid a head-on collision with the authorities. But he was surrounded by a powerful group of men who shared O'Dwyer's view that the time was ripe for firm and decisive action. Foremost among these was Lieutenant-Colonel Henry Smith, the Civil Surgeon. He was an extremely able surgeon who was unable, or did not feel the need, to curb his anti-Indian feelings; two sub-assistant surgeons in the hospital had resigned in protest over his attitude towards native subordinates. The native population, although appreciative of his skills, disliked and feared him, and stories were circulated to show him as a mercenary man rather than a dedicated medical practitioner.

Smith certainly did not conceal his strongly held views that a rebellion was in the offing and the agitators were Bolsheviks and part of a Russian-German organization. His views were shared by a large number of the British community who supported him in his demands that the time for talking was over. It was obvious that he managed to convince Miles Irving of the impending danger for Irving suffered a dramatic conversion. The day after O'Dwyer's warning he sent off a long and detailed report to Mr A. J. W. Kitchin, who immediately forwarded a copy to the Punjab Government.

Irving was clearly under a great strain and his nerve was beginning to crack:

> The Khan Bahadurs and Rai Sahibs are dead, and not fresh corpses at that. I am trying to get in touch with the new leaders who have influence. I was wrong in thinking I could influence Kitchlew — he is too deep in it. I may get hold of some of the outer circle. But I have not much hope for them. I think that things will be worse before they are better and that for the present we must rely on ourselves alone.

Kitchlew, he feared, was just a pawn in the hands of much bigger fish but he did not know who they were. There was an urgent need, he insisted, for an increased military presence in the city:

> It is absurd to attempt to hold Amritsar City with a company of British infantry and half a company of Garrison artillery. Any resolute action in the city would leave the city lines almost undefended. I know what the situation as regards British troops in India is, but another company would be of enormous value.

With the limited forces at his disposal it would be difficult to defend the railway station and civil lines, and in the event of a riot nine-tenths of the city would have to be abandoned.

Suddenly a day which would have been a picnic for a London bobby had assumed terrifying proportions.

Irving's conversion was complete and total. His earlier complacency had vanished completely and he rather strangely managed to suggest that all along he had been aware of the dangers:

> We cannot go on indefinitely with the policy of keeping out of the way, and congratulating ourselves that the mob has not forced us to interfere. Every time we do this the confidence of the mob increases; yet with our present force we have no alternative. I think we shall have to stand up for our authority sooner or later by prohibiting some strike or procession which endangers the public peace. But for this a really strong force will have to be brought in and we shall

have to be ready to try conclusions to the end to see who governs Amritsar.

Irving had at last seen the danger signals which had been visible to others for some considerable time. Even so, in the opinion of some British, he had still reacted too slowly and too late.

The day after Irving sent his long rambling despatch was the annual religious festival of Ram Naumi when the Hindus paraded their garlanded deities through the streets to the beat of drums and the music of bands. It was always a big occasion in Amritsar, only this time there was a marked difference in the celebrations. Although the British, who always enjoyed the spectacle, moved through the streets unmolested, there was a perceptible undercurrent of unease. What was normally a purely Hindu occasion was being shared by the Muslims. Kitchlew and Satyapal were both staunch supporters of Hindu/Muslim unity and many of their followers had taken a vow to bury their religious differences.

> We, Hindus and Mussalmans, swear before God that here-after we will consider ourselves brothers, forgetting all distinctions of caste or creed etc.and will suffer alike all the misfortunes. We will never do anything to annoy the religious feelings of each other and will never interfere with the religion of each other and will never hurt or kill each other for the sake of religion.

It was a unity that the British had always claimed was impossible, yet the day of Ram Naumi proved it could happen, and it was very disturbing to those who watched the festivities. Miles Irving, who was observing the procession from the balcony of the Allahabad Bank, was unable to conceal his concern. The vast crowds were chanting 'Mahatma Gandhi ki jai',* and 'Hindu-Mussalman ki jai'. Similar slogans were shouted in support of Kitchlew and Satyapal who were watching the procession from different spots. They acknowledged the cheers with silent approval.

When the procession passed Irving, there were loud cheers and every vehicle stopped below the balcony while its occupants paid their respects. Even the bands halted to play 'God Save the King'. It all seemed jovial and relaxed, but Irving was

*ki jai = long live.

aware of the menacing undertones. Hindus and Muslims were drinking out of the same vessels, an unprecedented breach of custom. There was another disturbing feature: when a group of Muhammadan students dressed in Turkish uniforms halted below the balcony they started clapping — a mark of disrespect in the eyes of the British. The Deputy Commissioner was visibly agitated.

Earlier in the day he had called a meeting at his bungalow which was attended by Captain Massey, the officer commanding the Amritsar Garrison, Mr J. F. Rehill, Superintendent of Police, Mr Plomer, his deputy, and Lieutenant-Colonel Smith, to discuss the situation in the city.

What transpired has never been satisfactorily explained, but what is known suggests that the Deputy Commissioner did not command the entire confidence of the British, for Smith made a hurried visit to Lahore to see Sir Michael O'Dwyer. It could be reached in a couple of hours by motor car. Irving was attending the Ram Naumi festivities when Smith made his trip. What passed between the two men who were so alike in their thoughts and feelings can only be conjectured, although Smith dropped a clear hint much later when he said:

> I told an important official on the 9 April that in my opinion these hartals had nothing to do with religion, but that they were designed and organized by Mr Gandhi or by a revolutionary organization behind him for the purpose of developing a little discipline and a revolutionary spirit, and that I had no doubt from the great success of the hartal on 6 April 1919, that they intended to have another hartal at no distant date on which the red flag would be heaved up everywhere at the same time, but that the saving of the situation would be in the fact that they developed the revolutionary spirit to such an extent that it was certain to get out of hand somewhere at any moment in which case the whole organization would go astray if dealt with with promptness and firmness, and that once it went out of hand I was confident that reasoning with these people would be of no avail — that prompt force would be necessary.

Smith's reluctance to name his 'high official' convinced a strong body of Indian opinion that during his visit to Lahore a deliberate plot was hatched to spark off a chain of events that was to end with the massacre in the Jallianwala Bagh. It was the day of reckoning O'Dwyer had warned of.

At 7 p.m., soon after he had returned from the festivities, Irving was visited by Colonel Smith who handed him orders for the detention and deportation of Kitchlew and Satyapal to Dharmsala, a hundred miles away. At the same time Sir Michael O'Dwyer, who had learned that Gandhi was planning to visit the Punjab, issued instructions that he was to be halted on his way from Bombay to Delhi and told he could not enter the Province. O'Dwyer had originally planned to deport him to Burma but this was countermanded by the Viceroy, and instead he was confined to the Presidency of Bombay.

Gandhi accepted it with that quiet resignation which so exasperated the British. It was to him a vital part of passive resistance and he issued a long open letter, 'To my Countrymen', urging them not to resort to violence of any kind, especially over his arrest:

> A departure from the truth by a hair's breadth or violence committed against anybody, whether Englishman or Indian, will surely damn the great cause the Satyagrahis are handling.

He explained that he could never permit himself to remain free whilst the Rowlatt legislation disfigured the Statute Book. 'My arrest makes me free.' Even so the Mahatma found it necessary to sound a note of warning.

> The English are a greater nation but the weaker also go to the wall, if they come in contact with them. When they are themselves courageous they have borne untold sufferings and they only respond to courage and sufferings and the partnership with them is only possible after we have developed indomitable courage and the faculty for unlimited suffering. There is a fundamental difference between their civilization and ours. They believe in the doctrine of violence or brute force as the final arbiter. My reading of our civilization is that we are expected to believe in soul-force or moral force as the final arbiter and that is Satyagraha.

The British believed that the appeal, even if the uneducated Indians to whom it was addressed could understand it, would not be observed and it only served to confirm Gandhi's unworldliness and political naivety.

As soon as Irving received his instructions from O'Dwyer he called another meeting and plans were drawn up for the secret arrest of the two doctors. Arrest and deportation were measures that were frequently adopted in India to silence hostile critics, and they were usually accepted with resignation by the victims and indifference by the majority of people. Therefore no one contemplated any real trouble over the arrest of Kitchlew and Satyapal. Nevertheless, it was decided to carry them out in a clandestine manner so that the two doctors would be well clear of the city before the news leaked out.

It was a disastrous miscalculation, as the events of the next twenty-four hours were to prove.

3. Murder, Looting and Arson

'Our duty is quietly to submit to being arrested.' —
Mahatma Gandhi.

April is a punishing month in Amritsar. The working day begins and ends early, with the sun, not the hands of the clock, dictating the day's routine. By midday the sun turned the dusty city into a smelting house, coating it with a heat shimmer that dulled the capacity for clear thinking and gave objects a double image. By noon the most productive part of the day had gone, at least as far as the British were concerned. For those fortunate enough not to be restricted to an inflexible schedule it was a time to change from sweat-stained clothes into something cooler. Even the Indians who were born to it sought the welcoming shade of trees and awnings.

It was probably for this reason that Miles Irving decided that ten o'clock was an excellent time to send the two doctors a polite request to call on him at his bungalow. Unaware of the trap about to be sprung, they summoned tongas and set off without saying anything to their families, except that they would be back shortly.

In two hours' time many Europeans would be seeking relief from the heat under slowly moving punkahs. The clock was simply halted for a brief spell; life would return to normal when the temperature began to drop. Most important, there would be no white women in the streets. By the time the streets began to come to life again the two men would be well on the way to a secret destination. There would be a few noisy protests from their supporters when the news leaked out, but they would be confronted with a *fait accompli*. And without the two doctors present to mastermind events, the agitation

55

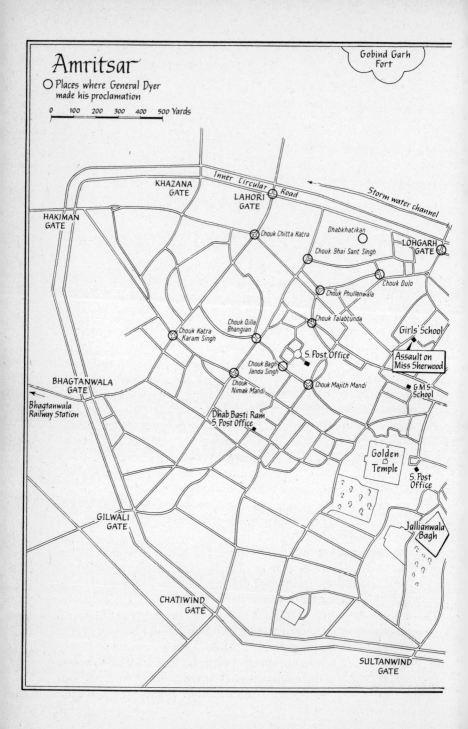

Amritsar

○ Places where General Dyer
made his proclamation

0   100   200   300   400   500 Yards

Gobind Garh
Fort

KHAZANA
GATE

Inner Circular Road

LAHORI
GATE

Storm water channel

HAKIMAN
GATE

Chouk Chitta Katra

Dhabkhatikan

Chouk Bhai Sant Singh

LOHGARH
GATE

Chouk Dulo

Chouk Phullenwala

Chouk Qilla
Bhangian

Chouk Talabtunda

Girls' School

Chouk Katra
Karam Singh

S. Post Office

Assault on
Miss Sherwood

Chouk Bagh
Janda Singh

Chouk
Nimak Mandi

Chouk Majith Mandi

G.M.S.
School

BHAGTANWALA
GATE

Bhagtanwala
Railway Station

Dhab Basti Ram
S. Post Office

Golden
Temple

S. Post
Office

GILWALI
GATE

Jallianwala
Bagh

CHATIWIND
GATE

SULTANWIND
GATE

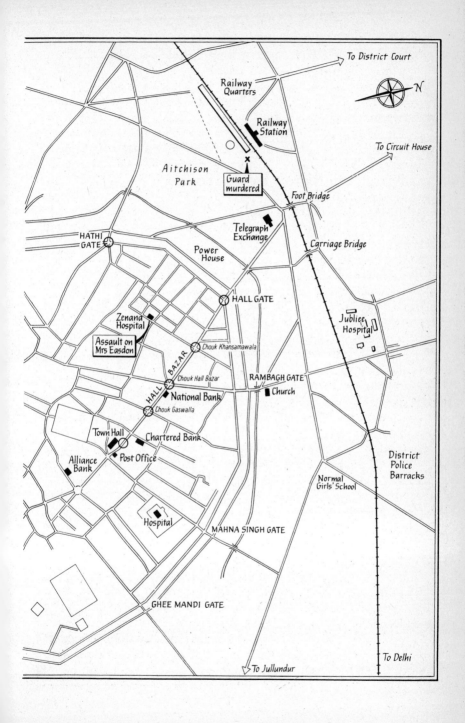

that had marred the past few weeks would evaporate and life in Amritsar would return to normal.

When Kitchlew left his house at Dhab Khatikan, he was met by Hans Raj, a good-looking but feckless young man of twenty-three, and when the doctor called for a carriage Raj asked if he could accompany him. The barrister was not surprised to find him there, for when he was not with him Raj was hard on the heels of Satyapal. He was like a shadow which divided itself between the two men, never too obtrusive but impossible to shake off.

Not that Kitchlew had any objection to the young man travelling with him, for he was one of his most ardent and active supporters. He had been a late convert to the movement, but he had more than made up for this with his seemingly boundless energy and enthusiasm. Apart from taking an active and leading role in the agitation he was ever ready to play his part behind the scenes with the host of humdrum chores that others found so irksome. Only forty-eight hours previously he had been appointed joint secretary of the Satyagraha Subha and was responsible for keeping the register of those who had taken the vow of passive resistance.

Hans Raj's interest in politics had been as sudden as it was unexpected. Until the previous month he had been considered something of a ne'er-do-well, and there were behind-the-hand whispers that he lived off the immoral earnings of his mother who was a bazaar prostitute. He was not an unintelligent young man for he had matriculated from a local school, but he was light-fingered and seemed to prefer helping himself to other people's cash rather than working for it. Twice he had been fired for embezzlement — first from the N.W. Railway where he was a ticket collector, and secondly from the Union Club.

Hans Raj had first emerged as a supporter of the two doctors when he joined the agitation over the issue of platform tickets, and since then he had devoted his time to supporting their aims. Although until 23 March Kitchlew had only been known to him by sight, he had helped to organize meetings and figured prominently in the two successful hartals, had done more than his share of clerical work, and was always available at the drop of a hat to run the odd errand and supervise the printing of leaflets and resolutions. His obvious enthusiasm tended to stifle any suggestion that he was a bit ingratiating.

There were, however, some who openly mistrusted him. The almost overnight conversion seemed quite out of character. As they were never reluctant to point out, it was not so long ago that he had tried unsuccessfully to join the local police, a force that did not command the greatest respect among the people of Amritsar. He had been interviewed by Mr Rehill, the Superintendent of Police, and, although turned down, had been placed on the waiting list.

Kitchlew certainly had no misgivings about his energetic and courageous disciple who had been bold enough openly to carry a Home Rule banner at the Ram Naumi procession and had been to the forefront when the hartal of 6 April was planned. In his enthusiasm he had come perilously close to forgetting that the movement advocated non-violence.

When Kitchlew invited him to jump into his tonga he was convinced that the meeting would result in a lecture from Irving and a request not to stir things up.

Satyapal, who lived near Hall Gate, was more restrained in his relations with Hans Raj; he welcomed his support but he did not encourage his company.

Although Irving was convinced that his well-prepared plan would go off without a hitch, he was wise enough to agree with those who were involved in the deportation that nothing would be lost by taking a few precautions. So steps were taken to deal with any trouble that might arise when the news leaked out.

Captain Massey gave orders to the officers at Amritsar Fort to have their ancient artillery in position and a machine-gun mounted; their mere presence would deter any crowd from marching on the railway station and other strategic points nearby. To prevent any demonstrations in the Civil Lines, steps were also taken to stop people crossing the railway lines. Mounted troops and policemen, accompanied by three European magistrates, were posted at the main crossing points. A force of British infantry was kept in reserve in the Ram Bagh, and seventy-five armed policemen under the command of an Indian Deputy Superintendent were posted in the Kotwali, the main police station, to deal with any trouble in the centre of the city. The danger seemed so remote that it was not thought necessary to issue any special warning to those Europeans who might still be at their desks.

Amritsar also had an Internal Defence Scheme which involved the evacuation of women and children to places of safety in the event of widespread riots, and this was placed on standby.

Soon after ten o'clock the two doctors arrived at Irving's bungalow. Once inside they must have realized that this was clearly more than an invitation to talk things over. Mr Rehill was there in mufti, standing with a group of soldiers dressed as if they were going on a *shikar*. Without any formalities they were told their presence in Amritsar was prejudicial to public safety and they were being deported to a secret destination. The two men began to protest, but they were told it was a waste of time as the orders came from the Lieutenant-Governor himself. They then asked if they could send messages to their families, and to this Irving agreed, assuring them that he would see they were delivered.

The doctors were given paper and pens and they sat down and wrote brief notes. They both seemed calm, composed and resigned to their fate. To an Indian politician, deportation was almost an accolade.

Satyapal wrote two letters, one to a family friend and another to his father. To his father he wrote:

There need be no anxiety about me. I am being sent to an unknown destination. I shall be writing from that place. Please keep a very cool mind and don't disturb yourself. I am quite happy.

Satyapal and Kitchlew were then escorted to two waiting cars which set off for Dharmsala with a military escort disguised as a hunting party.

The letters were then handed to Hans Raj who made copies of them before passing them over. When he called at the two houses he said that Kitchlew had told him when setting out for Irving's bungalow to see that the people took their revenge if he was deported. Satyapal had made a similar remark. Satyapal's father was surprised at this, for the letter from his son did not suggest there should be reprisals for their arrests.

Hans Raj returned to the centre of the city and sent telegrams to Gandhi and the Indian press reporting the deportations. Just before noon he hired a gharry and, with two other men, toured the city telling people what had happened. He said that Doctor Hafiz Mohammad Bashir had given instructions for a crowd to go to Irving's home and demand their release. Previously the two men had been held in high esteem; now they were being proclaimed as martyrs. At 11.30 a.m. Plomer, the Deputy Superintendent of Police, received a phone call informing him that a large crowd was heading towards Aitchison Park, and he immediately passed on the news to Miles Irving. Plomer promptly mounted his horse and took an armed party of twenty-five men to reinforce the picket at the railway foot-bridge. Irving still had no reason to fear that his plan had misfired; the crowd was noisy, but all Indian crowds were, and, although it was moving towards the Civil Lines, the Europeans it had passed on the way had not been subjected to any violence. Even so, he decided to ride down to the picket at the Hall Gate where there were two bridges, one for pedestrians and the other for traffic.

When he arrived the crowd was comparatively small and included a lot of youngsters who were clearly enjoying the sheer devilry of the situation. Irving urged the crowd to disperse but it continued to press forward, loudly demanding to know where their leaders were. Second by second the crowd increased until it numbered thousands. Although the crowd was unarmed the sheer momentum with which it slowly advanced forced the mounted soldiers to retreat. Someone removed his turban and brandished it under the nostrils of one of the horses, causing it to rear. Mr R. B. Beckett, the Assistant Commissioner who was on duty at the carriage bridge, pleaded with the crowd to withdraw, but he was howled down and several of the demonstrators sat on the road and beat their chests. One man seized a cane and struck Beckett's horse across the nose, causing it to whinny and rear in panic. The mounted soldiers were forced to retire over the bridge as the crowd began to pelt them with stones. The crowd had now grown to terrifying proportions and Beckett estimated that it numbered 40,000. Stones literally rained down on the troops from all angles.

Irving, meanwhile, had galloped off to the Ram Bagh to summon reinforcements. As this was all happening Plomer had arrived with his armed policemen and was holding a crowd at bay at the nearby railway footbridge.

Beckett was still trying to reason with the crowd which was chanting, 'Where is Satyapal? Where is Kitchlew?' He tried to convince them that he honestly did not know, but the stoning increased in intensity and the situation became so desperate that Beckett ordered the mounted soldiers to open fire. Three or four people were killed and several wounded.

From that moment the situation got out of hand. No longer was it a crowd of angry stone-throwing people but an unruly mob seeking revenge, as Hans Raj had urged.

Someone shouted, 'Where is the Deputy Commissioner? We will tear him to pieces.'

People from the crowd began picking up the dead and wounded and dragging them away. Some were put into tongas, others put on charpoys taken from nearby houses and carried to Doctor Bashir's house in the Fazid Bazaar.

If the crowd had originally started out with peaceful intentions it had now abandoned them. Soon after the first firing people descended on shops in the Hall Gate area and armed themselves with stout sticks.

A second and more determined attempt was made to cross the railway bridge. Mr F. A. Connor, an extra Assistant Commissioner, had seen the mounted soldiers trotting back at a very fast pace followed by a stone-throwing mob yelling slogans and full of murderous intent. He saw one man bare his chest and proclaim that he was prepared to die unless the two doctors were released.

Soon afterwards Irving appeared on the scene but his entreaties to the crowd to disperse peacefully were ignored. Instead he became the target for a volley of sticks. There were piles of large stones by the roadside where resurfacing work was being carried out, and these were picked up and hurled at the picket.

One small picket of three mounted British soldiers and three Indians led by Lieutenant Dickie was in grave danger of being swamped, and Connor reluctantly gave him orders to open fire. The young officer told two of the soldiers to dismount and take cover behind some culverts and open fire. They fired five or six shots, but they were enough to momentarily halt the crowd; several people were seen to fall.

During all the turmoil two members of the local Bar, Mr Maqbool Mahmood and Gurdial Singh Salaria, were in the middle of the crowd trying to restrain the mob from further violence while at the same time pleading with the soldiers to stop shooting. Plomer had provided Salaria with a horse in order that he could get to the crowd. Followed by his colleague, who was on foot, he edged his mount to the front of the rioters and the two lawyers found themselves dangerously positioned between the stone-throwers and the troops. Someone shouted that they would only retire if they were allowed to take the dead and wounded away. Salaria called out to the Deputy Commissioner that he believed he could get the crowd to listen to reason. The answer was a further volley of stones and sticks. Irving, who feared for the safety of the small force, was now in a terrifying quandary. If he gave an order for the firing to be resumed there was a danger of the two peace-making lawyers being killed, but as more missiles were showered on the troops he was forced to act. The soldiers promptly opened fire again and people began to fall under the feet of the rioters. Maqbool Mahmood estimated that around twenty to twenty-five people were shot, some of them in the back while attempting to run away. He ran up to the soldiers and asked them if they had any transport available — an ambulance, a car, anything to take the wounded to hospital. He was told there was nothing. He then offered to go to the hospital and obtain help. At first he was told he could not, then he was granted permission. By then the road was a scene of carnage. Bodies lay everywhere. One dead man lay with an eye blown out and his brains spilling on to the road. The groans of the dying and wounded filled the air. One man's last words were heard above it all, 'Hindu Mussalman ki jai.' A 16-year-old boy with his entrails protruding from a stomach wound refused the aid of Doctor Dhanpat Rai, who was administering medical aid. 'I am dying, don't trouble about me, attend to my brethen. Hindu Mussalman ki jai.'

As the crowd began to fall back, Doctor Rai tried to get hold of some stretchers for the wounded but he was unable to do so and eventually gharries were halted and charpoys brought from nearby houses to take the bodies away. The two lawyers walked away dejectedly, firmly convinced that if they had been given a little more time they could have got the crowd to disperse without further bloodshed.

By now crowds were gathering throughout the city and, as news of the shootings spread, thousands went on the rampage. Kitchlew and Satyapal were forgotten. Their target was now any European they might come across. The air was filled with shouts of 'They have killed our brothers and we will kill them' and, 'Come on, let us wreck their offices and banks'.

Within a short time Amritsar was being overrun. Incident piled upon incident and the situation in the city was changing so fast that it was almost impossible to obtain a coherent picture of what was going on. Not one of the fifteen C.I.D. officers on duty in the streets that day sent in a report to headquarters. They preferred to maintain a low profile; they were all well known by sight and moved in fear of their lives. Later, when all was quiet, they outdid each other with their accounts of what they had done in the crisis.

The Telegraph Exchange was destroyed, but before the mob could do further damage they were beaten off by a detachment of men who were guarding the railway station. The Telegraph Master was seized and dragged from his bedroom when he was dramatically rescued by a Jemadar of the 54th Sikhs. An attack was made on the goods yard and a considerable amount of damage done. Guard Robinson was chased, overtaken and beaten to death. When his body was recovered, 'it bore no resemblance to a human being.' Telephone wires and electric cables were torn down and parts of the railway line ripped up. A finger on the statue of Queen Victoria was broken off, but further damage was avoided when someone shouted, 'Do not attack her. She was a good Queen.'

The bodies of some of those killed in the shooting were taken to mosques and there the crowds were inflamed to further violence. Someone called above the din that he had seen innocent men shot down, many of them while running away. In one street a picture of the King and Queen was ripped down.

A mob, alleged to be led by two Hindus, Rattan Chand and Bugga Mal, lieutenants of Kitchlew and Satyapal, attacked the National Bank. The Manager, Mr Stewart, and his assistant, Mr Scott, both popular men who had done much for the Indian community, were bludgeoned to death and their bodies tossed on a pile of office furniture which was then saturated with kerosene and set on fire. Before the Bank was razed to the ground it was looted and cloth and other goods worth several lakhs of rupees were stolen from an adjoining store. While the funeral pyres were still burning the mob moved on to the Chartered Bank where the door and windows were set on fire. The European Manager, Mr J. W. Thomson, and his assistant, Mr Ross, hid in an upstairs room and their lives were saved by the arrival of policemen from the Kotwali less than fifty yards away.

The frenzied mob then turned its attention to the Alliance Bank. Inside the besieged building the Manager, Mr G. M. Thompson, hid in a small cubicle and as the mob broke in he fired his revolver through a gap, killing one man. He then raced up the stairs on to the roof where he was pursued by the yelling mob. He ran down and tried to lock himself in his office where he was overwhelmed and clubbed to death. When someone called out that he was still breathing his killers returned and smashed his body to pulp. It was then hurled off the balcony into the street below and cremated on a pile of bank furniture soaked in kerosene. The safe was broken open and the contents looted.

A group of rioters then headed for the Zenana Hospital and began a systematic search for Mrs Easdon, the doctor in charge. Like the bank staff she was a popular figure, but someone had started a rumour that she had said those who had been killed deserved it. They broke down doors and smashed open cupboards in their search, but the doctor had hidden in a rooftop toilet. Mrs Nelly Benjamin, a Sub-Assistant Surgeon, and a friend of Mrs Easdon, managed to convince the mob that she was not in the hospital. The frustrated rioters withdrew when they could not find her, but they hurried back when one of the servants told them where she was. Still unable to find her they left to take part in further looting. Mrs Easdon was finally helped to escape by Mrs Benjamin and a loyal chaprassi who provided her with some Indian clothes and helped her to darken her face with a bottle of ink.

The looting, rioting, arson and murder had all happened so quickly that many were caught completely unawares. Among them was Miss Marcia Sherwood, a woman doctor who had spent fifteen years helping the people of Amritsar. She was well liked and respected for the devoted work she did for the Zenana Missionary Society, and as soon as she heard of the rioting she mounted her bicycle and rode to the five schools where she was superintendent with the intention of closing them and sending the 600 Hindu and Muhammadan girl students home. As she turned a corner she was suddenly confronted by a group of young men. Someone bellowed 'Kill her, she is English.' Above the clamour she heard someone else cry out, 'No. She is one of God's chosen who is educating our children and doing God's work of charity.' She spun her machine round and pedalled away, but unfortunately rode down a blind alley and had to retrace her steps. Pedalling frantically she reached a street where she was well known and slowed down, feeling she had reached friendly territory. Doors were opened and she was invited inside, but she was concerned about the safety of two teachers she had left alone at one of the schools and she insisted on going to them. By then the mob had caught up with her. One man aimed a blow with his fist and missed, another struck out a foot to topple her from her cycle. A blow from a stick knocked her to the ground and as she struggled to her feet she was felled with another rain of blows. Incredibly she managed to regain her feet and stagger to an open door, but it was slammed in her face. The crowd of youths promptly renewed their attack. Eventually she collapsed with exhaustion, but with astonishing willpower got to her feet again. A youth grabbed her dress and flung her down, another struck her with his fist. Her hair was grabbed as she once more regained her feet and she was then struck several blows on the head with a shoe. A savage blow knocked her unconscious and the youths retreated shouting, 'She is dead', 'Victory to Gandhi', 'Victory to Kitchlew'.

Seeing the gang withdraw some Hindu shopkeepers crept out of their house and carried her indoors. Her scalp was lacerated and there were deep cuts on her head and body. Primitive Indian remedies were applied and silk, burned to a powder, was rubbed into the deep cuts to staunch the bleeding.

Somehow or other the youths had heard that she had survived and began pounding on the door and demanding for her to be handed over. With remarkable courage an elderly Indian lady went out to them and swore that Miss Sherwood was not inside.

When darkness came she was laid on a stretcher and put in a cart, concealed with blankets, and taken to her own home, where a doctor treated her. If treatment had been delayed any longer he said she would have died. The next morning she was taken to the safety of the Fort.

Sergeant Rowlands, the electrician at the Military Power Station, was waylaid at Rego Bridge on his way to the Fort and his skull battered in.

The military strength in Amritsar was further reinforced by the unexpected arrival of fifty men from the 1/9th Gurkha Rifles who were on their way from Dehra Dun to join their battalion at Peshawar. They were commanded by Captain G. P. Crampton who was sharing a compartment with young Frank McCallum who had recently arrived from Sandhurst. As the train drew slowly into Amritsar, Crampton and McCallum heard a lot of shouting and when they lowered the window and looked out they saw a large crowd massing at the level crossing and on the overhead footbridge. Crampton shouted 'Look out' as a heavy stave came through the open window like a well-aimed arrow. When the train stopped at the platform an agitated Major told them there had been serious riots in the city; that one woman had been knocked off her cycle and left for dead, buildings set on fire and banks looted. There was a welcoming look of relief on the Major's face when he saw the Gurkhas but it vanished when he was told that they had no rifles.

The train was shunted into a siding and the Gurkhas made their way to the Fort where they were issued with fifty rifles. McCallum was shocked at the condition in which the women and children were living:

> There was a terrible quietness in that barrack room. The ladies seemed so bemused and sad. Imagine leaving your own comfortable bungalows and quarters to be put in a room with a long line of beds, cots, camp beds or floor, and no privacy.

McCallum and a handful of Gurkhas were taken by a civilian to a crossroad near the Civil Lines where they kept guard. The nameless civilian proved a tower of strength to the young officer:

> He knew the language and he had a wonderful .22 long cartridge rifle which he led me to believe was worth all my men and their rifles, and I was very young.

It was a boring spell of duty for the Gurkhas who sat in a ditch for several hours. Apart from halting the odd looter and confiscating the bales of cloth, nothing happened. When McCallum returned to the station he saw the rather strange spectacle of two English ladies with blackened faces and wearing Indian clothes brought in by Indian friends.

During the two hours that the mob overran the city, the Indian Christian Church was burned down; the Church Missionary Society's Normal Girls' School was fired, and all the books, clothes and furniture destroyed. Four women trapped inside were rescued by police who arrived unexpectedly and drove off the mob.

An attempt was made to stop the Calcutta mail train as it passed through on its way to Lahore. The Religious Book Society and hall were burned down, although the native Christians inside managed to escape. The sub-Post Office at the Golden Temple was destroyed and two other sub-offices gutted. The Town Hall adjoining the Kotwali was a blazing ruin. By the time the mob was satiated Amritsar was virtually isolated for most of the telephone wires had been cut.

Seventy-three shots had been fired which did not include those fired by the police. If the police had fired a few more rounds the situation might well have been very different. Amritsar would not have witnessed so much violence and devastation.

Ironically when the Town Hall had been set ablaze the armed police in the adjoining Kotwali had watched it happen without firing a round. Apart from rescuing the two Europeans from the Chartered Bank the seventy-five armed men had watched the town being burned, looted and ransacked without leaving the safety of the Kotwali. The most decisive action had amounted to no more than an empty threat to open fire. Witnessing the inactivity of the police, the mob did more or less as they pleased. They formed the opinion that the police approved of their actions.

The bitterness of the authorities and the European community was understandable; during the rioting and killings the two principal Indian officers had spent their time bickering over their respective seniority. City Inspector Muhammad Ashraf Khan stubbornly refused to take orders from Deputy Superintendent Sahaib Jan, and so the two men who could have saved the city remained idle and waited for orders from outside.

*   *   *

When the first shots were fired, Lieutenant-Colonel Henry Smith was performing a cataract operation. They confirmed what he had repeatedly stressed to Irving — that a rebellion was liable to break out any minute. He rushed out of the operating theatre and tried to telephone the Deputy Commissioner, but the line had been cut. Smith had been in the Punjab since 1895 and in Amritsar ten years, and he knew that many people who had arrived from outlying villages to attend the annual Baisakhi horse fair would seize the opportunity to loot whatever they could lay their hands on.

With complete disregard for his own safety, he filled his ambulance with nurses and drove into the smouldering city to evacuate European women and their children and drive them to the safety of the Fort of Gobindgarh. By then the Internal Defence Scheme was well under way and every conceivable form of transportation was utilized to evacuate the Civil Lines. Collecting points were established in a number of bungalows and buildings, and women and children descended on them with just the few personal belongings they had managed to pack. Many of them had to cross the railway lines at Rego Bridge which the soldiers were holding against the mob. Men with staves escorted the women to the waiting vehicles. But no attempt was made to molest them. Pickets were mounted on the routes to the Fort in case an attack was made on the fleeing Europeans. The streets leading to the Fort were so congested that it reminded one woman of Epsom Downs on Derby Day. It was an odd comparison.

Incredibly, some of the women were still resting when the evacuation began. One, Mrs Beckett, who was seeking relief under the punkah, recalled her anger at being disturbed: 'I rose reluctantly, annoyed with my bearer for having admitted a visitor after my order that I was not to be disturbed.' Seconds later her house was invaded by people and crying babies, and all she could hear above the din was her servant shouting something about 'badmashes' and 'bazaar'. It then occurred to her that her house was designated as a collecting place in the Emergency scheme. Within minutes her drawing-room was packed. In the distance the cries of the mob could be heard like the howling of wolves. And every second the spine-chilling sound got closer and closer. Those who had fled their homes without even packing the bare essentials helped themselves to anything that would serve as bed linen. Even with the crowds gradually encircling the Civil Lines and the sound of gunfire filling the air, some women were reluctant to leave their homes: one protested that she did not wish to disturb her child.

As the convoy of tongas, gharries, rickshaws and the occasional car headed for the Fort, men galloped past on horseback and bellowed the latest news: the Banks were burning, Europeans were being slaughtered.

The Fort itself had been built more than a century earlier by the Rajah Ranjit Singh as a security vault to house his treasures. It was ideal for that purpose, but totally inadequate as a haven for a large number of women and children.

The heat was stifling and made worse by an acute shortage of fans. A quick count established that there were only a dozen fans and some of those had to be allocated to the makeshift hospital.

It was half an hour before sunset when the last evacuees reached its safety. Most of them were packed into the Cavalier Block which was in the centre of the dusty quadrangle. It was so overcrowded that many of the women had to sleep outside. In some respects they were better off; at least the air was breathable.

A few of the women had managed to get their servants to bring in extra bedding, and this was shared out as fairly as possible. Others had to make do with heavy clothing and floor rugs as bed covers. The soldiers, moved by the plight of the women and children, readily handed over their own blankets.

A hasty roll-call established that there were 130 women and children inside the Fort, excluding the very small babies. The men who had managed to reach the safety of the Fort were immediately posted on sentry duty.

The shortage of food created a problem; many of the women and children had not eaten for hours and were ravenous, and the walls echoed with the cries of hungry babies. The presence of a number of servants further aggravated the situation, for they insisted on having their own special food.

As darkness fell conditions became intolerable for the

women, who were accustomed to being waited on hand and foot. The Fort was filthy, there was no sanitation, and the lack of protective nets made them the victims of non-stop attacks from the voracious sandflies and mosquitoes which bred in their millions in the stagnant moat. Sixteen women were crammed into one tiny room in which there was no privacy at all. Yet they withstood the hardship with amazing fortitude. Overcrowded as they were a fresh danger emerged: one of the babies developed typhoid.

At 4.15 p.m. a desperate Irving had managed to get a message through to Lahore over the railway telephone which was the sole remaining source of communication. The Deputy Commissioner urgently called for more men and an aeroplane. O'Dwyer read the brief report and promptly ordered Kitchin to drive the thirty-five miles to Amritsar and make an on-the-spot investigation. Kitchin made the trip without any trouble and within a relatively short time arrived at the Fort.

Despite Irving's earlier warning, 10 April was still a holiday in Lahore. It was the day the mail arrived and letters were sent home. The Indian battalions, not affected by the mail, were holding a cross-country run. Lieutenant-Colonel M. H. Morgan, commanding the 124th Baluchis, was called into the Brigade Office along with other COs and told of the troubles in Amritsar. Morgan was ordered to send his second-in-command, Major MacDonald, to the city with a force of British and Indian soldiers.

At about 11 p.m. MacDonald's train arrived from Lahore with a detachment of the 2/6th Royal Sussex Regiment. When he reported to Kitchin at the Fort he was told the situation was now out of control and he should take any action necessary to restore order.

Meanwhile people who had been unable to reach the rallying points continued to arrive at the Fort. Some only managed to get through the streets by dressing as Indians. They all had horrifying tales to recount: the streets were filled with a half-crazed mob demanding 'white blood' and rioters were openly displaying the loot they had plundered from the National Bank. A detective who managed to dodge the crowd said people were shouting, 'Murder the Europeans. This is the time we should rise.'

At midnight, under cover of darkness but still at great

71

personal risk, Major MacDonald, with Mr Plomer as a guide, took a force of men into the city. They entered by the Ram Bagh Gate and Hall Gate and went to the Kotwali where they brought out the two men who had been rescued from the Chartered Bank along with three other civilians who had sought shelter there. They also found Mrs Easdon. Strategic points on the railway and Civil Lines were reinforced with the newly arrived soldiers, and during their patrol of the city they recovered the charred remains of the three men who had been cremated by the mob. Miss Sherwood, swathed from head to toe in bandages, arrived on a stretcher.

By then the streets of Amritsar were deserted and an uncanny silence made the scene even more unnerving. There was debris everwhere and the flickering flames lit up the discarded plunder from the Banks, the godowns and other gutted buildings. The overhead telegraph wires trailed down as if a gigantic spider's web had been destroyed. Amritsar was virtually cut off. The situation was desperate. As Kitchin reported, 'For all we knew, we were the only white men left in India.'

4. Dyer Arrives at Amritsar

'I have been expecting this, there is a very big show coming.'—General Dyer.

While Amritsar was burning and the refugees were flooding into the Fort, General and Mrs Dyer were giving a dinner party at Flagstaff House in Jullundur. Dyer appeared relaxed and calm as he chatted to his guests over pre-dinner drinks, although one or two could not help noticing that some of his staff seemed a trifle preoccupied. In India, appearances were extremely important and Dyer's outwardly unruffled exterior gave no hint that his thoughts were in Amritsar, a three-hour car journey to the south. A message from Lahore at 6 p.m. had alerted him to the seriousness of the situation in the holy city and he had been ordered to send a force of men there as quickly as possible.

Minutes later a hundred men from the London Regiment who had not so long ago been chatting cheerfully about returning home to Blighty were ordered to be prepared for an immediate move and to muster on the guardroom veranda in full marching order. They were supported by 230 Indian soldiers, plus a medical officer and staff.

Shortly after 9 p.m. the party, under the command of Major F. S. Clarke DSO, was marching to Jullundur station.

In Flagstaff House the dinner party continued, although the telephone and telegraph wire were continuously manned and from time to time Dyer slipped out to be briefed on the latest developments. By late evening he knew that the situation was extremely grave and several Europeans had been murdered. It was not, however, until 2 p.m. the following day that Dyer received orders to go personally to Amritsar. For some unex-

73

plained reason he did not set off until 6 p.m. This lack of urgency seemed strange, for just before he left he told his son, 'Mussulmans and Hindus are united. I have been expecting this, there is a very big show coming.' He instructed his son to sleep on the veranda and guard his mother and his cousin Alice.

It took Major Clarke's party five hours to reach Amritsar as the train was repeatedly halted while an armoured train, manned by members of the Indian Defence Force, went ahead and repaired sections of the track which had been torn up. When they detrained they learned that the Fort and the station were the only parts of the city remaining in British hands. The waiting rooms and refreshment rooms were packed with exhausted women and children, and some other soldiers told them that conditions in the Fort were worse.

The Londons were dog-tired themselves, but there was no time to take their boots off, let alone put their feet up. As soon as the sky began to brighten they were marched off to guard the European side of the city and prevent any recurrence of the previous day's violence.

*   *   *

Dyer, travelling by car with his Brigade Major, Captain Briggs, and Captain Bostock, had plenty of time to contemplate what lay ahead. The warning given to his son was based on personal experience, for he had been on leave in Delhi during the hartal of 6 April. There he had witnessed the rare spectacle of Hindus and Muslims fraternizing and seen people ordered to dismount from tongas and pony carts, and forced to get out of their motor cars. His own car had been stoned and its passage blocked by a fallen tree, and several people had been killed during the rioting. Although Jullundur had remained unaffected, Dyer knew there had been disturbances elsewhere. It was a clear-cut issue: the disturbances had to be put down as swiftly and rigorously as possible.

He was a soldier first and foremost with a tendency towards over-simplification. Life to him was made up of clearly defined blacks and whites; there were no subtle shades. Politically he was even more intransigent than his civil boss, O'Dwyer. It was summed up in the phrase 'There should be an Eleventh Commandment in India — Thou shalt not agitate'. He sincerely believed that Indians did not understand self-government, neither did they want it. To them 'the Raj was immaculate, just and strong; to them the British officer is a Sahib who will do them right and protect them from enemies of all kinds.'

While he approved of free speech and a free press, they should be restricted to enlightened people, and that excluded the Indian. It would be generations before they were capable of governing themselves. Like O'Dwyer, he considered the Indian politician a dangerous agitator who stirred up trouble, then discreetly withdrew from the results of his handiwork. Therefore, it was his duty to protect the simple, honest peasant from the evil machinations of the educated minority. If, however, they were foolish enough to listen to the political harangues of the trouble-makers and think they could challenge the authority of the Raj, then they had to be taught a lesson.

*   *   *

Amritsar on the morning following the riots was like a ghost city. The deserted streets were littered with debris and several of the buildings were gutted shells; others were still smouldering. The shops and bazaars were closed and a sullen and subdued population was making preparations for the burial and burning of the dead.

Miles Irving, who had established himself at the railway station, summoned two lawyers, Mr Maqbool Mahmood, who had tried, at the risk of his own life, to get the rioters to disperse, and Mr Yasim, and told them that not more than four persons would be permitted to follow each body. The two men protested that this would only inflame the people, for a funeral was a religious occasion and certain rites had to be observed. But the Deputy Commissioner was adamant and, when the two men continued to press the matter, Irving, who had been without rest for a considerable time, lost his temper. Trembling with rage he shouted, 'No more talking. We have seen our bodies charred. Our temper is changed.' When the two men expressed their sorrow at the murders he retorted, 'You are sorry now. You ought to have been sorry when you were attending those foolish meetings of yours, and you may be sorry before you leave.' The cowed lawyers tried to explain that they had not attended any of the meetings, but they sensed that the time was not opportune for an argument and so they withdrew, but not before they had heard Colonel Smith suggest that the mob should be bombed by aircraft. The surgeon was not alone in thinking that there should be reprisals.

Later, at the hospital, Doctor Balmokand, the Sub-Assistant Surgeon, was told by Smith that General Dyer was on his way from Jullundur to bombard the city and drew diagrams to illustrate how and where the city would be shelled and destroyed in half an hour. The doctor, who lived in the city, not unnaturally expressed fears for his personal safety, and Smith advised him to leave his home and take shelter in the hospital.

Crowds of waiting mourners followed the funeral parties to the city gates, but, as ordered, only a handful went out to the burning ghats and burial grounds.

Kitchin, meanwhile, had accumulated as much evidence as he could about the previous day's rioting and was of the firm opinion that a state of war existed. He decided to return to Lahore and report his views to O'Dwyer and suggest that martial law should be proclaimed.

Dyer arrived at 9 p.m., but, hot and dusty as he was, he went direct to the railway station. There he immediately called a conference in a railway carriage which was attended by Irving and the Superintendent of Police. Irving gave him a complete rundown on the situation and expressed the view that the crowd was still impenitently hostile, and that a second Mutiny was in the offing. When Dyer was told of the cowardly assault on Miss Sherwood he was visibly moved: the protection of women was almost an obsession with him. As they talked things over, Dyer became convinced that Miles Irving was cracking under the strain; he looked a broken man, utterly worn out by the heavy burden of his responsibilities. His fears were confirmed when the Deputy Commissioner confessed that he could no longer cope with the situation which was now beyond the control of the civil authorities.

At the conclusion of the conference a document was drawn up which was handed to a number of leading citizens for distribution throughout the city. Irving had more or less thrown in the towel:

Handed over to G.O.C. 45th Brigade and signed by the Deputy Commissioner midnight 11-12 April 1919.
The troops have orders to restore order in Amritsar and to

use all force necessary. No gathering of persons or processions of any sort will be allowed. All gatherings will be fired on. Any persons leaving the city in groups of more than four will be fired on. Respectable persons should keep indoors.

The city had been handed over to Dyer, who stated that he would continue to consult Irving and seek his advice.

Within minutes of being handed the signed document, Dyer was leading a force of men through the streets of Amritsar to the Kotwali. There he saw Inspector Ashraf Khan and asked him to supply a list of the ringleaders. The policeman, whose inactivity had been so marked during the rioting, readily produced a list of about a dozen names, and Dyer ordered them to be rounded up as soon as possible. He then returned to the railway station where he began to prepare his plans for the approaching day.

He now had at his disposal: 474 British troops and 710 Indian, consisting of the original garrison force of 184 officers and men of the Somerset Light Infantry; 41 men of the 12th Ammunition Column; the Gurkhas who had been halted on their way to Peshawar; 130 men from the 2/6th Battalion of the Royal Sussex Regiment; 12 men manning the two armoured cars; 181 men from the 1/124th Baluchis; 107 men from the 1/25th London Regiment; 21 men from the 54th Sikhs; 101 men from the 59th Rifles, and 130 men from the 2/151st Infantry. They were not all front line troops; some were raw and untrained, others lacked battle experience.

At first light Dyer moved his headquarters from the railway station to the Ram Bagh, a much better and more comfortable place as far as the soldiers were concerned. The gardens were spacious and attractive, having been laid out as a pleasure garden by the Rajah Ranjit Singh. There was plenty of shade and fresh water and ample room for the men to pitch their tents. The Ammunition Column and the Somerset Light Infantry remained on duty in the Fort where the ancient guns were trained towards the city.

At 10.30 a.m. Dyer marched through the city with a force of 125 British and 310 Indian troops, followed by the two armoured cars. At the Sultanwind Gate he encountered a belligerent crowd which was openly hostile and insolent. They jeered and showed their disrespect by spitting on the ground when he

77

passed and refused to disperse when ordered to; instead they shouted the by now familiar cry, 'Hindu Mussalman ki jai'. Dyer was furious and considered he would be justified in opening fire, but he decided against it, thinking it would be more proper to issue a further proclamation before he resorted to such drastic action.

At the Kotwali he asked for the arrested ringleaders to be brought before him for interrogation. While the troops rested he questioned them closely about others who might have been involved in the riots.

Several of the people who had been arrested on Dyer's orders were handcuffed and marched back to the Ram Bagh where they were chained round a tree in the centre and guarded by a strong force of Gurkhas until such time as they could be questioned again.

Lieutenant McCallum was ordered to remain at the Kotwali with a handful of Gurkhas to keep an eye on a number of rioters who were locked in the cells, in case an attempt was made to rescue them.

'If that happens, am I to open fire?' he asked Dyer.

'Yes, and just you . . . well see that you do,' replied the General.

By the time the column arrived back at the Ram Bagh, Kitchin had returned from his visit to Lahore where he had reported to O'Dwyer. The Lieutenant-Governor had contacted Simla by telephone and outlined the grave situation to the Indian Government. He was told that if the troops were forced to open fire 'they should make an example'. He carefully jotted this down in his diary.

It seemed, however, that this need would not arise, for Kitchin said that his trip back from Lahore had been uneventful and he had encountered no trouble. But it was a short-lived period of relief. Soon afterwards Dyer received an unconfirmed report that Indian troops had rioted in Lahore and that the Lieutenant-Governor had been killed. But a further report from O'Dwyer's headquarters said that the original rumours were untrue; the Lieutenant-Governor was unharmed, and the situation was now under control. But trouble had also broken out at Kasur where the station had been looted and two Europeans killed.

To Dyer the brief lull was just the calm before the storm and he prepared a further statement for distribution by the police to the citizens of Amritsar:

> The inhabitants of Amritsar are hereby warned that if they cause damage to any property or commit any acts of violence in the environments of Amritsar, it will be taken for granted that such acts have been committed in the Amritsar City itself and the offenders will be punished according to military law. All meetings are hereby prohibited and will be dispersed at once under military law.

When Kitchin returned to Lahore to report to O'Dwyer he expressed the opinion that Major MacDonald was not being firm enough and should be replaced. Lieutenant-Colonel Morgan was promptly summoned by General Sir William Beynon, the Divisional Commander, who handed him a message he had received from Kitchin: 'Major MacDonald has done nothing to quell the rebellion. Please send an officer who is not afraid to act.' Beynon promptly ordered Morgan to go to the city. 'Amritsar is in the hands of the rebels. It is your job to get it back,' he told him.

But when Morgan arrived on the night of the 12th-13th he found Dyer already in control. 'I am the senior officer here so I must take command,' Dyer said, but he added, 'I would like you to remain with me for the present.'

✻ ✻ ✻

While General Dyer was preparing his plan of operation on the 12th, a meeting was being held at the home of Doctor Bashir and a crowd of some 20,000 people gathered outside. Some were in favour of calling a hartal next day but were prepared to cancel it if they were given an assurance that there would be no reprisals taken against anyone for the looting and loss of life the previous day. Bashir urged them to call it off in any case, as they would certainly not be able to get the assurance they wanted. The crimes could not go unpunished.

Hans Raj, on the other hand, was adamantly opposed to any stepping down. At a meeting he convened in the Hindu Subha High School he said that as their leaders had been arrested it was now up to everyone to be his own leader. He announced that a meeting *would* be held next day in the Jallianwala Bagh under the chairmanship of Lala Kanheya Lal, an elderly and most respected resident of Amritsar, at which letters from Doctors Kitchlew and Satyapal would be read out. The fact that Lala Kanheya Lal had not been told that he was to preside over the meeting did not worry Hans Raj unduly. He exhorted his audience to be prepared to make more sacrifices and he called for volunteers to find out the names of those who had been arrested so that their release could be called for. A hartal would be proclaimed on the 13th and all business suspended until Kitchlew and Satyapal were released from detention.

*   *   *

Unaware of what was taking place in the Punjab, Gandhi, who had been released from detention, addressed a mass meeting of followers near Bombay and reminded them once again of the importance of non-violence in their campaign and he reiterated his firm conviction that it was the duty of the Satyagrahis to submit to arrest and that there should be no demonstrations demanding their release. It was far too late for the message to be heeded in Amritsar.

*   *   *

Sunday 13 April was Baisakhi Day and marked the beginning of one of the most important religious festivals in the Punjab. The roads approaching the city were thronged with thousands of pilgrims from outlying districts who descended on the city to bathe in 'the pool of immortality' and worship in the Golden Temple. Equally large numbers came in for the horse and cattle fairs which figured prominently in the festival which lasted for several days.

Hotels were luxuries that few of them could afford, and the Jallianwala Bagh was a popular meeting and resting place. It was hardly comfortable, but most of the villagers were used to discomfort, and so long as they had a blanket to wrap round them to keep the night chill out they were happy. By nightfall the eight acres of dry earth were dotted with sleeping figures. The Jallianwala Bagh was a garden in name only, for it was more like an empty swimming pool. There were no flowers or lawns, pi-dogs scavenged for discarded scraps of food, and mudcaked buffaloes drowsed in any convenient spot of shade. A low wall surrounded the 200 yard oblong-shaped plot and houses over-jutted the wall. On one side, not far from a tall peepul tree, was a large well, and almost in the centre there was an old samadhi, or shrine, fringed by four small trees.

In his Ram Bagh headquarters, Dyer was told of the large numbers of people flocking into the city, some of whom had carts because they had been told there was plenty of loot in the city and the sooner they got their share the better. Church parade was held in the garden and Dyer took the opportunity to address the men and warn them of the dangers of seeking personal reprisals against anyone for the murders and the assault on Miss Sherwood. He then decided to enter the city with an impressive force of men and issue a proclamation about which there could be no possible doubt. Captain Briggs drafted it and Dyer approved of the wording. It was then handed to Miles Irving who translated it into Urdu. He made one slight but extremely important addition: he inserted the two words 'if necessary' at the end.

At 10.30 a.m. Dyer went through the city with a formidable show of force. The column of British and Indian soldiers marched ahead of a car containing Dyer, his Brigade Major and Miles Irving. Following in a police car were Rehill and Plomer. The two armoured cars made up the rear.

Dyer told Lieutenant-Colonel Morgan, 'If we are not back by 2 p.m. you must come into the city with the rest of the troops and look for us.'

Heading the column of marching soldiers was Inspector Khan mounted on a white horse, and behind him trundled a bamboo cart which contained a drummer and the Naib-Tahsildar, the official town crier who would read the proclamation aloud in Urdu, and a second man who would make an on-the-spot translation into Punjabi.

The column halted at nineteen places in the city and the drummer summoned the crowd to gather around while the proclamation was read out:

1 It is hereby proclaimed to all whom it may concern, that no person residing in the city is permitted or allowed to leave the city in his own private or hired conveyance, or on foot, without a pass from one of the following officers:
The Deputy Commissioner
The Superintendent of Police, Mr Rehill
The Deputy Commissioner, Mr Beckett

     Mr Connor, Magistrate
     Mr Seymour, Magistrate
     Agher Mohammad Hussain, Magistrate
     The Police Officer in charge of the city Kotwali
     This will be a special form and pass.

2 No person residing in Amritsar City is permitted to leave his house after 8 p.m. Any persons found in the streets after 8 p.m. are liable to be shot.

3 No procession of any kind is permitted to parade the streets in the city or any part of the city or outside of it at any time. Any such processions or gatherings of four men will be looked upon and treated as an unlawful assembly and dispersed by force of arms if necessary.

A great many heard the summons by drum-beat, but the mere sight of the soldiers and the armoured vehicles was enough to send them scampering to safety. Thousands who did hear the proclamation were arrogantly defiant. Some banged empty kerosene tins and shouted, 'The British Raj is at an end'. A voice was heard above the hubbub shouting, 'We will hold a meeting, let us be fired at'.

The procession took more than two hours to tour the city, and by then the heat was like a furnace when the door is opened. Dyer ordered the column to return to the Ram Bagh. It was too hot, he decided, to go any further. In any case, he reasoned, the news of the proclamation would soon be spreading by word of mouth to those who had not actually heard it.

During the tour Dyer and the police officers were receiving reports from informers and C.I.D. officers, and at 12.40 p.m. the General was told that a meeting was to be held in the Jallianwala Bagh later that afternoon.

Surprisingly he decided not to visit the Jallianwala Bagh or the Golden Temple, the two places where the proclamation would have been most effective. Admittedly he was a stranger in the town, but that did not explain why neither Rehill nor Plomer pointed out the omissions. Soon afterwards Rehill informed Dyer that a large crowd was already beginning to gather in the Jallianwala Bagh in defiance of the proclamation. At 4 p.m. Mr Lewis, the manager of the Crown Cinema, suspected by many Indians to be an undercover agent, arrived at Dyer's headquarters. He had been touring the streets disguised as a native, and he confirmed that the meeting was definitely going to be held.

Dyer, meantime, had been working out his plan of action, and by the time Lewis had reported to him it had matured. He ordered a small force of men to be mustered, consisting of twenty-five armed men from the 1/9th Gurkhas, twenty-five from the 54th Sikhs Frontier Force and 59th Rifles Frontier Force, and forty Gurkhas armed only with kukris. In addition, extra men were detailed to be dropped off at various picket points.

Within a few minutes Amritsar witnessed the now familiar sight of a column of men marching through the streets. Dyer followed the marching men in his car which contained his personal bodyguard, Sergeant William Anderson of the Londons, and Captain Briggs, his Brigade Major. In a second car were the police officers, Rehill and Plomer. The two armoured cars made up the rear of the column.

If it crossed the minds of any of the Europeans that it seemed a trifle odd that the General should have taken personal control of the operation, no one spoke his thoughts aloud. Neither did anyone comment that it seemed even stranger that with all the soldiers at his disposal he should have selected the relatively raw Gurkhas, many of whom had never fired a rifle before. Even more remarkable was the absence of the most important civilian official in Amritsar, Mr Miles Irving, the Deputy Commissioner. Although Dyer had in his pocket written evidence that Irving had handed over responsibility, it had been agreed that he would still consult him. But Irving was at that moment catching up on his sleep.

Only a few minutes remained before sunset when the column approached the narrow entrance to the Jallianwala Bagh. Dyer immediately ordered the fifty riflemen and forty Gurkhas with kukris to enter at the double. He followed close behind with Briggs and Anderson at his side. The two armoured cars remained in the street outside: the entrance was too narrow for them to enter.

5. The Massacre

'But this unexpected gift of fortune, this unhoped for defiance, this concentration of the rebels in an open space — it gave him such an opportunity as he could not have devised. It separated the guilty from the innocent, it placed them where he would have wished them to be — within reach of his sword.' — Ian Colvin, The Life of General Dyer.

Hans Raj had had an extremely busy morning making the final arrangements for the mass meeting in the Jallianwala Bagh. A platform for the speakers and poets had been erected near the well and a squad of hired sweepers had scurried across the dusty surface trying to make it as clean as possible. The energetic Raj had even had the foresight to arrange for water carriers to move among the crowd dispensing drinks. Among them was Udham Singh from the nearby Sikh Orphanage. Long before the appointed time people began drifting into the garden, seeking out spots under the few trees.

Just before the meeting was due to start Hans Raj was observed to be in whispered conversation with two detectives from the C.I.D. who had beckoned him aside. No one paid too much attention to the fact that, despite his political activities and the prominent part he had played in calling the illegal meeting, the young man seemed able to remain on amiable terms with the C.I.D. Several other police officers were noticed in and around the Bagh and three had set up an observation post in the house of Mr Raiz-ul-Hasan which overlooked the Bagh. They were uninvited guests, and the unfortunate owner was forced to keep guard outside his own premises while they maintained their watch. The presence of so many policemen had a disquieting effect on some of the people, but there were others who had reason to be grateful for their attendance; they were tipped off to beat a hasty retreat and not hang around for the meeting to start. Among them was Khusal Singh who was on his way to the garden when he encountered a

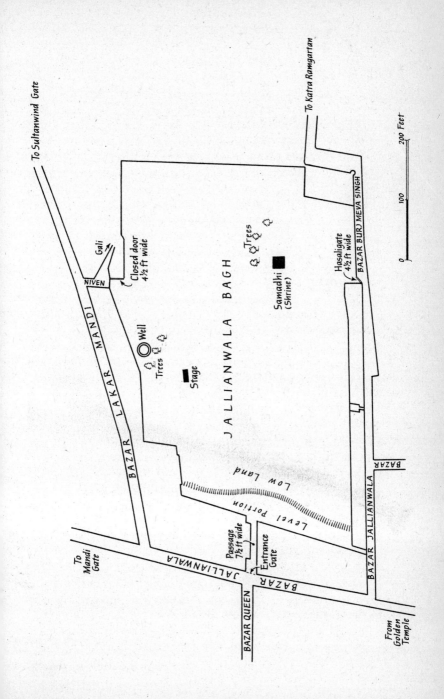

friend who was standing chatting to Raiz-ul-Hasan. He advised him to leave as he had been told the soldiers would be arriving soon and would open fire. He wisely took the hint and went home.

When the meeting opened a picture of Doctor Kitchlew was prominently displayed and two resolutions were passed. One called for the repeal of the Rowlatt Acts, the other condemned the firings of the previous day and expressed profound sympathy for the dead and bereaved. A few poems more marked by fervour than talent were recited, and a number of speeches were made.

The crowd in the garden was vast. No one was sure just how many people were present and estimates varied from 15,000 to 50,000. But they were by no means a captive audience; some were only half-listening, while others showed a total disinterest in politics, preferring to sleep, play cards and dice, or simply gossip. Others kept guard over piles of shoes and sandals and other personal belongings placed in their custody by friends who had gone to the Temple.

Soon afterwards a strange noise was heard overhead, and as it got louder they gazed up and saw the unfamiliar spectacle of a spotter plane flying low over the garden. A small flag fluttered in its slipstream and some people swore they saw Hans Raj wave a handkerchief towards it. Others claimed that with its appearance the police officers in the garden made a rapid departure. Few had ever seen an aeroplane before and its sudden and unexpected appearance had a distressing effect and many decided to leave. Among them was Mulchand, son of Lala Mohanlal Khatri, but he was dissuaded by Hans Raj who told him it was only doing its job and they should remain in their places and do theirs. The panic was short-lived for the plane gained height and was soon out of sight.

The arrival of the plane had made Durgas Dass, the editor of *Waqt*, pause while moving a third resolution which criticized the repressive measures adopted by the Punjab Government. With its departure he carried on. Suddenly the sound of heavy boots was heard in the Bagh and soldiers appeared at the double through the narrow passageway at one end of the garden and began to spread out along the raised earth platform on either side. People close to the stage said that the arrival of the soldiers seemed to coincide with Hans Raj again waving his handkerchief. The time was roughly 5.15 p.m.

A section of the crowd began to chant '*Agaye, agaye*' (They have come, they have come), and rose as if about to leave; but Hans Raj shouted at the top of his voice urging them to remain. 'Don't be afraid. Sit down. Government will never fire.'

Dyer shouted, 'Gurkhas right, 59th left. Fire' The order was immediately repeated by the young British subaltern in command of the Indians. The fifty soldiers knelt, raised their rifles, took aim and fired a volley into the heart of the crowd gathered near the platform. Hans Raj leapt down and shouted, 'They are only blanks.' Then he vanished.

As people began to fall dead and wounded, the crowd rose and ran in all directions in a desperate attempt to escape the hail of bullets. There was total panic as people fought to find a way out.

William Anderson was standing behind the General and a little to his right when the first volley was fired. He glanced around and noticed that Captain Briggs was just ahead of him while Mr Plomer was standing on the left of Dyer. As the shots rang out the whole crowd seemed to sink to the ground in a flurry of white garments. Seconds later the horror of the situation struck home and people began running for the walls and clambering over while others streamed towards the entrance through which the troops had emerged. Anderson particularly noticed that there was no attempt to rush the troops and that the subaltern kept his eyes firmly on the General and when he repeated his orders the men obeyed him implicitly. The kneeling soldiers continued to fire with accuracy and deliberation, carefully selecting their targets and making each round tell. When the soldiers had emptied their magazines, Dyer ordered them to reload and continue independent rapid fire, and to direct their fire where the crowd was densest. Anderson glanced at Briggs and noticed that he was puckering his face as if in pain and plucking at Dyer's sleeve, but he did not speak and the General ignored him and did not divert his attention from the slaughter that was taking place a few yards below and in front of him. An eerie silence filled the Bagh when the magazines were once again empty, and in the brief lull during which the soldiers replenished them Anderson heard Plomer remark to Dyer that he had taught the crowd a lesson it would never forget.

Dyer was so totally absorbed that he did not hear the policeman; instead he cast his eyes around the scene of confusion below and ordered the soldiers to fire towards the peepul trees where a large number of people were seeking shelter. The soldiers were as disciplined and calm as marksmen at the butts, and there was no wild or sporadic firing. William Anderson was bewildered by what was going on. Briggs was most impressed that not one man had hesitated and none had fired high. It was a point he stressed afterwards, for some people later swore that they heard an officer shout, 'Why are you firing high? Fire low. For what else have you been brought here?'

People who were watching from the windows and roofs of houses overlooking the garden were in no doubt that some of the soldiers had also fired at them, and they pointed out in proof that people in second- and third-storey rooms were wounded and that the walls of many houses were pock-marked with bullet holes.

But there was no dispute about the effectiveness of the firing into the heart of the crowd in the Jallianwala Bagh. The people were trapped and no matter which way they ran there was no escape from the firing. Some bullets tore through soft flesh and exited to claim other victims. And so concentrated was the fire that several people received numerous wounds, each of which would have been fatal.

Several buffaloes died as the bullets smacked home. As people fell others collapsed on top of them, and many who escaped the rain of bullets died agonizingly of suffocation. Others owed their lives to the protective shield of fallen bodies. Among them was the orphan Udham Singh who was struck in the arm but saved from further injury by sheltering under a pile of dead and wounded.

From his vantage point on the platform of stamped-down earth, General Dyer continued to direct the fire towards people trying to scale the walls and those who were scrambling blindly for the few narrow exits. Some sought shelter behind the small samadhi (shrine), but they were ruthlessly cut down. Many of those who had managed to scramble over the walls dropped dead from their injuries and the narrow alleys outside the Bagh were soon choked with corpses. In one narrow passageway 150 bodies were heaped on each other like carcasses in an abattoir.

Incredibly, despite the danger from wayward bullets, people continued to watch the slaughter from the windows of their homes.

For many trapped in the garden, the deadly fire meant the slaughter of the totally innocent, for they had arrived in Amritsar to celebrate Baisakhi and had made their way to the Jallianwala Bagh totally ignorant of Dyer's proclamation or the protest meeting. Atma Singh Sidhu, a teacher from the O'Brien High School at Mianawali, was one. He was on a fortnight's holiday and had not even arrived in Amritsar when the proclamation was made. He had gone to the Bagh out of sheer curiosity. He was standing by the platform when the first shots rang out and as he dived for cover he saw people toppling into the well and others diving in after them. The well provided shelter from the bullets but not safety, and many drowned. The terrified schoolmaster was hurled to the ground by the weight of falling bodies and was one of the fortunate people who survived unscathed.

Daulat Ram Bhatia had gone with his school friend Ram Nath to listen to the speeches. As he sat on the ground, he heard shouts of 'Army here, Army here'. Immediately the rifles opened fire and he heard someone shout out that the soldiers were only firing blanks. Seconds later a bullet ploughed through his leg and another went through the upper jaw of his classmate killing him instantly. He found shelter behind the peepul tree and stayed there, drenched with blood, until the firing ceased and the soldiers departed. It was his fifteenth birthday.

Pratap Singh was one of many who had foolishly taken his small son to the meeting and got trapped in the lethal cross-fire, but by some miracle he and his son were not hit. They began to scramble over the mounting pile of bodies in a desperate attempt to get clear. Then he lost hold of the child and was knocked down. People clambered over him in the mad mêlée and he was soon a mass of cuts and bruises. Unable to breathe under the stifling blanket of corpses he resigned himself to dying, but somehow he managed to wriggle free and clamber over a wall into a lane. Then he heard a terrified voice screaming, 'They are coming again. They are coming again'. In a blind panic he started to run. 'Has anyone seen my child?' he cried.

89

No one had. He ran home, but there was no sign of his son and he began to organize a search party. The child then appeared at the door, terrified but unharmed.

As the soldiers fired, reloaded and fired again, the panic was indescribable. A boy of twelve lay with a dead baby in his arms. The corpses of many children littered the ground.

Girdhari Lal, the deputy chairman of the Punjab Chamber of Commerce, watched the scene through a pair of binoculars from the roof of an overlooking house. He was one of the fortunate; he had intended going to the meeting but first he had gone to pray and just as he was heading for the Jallianwala Bagh he saw the soldiers arrive.

Outside the Bagh escapers ran naked through the streets. Some dropped dead in their tracks. The Navi Gali, close to the Sultanwind Gate, was blocked with bodies, and corpses choked the Hansli, a narrow lane with a drainage trench beside it.

For ten minutes the firing continued, broken only by the occasional pause as the soldiers reloaded. When the soldiers had almost expended their ammunition, Dyer ordered them to cease fire: 1,650 rounds of .303 Mark VI ammunition had been fired into the crowd.

Those Gurkhas who were armed only with kukris were ordered down on to the flat where they drew their knives and advanced in extended order for a few yards before being ordered to withdraw by the European subaltern in command.

Dyer calmly gave the order for the force to withdraw. They left by the same narrow entrance, sloped their weapons and began the march back to the Ram Bagh. Dyer strode briskly to his waiting car without so much as a backward glance at the scene of carnage in the garden. He was glad that some had escaped for they would serve as messengers to warn others of the dire consequences of rebellion.

The Jallianwala Bagh now resembled a deserted battlefield. The dead were deepest by the walls and the exits where people had tried to get out. Among them were a great many peasants and their children who had come from outside villages for the Baisakhi fair. The water in the overflowing well had turned crimson.

The nameless Gurkhas had performed their duty with a relish that characterized the bitterness and rivalry that existed between the hill men and the people from the plains. If they had disobeyed Dyer's orders they would have been court-martialled, but that fear was never uppermost in their minds for much later two of them gloatingly told a British official, 'Sahib, while it lasted it was splendid: we fired every round we had'. They remained nameless; none of them was ever asked to give evidence at the Hunter Inquiry.

✻   ✻   ✻

People living in the labyrinth of narrow streets that surrounded the Jallianwala Bagh had heard the crash of the first volley which sounded like the single crack from a big cannon, and immediately realized something awful was happening in the heart of the city. Crowds of women who knew their men and children were inside the garden began to hurry towards the sound. They stopped as they neared the Jallianwala Bagh and stood terror-stricken as the crack of rifles echoed in the evening air. It was not until the armoured vehicles and motor cars moved off, followed by the soldiers, that they ventured into the Bagh.

Sardhar Partap Singh, a bookseller, ran towards the scene with a heavy heart for he knew his son had gone there. Men with blood streaming from gaping wounds rushed past him, others crawled along like stricken animals. Those less seriously injured managed to reach a doctor, but the surgeries of the local medical men were overcrowded and facilities were totally inadequate for the treatment of many of the wounds.

The bookseller passed the Hansli ditch, a feed stream from the nearby canal. Part of it was covered but a large hole at an intersection was exposed. Breathless from his exertions he paused for a drink but recoiled in horror when he saw it was choked with bodies. Suddenly a head emerged and a voice enquired, 'Are the soldiers gone?' and he realized that several people had sought the company of the dead in order to remain alive.

Desperately anxious for the safety of his son, he hauled himself over a wall, using the bodies at the base as a ladder, and began his grisly search. He turned over the dead and rummaged among the wounded, pulling them aside to expose those buried underneath. All the time he was calling out his son's name, but his voice was drowned by the cries of the injured.

He spent twenty minutes looking for him, but by then the sky was darkening and further searching was pointless. He returned home to find his son safe and unharmed.

In the city itself there were many who were prepared to die rather than wait until daylight and the lifting of the curfew. So, under cover of the sheltering darkness, they began to creep into the garden. Those who were lucky enough to recover the dead or wounded bodies of their loved ones bundled them on to charpoys and hurried away. The searchers worked feverishly, fearful that the soldiers would return and open fire on them for breaking the curfew.

No such fears inhibited the jackals, pi-dogs and vultures attracted by the stench of blood and this unexpected banquet of human flesh. The ever-ravenous kites were so anxious to gorge themselves that in their haste they swooped down and soared off with the turbans of the searchers dangling from their talons.

Not all the people who went inside were searching for members of their families; some were prompted by humanitarian reasons. The tormented cries of those pleading for water so moved them that they risked their lives to give some temporary relief to their suffering. The wounded Udham Singh, who had gone there as a water-carrier, remained behind to continue his task.

As night drew on more and more people began to leave the garden. Unable to locate those they were seeking, they decided it was foolhardy to risk being shot down when the patrols toured the city to see that the curfew was being observed. And so they returned home, not knowing whether they had left behind a corpse or abandoned a badly wounded relative.

Several women, however, remained totally indifferent to personal danger and continued their heartbreaking search. Attaur Kaur, the twenty-five-year-old wife of a firewood dealer, had last seen her husband when he left home that morning with 700 rupees for a business transaction. Although she had heard the firing she was not unduly worried. He had not said he was going to the meeting. But her apprehension increased as the hours passed and he did not return home. Finally she set off to search for him in the Jallianwala Bagh. Eventually she found her husband lying at the base of one of the walls. He had been shot in the legs and chest and one ear was missing, but his eyes were open as if still capable of sight. She repeatedly massaged his feet and hands before finally accepting that he was dead and giving vent to her grief. A water boy — some said it was Udham Singh — hastened to her side and she asked him to keep watch while she went off to fetch a charpoy. When she returned with the cot they carried the body home.

Rattan Devi was lying down in her home near the Jallianwala Bagh when the first shots were fired. There was no agonizing period of suspense for her; she knew her husband had gone to the meeting at 4 p.m., so as soon as the soldiers had left she went to the Bagh and in a very short time she found her husband's dead body. She called out to two boys to hurry to her home and bring back a charpoy, but by then the curfew was in operation and they were scared to return to the Bagh. So she remained there in the pitch dark, weeping and waiting for daylight. As snarling dogs encircled her she groped around and found a stout bamboo stick with which to beat them away from the corpse of her husband. A twelve-year-old boy who was lying close by begged her not to leave him alone, and she consoled him by saying that she would not leave as she had to watch over her husband. A clock nearby struck the hours informing her of the passage of time. At 2 a.m. a Jat who was trapped near a wall asked her to help him free his legs; she did so and got soaked with his blood. It was nearly dawn when people began to converge on the garden once more. At 6 a.m. the boys who had gone to collect a charpoy returned with it and helped her carry her husband home.

'What I experienced that night is known only to me and God,' said Rattan Devi. (Months later a Government official called on the two women and offered them 25,000 rupees in compensation for the loss of their husbands. Both declined.)

Those who had refused to venture out to succour the wounded justified their action by pointing out that General Dyer had not issued an empty threat against anyone defying his curfew orders. That night he had set out from the Ram Bagh with an armed force, visited the pickets and city gates and toured the streets to make sure that it was being observed. He found the streets deserted and the city absolutely quiet. Fortunately the soldiers did not consider it necessary to visit the Jallianwala Bagh. If they had they would have been faced with a decision of horrific proportions.

❖   ❖   ❖

At 11.15 p.m. Lahore received the first news of the shooting but the reports were vague and confused. It was not until 3 a.m. the following day that O'Dwyer was roused from his sleep by the arrival of Mr G. A. Wathen, the Principal of Khalsa College, and Mr Jacob, a member of the Indian Civil Service who had raced from Amritsar on a motor-cycle to deliver a personal despatch from Miles Irving. The Deputy Commissioner had not been told of Dyer's proposed action and his terse message conveyed the alarm and surprise he felt:

> The military found a large meeting of some five thousand men and opened fire without warning, killing about 200. Firing went on for ten minutes. I much regret I was not present.

O'Dwyer seemed far more concerned about the incorrect information the two men imparted — namely that the firing had been carried out by British troops. He had told Dyer to use Indian troops as much as possible during the disturbances.

Mr Wathen's dramatic ride through the night did not impress him; he thought he had panicked. Neither did it occur to him to ask why the news had been delivered in such an unconventional manner and by one of the few Europeans who had repeatedly counselled caution, or why Irving had been allowed to sleep through the shooting.

The Lieutenant-Governor immediately sent off a wireless message to the Government of India which contained the barest details:

> At Amritsar yesterday Brigadier-General Dyer and Deputy Commissioner read proclamation in city forbidding all public meetings. Prohibition proclaimed by beat of drum and read and explained at several places in city. In spite of this, meeting attended by six thousand was held at 4.30 contrary to Deputy Commissioner's expectations. Troops present under command of General Dyer fired, killing about two hundred. Deputy Commissioner not present. Military report not yet received.

He went on to say that the city was now quiet although the

political situation in the surrounding area was not certain and the loyalty of some Indian troops was in doubt. In view of that, extra troops were being drafted to Lahore. He added that a large mob had meanwhile attacked the railway station at Wagah, sections of the line had been uprooted and an armoured train which had left Lahore had also been derailed. The situation seemed serious but not explosive.

Within a short space of time O'Dwyer was painting a very different picture. After consultations with General Sir William Beynon and Sir Henry Rattigan, the Chief Justice, he sent another communication to Simla. Timed at 3 p.m. it reported that stations between Kasur and Amritsar had been looted and two British officers injured and a British soldier killed. Bands of marauding rebels were on the move and the treasuries at Kasur and Tarn Taran attacked:

> State of open rebellion exists in parts of districts of Lahore and Amritsar. Lieutenant-Governor, with concurrence of General Officer Commanding 16th Division and Chief Justice High Court, requests Governor-General in Council to suspend functions of ordinary Criminal Courts in Amritsar and Lahore districts to establish martial law therein.

The message went on to ask for special tribunals to be set up to try people accused of offences arising from the disturbances.

The Viceroy approved, but owing to the breakdown in communications the answer was not received in Lahore until the 14th and martial law was not proclaimed in Lahore and Amritsar districts until the following day. The delay was to assume considerable significance later and become part of a long-drawn-out controversy and a bitter legal wrangle.

※　　　※　　　※

On the 14th the streets of Amritsar came to life again. A deputation asked Dyer for permission to bury and burn the dead, and this he granted, with a stern warning that there must be no demonstrations of any kind and mourners must return to the city immediately after the ceremony.

Crowds of people began to leave their homes and make their way to the Jallianwala Bagh to collect the dead and wounded. Long processions of wailing mourners filed through the Chatiwind Gate behind carts piled high with bodies. There were so many corpses that religious observances were ignored and four or five bodies were cremated on the same pyre.

The mourners made no attempt to arrive at an accurate count of those killed: there seemed an almost indecent haste to destroy any evidence as to who was actually at the prohibited meeting for fear that relatives would be found guilty of an offence through association. As a result no one was sure of the death toll and estimates varied widely. The Indians who survived and chronicled their stories put the number of dead at around 500, although they claimed that 1,000 was a more realistic figure. The Government of India put the figure much lower, but did not initiate a detailed investigation into the casualties until four months after the shooting.

Later that day Dyer wrote his official report of the incident, which he sent to General Beynon. In formal military phrases he outlined all that had happened since his arrival in the city, ending with the news that a meeting held in defiance of his orders had been dispersed.

I entered the Jallianwala Bagh by a very narrow lane which necessitated leaving my armoured cars behind. On entering I saw a dense crowd, estimated at about 5,000 (those present put it at 15,000 to 20,000); a man on a raised platform addressing the audience and making gesticulations with his hands.

I realized that my force was small and to hesitate might induce attack. I immediately opened fire and dispersed the mob. I estimated that between 200 and 300 of the crowd were killed. My party fired 1650 rounds.

I returned to my headquarters about 1800 hours. At 2200 hours, accompanied by a force, I visited all my pickets and marched through the city in order to make sure that my order as to inhabitants not being out of their homes after 2000 hours had been obeyed. The city was absolutely quiet and not a soul was to be seen. I returned to headquarters at midnight. The inhabitants have asked permission to bury the dead in accordance with my orders. This I am allowing.

(Signed) R. E. H. Dyer, Brigadier-General. Commanding 45th Brigade

It did not give Beynon a true picture of what had taken place, and clearly showed that Dyer had left the dead and wounded

Brigadier-General R.E.H. Dyer, GOC Amritsar, 1919.

(*above*) Sir Michael O'Dwyer, Lieutenant-Governor of the Punjab in 1919.

(*below*) Lord Chelmsford, Viceroy of India.

(*above*) Sergeant Anderson, Dyer's personal bodyguard during the massacre.
(*below*) Edwin Montagu, Secretary of State for India.

(*above left*) Lord Hunter. He presided over the inquiry that censured Dyer.

(*above right*) Miss Marcia Sherwood, the missionary beaten by the Amritsar mob, from the *Daily Express* of 16 December 1919.

(*above*) The interior of the National Bank in Amritsar after the riots.
(*below left*) Udham Singh being led from Caxton Hall by detectives following O'Dwyer's murder.

(*below*) Amritsar, the administrative capital of the Punjab.

A contemporary photograph of the recess in which Miss Sherwood hid during the riots—the Indian is demonstrating her hiding place.

The 'crawling lane', where Miss Sherwood was beaten for the second time.

(*opposite inset*) The house in which Mrs Easdon took shelter from the mob.

Dyer ordered that Indians must crawl along the street in which Miss Sherwood was assaulted—three British soldiers enforce the order at bayonet point.

lying in the Jallianwala Bagh for several hours. This seemed to have escaped Beynon who turned to Sir Michael O'Dwyer and told him he was conveying his approval of the action and asked the Lieutenant-Governor to endorse it. O'Dwyer agreed and Sir William sent off a personal message by aeroplane:

Your action correct and Lieutenant-Governor approves.

It was one of the shortest yet most controversial signals of the thousands that were despatched during the Punjab disturbances. It was certainly to haunt O'Dwyer in the months to come. While he never denied giving his approval, he qualified it by saying he would not have done so if he had been fully aware of what had happened at the Jallianwala Bagh. But his Indian critics were quick to point out than no one took more care than O'Dwyer to ensure that the full facts were suppressed for as long as possible.

✻   ✻   ✻

General Dyer may have quashed the rebellion but he had not restored Amritsar to normality. The city grieved, the shops and businesses remained closed and the people stayed indoors. It was a situation that could not be permitted to continue. Irving, who had not been consulted or informed about the show of force at the Jallianwala Bagh, emerged to take an active interest in the life of the city. He summoned the leading Europeans to a meeting, and they arrived wearing their pistols at their sides. The bellicose Lieutenant-Colonel Smith was all in favour of a further dose of shooting and even gained some support for a suggestion that the town should be bombarded from the air to bring the population to its senses. Mr Wathen once again advocated caution by strenuously arguing against such a drastic step: if anything happened to the Golden Temple, the British would permanently alienate the Sikhs from whom the army drew a large proportion of its soldiers. But the meeting agreed that Amritsar must resume normal life without further delay.

Soon afterwards local magistrates, Ward Members, lawyers and prominent businessmen were ordered to attend a meeting at the Kotwali. There Mr Kitchin, speaking in Hindustani, berated them:

> Do you people want peace or war? We are prepared in every way. The Government is all-powerful . . . It is capable of doing anything. The General will give orders today. The city is in his possession. I can do nothing. You will have to obey orders.

He then walked out. At 5 p.m., according to the Indians present, Dyer, Irving and the two senior police officers, Rehill and Plomer, arrived. The leading citizens were left in no doubt that the patience of the British had run out, for they were then subjected to a further harangue by Irving who was unable to contain his bitterness:

> If anyone has any trouble, say so, I shall listen. You have committed a bad act in killing the English. Their revenge will be taken from you and from your children. You people must open shops at once. The Government is very angry with you. You cannot fight the Government. I shall severely punish anyone who will talk against the Government.

The stilted and clipped phrases were how the Indians present translated them into English.

But their verbal chastisement was still far from over. Dyer then launched into an angry tirade in Urdu:

> You people know well that I am a soldier and a military man. Do you want war or peace? And if you wish for war the Government is prepared for it, and if you want peace, then obey my orders and open all your shops, else I will shoot. For me the battlefield of France or Amritsar is the same. I am a military man, and will go straight. Neither shall I move to the right, nor to the left. Speak up if you want war. In case there is to be peace, my order is to open all shops at once. Your people talk against the Government, and persons educated in Germany and Bengal talk sedition. I shall uproot these all. Obey orders. I do not· wish to hear anything else. I have served in the military for over thirty years. I understand the Indian Sepoy and the Sikh people very well. You will have to observe peace, otherwise the shops will be opened by force and by rifles. You must all inform me of the badmashes. I will shoot them. Obey my orders and open shops, and speak up if you want war.

Within a short time the shops and businesses were open.

The police immediately began a round-up of people who were suspected of having taken part in the rioting and who had attended the meeting. Doctors who had treated the wounded were asked to submit lists of names and those who protested that they had been too busy to take names were arrested. Mrs Nelly Benjamin, who had helped Mrs Easdon to escape from the mob, was threatened with arrest when she refused to name a man suspected of being one of the attackers. When that approach failed she was offered a reward, but again she refused. Arrests were indiscriminate and caused a deep sense of resentment among the people, who protested that the police were being over-zealous and making widescale arrests without any real evidence to back them up.

Many of those who were detained protested that they were tortured and held in indescribably filthy cells, were deprived of food and threatened with all kinds of reprisals if they did not give false evidence.

Hans Raj was among the first to be arrested, although there were a number of people who complained that he seemed to be receiving preferential treatment and seemed 'quite jolly' in the police station.

The complaints of police ill-treatment and brutality fell on deaf ears; it was no time for kid-glove treatment and this was spelled out in no uncertain manner by Major R. Shirley, the Provost-Marshal:

> The reluctance of the people of Amritsar City to give evidence which would lead to the arrest and punishment of conspirators and rioters was very noticeable indeed, and if doubtful methods were used to obtain information or if persecution by the police took place, the inhabitants of Amritsar themselves are more to blame than anyone else.

In retrospect such comments show a total disregard for justice, but at the time they had the almost universal backing of the European community. Furthermore, O'Dwyer seemed in total agreement with any harsh measures that were introduced. To make certain that no suspect eluded the massive round-up, martial law was backdated to 30 March which meant that Satyapal and Kitchlew, who were actually under arrest at the time of the troubles, could be put on trial.

A clamp-down on all news relating to the disturbances was

imposed and what appeared was heavily censored; and although newspaper reporters flooded into the Punjab, they were hampered in trying to find out what had actually taken place. Nothing, however, could prevent the news being passed by word of mouth, and very soon the story of the massacre was spreading like wildfire.

The story in the *Civil and Military Gazette* on 16 April under a small headline, 'Meeting dispersed at Amritsar', considerably underplayed the incident, and was totally inaccurate on the vital point that no warning was given before the firing started:

> An attempt to hold a proscribed meeting at Amritsar was frustrated, after the arrest of some ringleaders. The General, with only Indian troops and police, gave the orders to disperse. As the crowd refused to go the order to fire was given. There were heavy casualties amongst the mob, several hundreds being killed and injured and there was no further trouble.

At the same time, readers were also informed that martial law had been proclaimed in the Lahore and Amritsar districts.

On the same day that the news item appeared General Dyer and the Lieutenant-Governor met for the first time in Lahore, and the General gave a verbal account of what had happened in the Bagh. Recalling the meeting later, Sir Michael said that Dyer told him that he only opened fire when he feared his small force was about to be attacked. It was an important point and its omission from the press hand-out is hard to understand as it went a long way towards answering those Indian critics who said he had fired without cause or warning.

The amount of space given to the news item was a clear indication that it did not merit too much importance and the life of the Europeans continued very much as before.

Support for O'Dwyer was unqualified, as a leading article a few days later underlined:

> At first sight it may seem a misfortune that the last days of a brilliant Lieutenant-Governsorship, in which the fame and status of the Punjab have been raised to greater height than they have ever reached before, should be clouded by grave and widespread disorders, but there can be little doubt that

the firmness and courage with which Sir Michael O'Dwyer has met the crisis will, when the verdict of history comes to be written, be found to be by no means the least brilliant part of his administration. At all events we can speak for the whole European community of the Province, and we believe for a very large section of Indian opinion as well, in expressing profound thankfulness that the moment of crisis found so strong a hand at the helm.

In Amritsar nothing could silence the increasing anger and bitterness of the people over Dyer's action; there was hardly a family that had not been affected and there was no reluctance on their part to retell the story of the Jallianwala Bagh to anyone who was willing to listen. Eventually, Irving was forced to issue a statement warning the citizens against spreading false rumours and aimed at putting the General's action in a less horrifying light. He reminded them that the meeting had been called in flagrant defiance of Dyer's proclamation and that he had no alternative but to fire when his small force was in danger of being attacked:

> The Government is sorry that some innocent persons were seduced by wicked people to go there and got killed. But everyone should bear in mind that the Sahib General will not in future put up with any kind of unrest.

It inflamed rather than soothed their feelings; no one had yet explained how several children had been seduced into going to a political meeting.

※   ※   ※

In London Edwin Montagu became the target of much political sniping and accusations that he was withholding information about the true extent of the disturbances, and no denials by him could silence his critics. But, as the Cabinet Records reveal, he could not really be blamed for appearing vague; the information sent to him by the Viceroy was very sparse indeed, and in fairness to Lord Chelmsford it could be said with some justification that he too was kept in the dark by Sir Michael O'Dwyer.

At a secret War Cabinet Meeting on 14 April, presided over by Mr Bonar Law, Montagu reported that he had received three telegrams reporting further rioting. 'Though the situation gave cause for anxiety, he did not consider it serious.' One dated 11 April said there had been a slight disturbance at Lahore the previous day in connection with passive resistance, and a few shots had been fired on a mob which attempted to reach the civil station. Another dated the same day reported an attack on the city telegraph office at Ahmedabad, while a third from Amritsar reported serious rioting in the city which had resulted in the death of some Europeans.

Mr Montagu then read a telegram which he had received from the Viceroy, dated 14 April. The Viceroy said that it was difficult to attribute the present outbreak to any particular cause. Racial feeling, Mohammedan soreness, Rowlatt Bills, high food prices — no doubt all contributed. It was noteworthy that outbreaks had occurred at places where our policy had been repressive (Punjab), laissez-faire (Bombay), and also from mere accidental collision (Delhi).

The Minutes went on to record that the Viceroy had no indications of active disturbances outside the Punjab or Bombay areas, and that so far the active hostility had been confined to the town rabble.

Mr Montagu then told the meeting that in reply to a private question in the House he proposed reading out the telegrams.

When he did so next day he had to inform Members: 'I have little to add to the information that has appeared in the press.' It was an observation that did little to satisfy Members or enhance his own reputation.

The Times, normally renowned for its Indian coverage, seemed as much in the dark as anyone else. That morning a small item had disclosed that there had been serious rioting in the Punjab and Europeans had been murdered, but order restored when the mob had been fired on.

During the days that followed dribs and drabs of news continued to trickle through to The Times: planes had dropped bombs at Gujranwala and machine-gunned rioters.

On the 19th a paragraph announced:

There is no news of any troubles at Amritsar since the troops dispersed the rioters on Sunday with very heavy casualties.

This was followed by a 'Report from the Punjab':

At Amritsar, on 13 April, the mob defied the proclamation forbidding public meetings. Firing ensued, and 200 casualties occurred.

None of the reports, official or otherwise, gave any true indication of the extent of the troubles and the explanation given to readers was that the telegraph wires had been cut.

A leading article, in an attempt to shed some light on the riots, said:

> The rising has little or nothing to do either with the reforms or the Rowlatt Act. In essence it is a deliberate attempt to overturn British rule altogether.

The *Times* correspondent seemed singularly ill-informed as to what had been the main reason for the original agitation, if not the bloodshed, but it provided the newspaper with an opportunity to attack Montagu and praise Sir Michael O'Dwyer:

> The strongest Lieutenant-Governor in India who is just relinquishing his control of the Punjab, should be asked to remain at his post for the present. We owe it to his firm administration that the Punjab was safely guided through the troublesome period of the war. There are times when plain speaking is required, and it is necessary to say that Sir Michael O'Dwyer's successor does not possess the same qualifications for dealing with 'open rebellion'.

Sir Michael was asked to stay on for a while.

✣   ✣   ✣

On 16 April Lord Chelmsford was able to send Montagu a much more detailed despatch, but even that showed how little he knew about the situation in the Punjab or what had led up to it. He was still referring to slight disturbances caused by

> a population in many parts inclined to be lawless; a large number of disbanded soldiery, some puffed up by victory, others discontented at being demobbed, (I am enquiring of O'Dwyer how far this is so) high prices of food and a reaction from all the strain which the war has put on them. O'Dwyer has asked me for powers under Regulations X of 1804, as throughout the Lahore, Amritsar and Gujranwala districts bands were perambulating the country looting and

destroying. I assented with modification that in place of courts martial composed of young officers inexperienced and possibly prone to 'see red', I gave him tribunals of Defence of India standing with court martial powers. I am afraid summary justice is the only thing for wandering bands of marauders . . . Amritsar had a severe lesson the other day at the hands of the military, but it remains to be seen how far it will have been efficacious. I am hopeful that the strong measures we have taken may result in order being restored within a few weeks, but there are bound to be smouldering embers left.

The Viceroy was also happy to be able to assure Montagu that there had not been the slightest evidence of any wavering or disloyalty on the part of Indian troops, many of whom had taken part in the repressive measures.

Sir Michael O'Dwyer, meanwhile, was totally unruffled by suggestions that he had not kept Chelmsford fully informed of events, and on the same day that the Viceroy sent off his report to London the Lieutenant-Governor was apologizing for not having written more often; he had in fact tried three times, 'but events were moving so fast I could not get one through'. Nevertheless he was optimistic over Dyer's action for, as he wrote two days later, 'The Amritsar business cleared the air, and if there was to be a holocaust anywhere, and one regrets there should be, it was best at Amritsar.'

Soon afterwards he wrote to Chelmsford to inform him that Sir Edward Maclagan would be taking over on 26 May and to apologize for not having passed on as much as he might have done:

We were usually so busy here in dealing with the difficulties that it was not always possible to put before the Government of India a clear picture of the situation and justify ourselves before hostile critics outside the Province.

He was less insensitive, however, to the mounting criticisms of what was taking place in the Punjab under martial law:

It's all very well for armchair politicians in Bombay and Allahabad to cry out about harsh measures but martial law cannot be carried out without taking the kid gloves off.

At times the methods which he had employed may have seemed drastic to outsiders, but the Punjab and its people were different to any other province.

The Viceroy agreed and assured him he would 'not examine meticulously what was done'. Even so he expressed concern over some of the things he had read and heard and advised Sir Michael that no more force than was necessary should be used and the military should not be given an absolutely free hand.

6. Martial Law

'The Punjab was isolated, cut off from the rest of India; a thick veil seemed to cover it and hide it from outside eyes. There was hardly any news, and people could not go there or come out from there. Odd individuals, who managed to escape from that inferno, were so terror struck that they could give no clear account.'—Nehru: An Autobiography.

When martial law was introduced into the Punjab, it appeared to many Indians to be a classic case of shutting the stable door after the horse had bolted, not to say a spurious excuse to exact revenge. The rebellion had been suppressed and General Dyer was already being acclaimed as the 'Saviour of the Punjab' for his ruthless action which had nipped the rising in the bud and more or less quelled the people into total submission; all this he had accomplished before martial law had been officially proclaimed.

The people were stunned by the punitive measures introduced and the seemingly senseless and bizarre punishments meted out that made no distinction between the innocent and the guilty. Nor was it ever adequately explained to them by the Government why a new type of administration was temporarily required in order 'to secure unquestioning obedience to its orders', although they suspected it was because they had had the temerity to challenge the authority of the white man.

The role that the people of the Punjab had played in the war was forgotten; they were now mistrusted and maligned. The demand was for revenge and humiliation.

In Amritsar anyone who passed Dyer or any other European had to salaam. People of all ranks were forced to dismount from their transport and make obeisance; if they did not, they were flogged or arrested and made to suffer other indignities, often trivial in European eyes but of immense significance in a country where caste, religion and social status were of paramount importance.

106

Dyer was almost paranoid in his insistence that the saluting should be done properly. Lala Har Gopal Khanna, a Bachelor of Arts, complained that he was walking along a street with some friends when they encountered General Dyer with Mr Plomer, the Superintendent of Police, and an escort of mounted policemen. He promptly saluted in the normal military manner and was surprised to see the General beckoning him over; he again saluted but was told he did not know how to salaam properly, and should present himself at the Ram Bagh next day. Next morning he was taken to the General's headquarters where he was kept waiting in the blazing sun for a considerable time before being given a lesson by a Havildar in how to salaam correctly.

To enable the troops to move about the city, while at the same time restricting the movement of the native population, an Order was passed commandeering every means of transport. All the tongas, tumtums and gharries had to report to a special parking place each morning where they were detailed for duty at various offices and military billets which had been established in Amritsar.

If he was indifferent to the needs of the Indians, the General made certain that his soldiers were well looked after. The Londons, who had been through a particularly rough period and had gone for days without taking their clothes off, had much reason to be grateful. Every effort was made to make them as comfortable as possible and ensure that they did not suffer unduly in the heat. Every available fan was confiscated and fitted to the ceilings of their quarters in such numbers that 'the blades only missed each other by a hair's breadth'.

If it was the General's intention to get the city to return to normality as quickly as possible, he went about it in a manner that bemused the people.

The ninety-three lawyers in the city were forced to act as special constables, were made to do the work of coolies and to witness people being flogged in public. Their enforced enlistment was explained as being necessary for the maintenance of law and order. They assumed they were being punished for expressing professional objections to the Rowlatt Acts.

The railways were virtually closed to the natives as the issue of all third-class and intermediate tickets was withdrawn, the explanation being that it was necessary to stop them spreading false information outside the Province. Not more than two persons were allowed to walk abreast on the pavements and all cycles, other than those owned by Europeans, were called in. The measure struck the Indians as being as stupid as it was pointless: the cycle was the major means of transportation for most of them, so it had the effect of partially paralysing the city.

The city's water and electricity supplies were cut off in the Indian quarters, causing incredible hardship to tens of thousands who had taken no part in the disturbances. And in addition to a daily mounting list of restrictive orders, a rigid curfew operated which made any return to a normal existence virtually impossible. The people were so bewildered and terrified that when Dyer ordered that all cudgels and lathis should be handed in, they surrendered walking sticks, riding crops, fancy canes and anything else that could possibly be construed as a weapon.

Dyer himself presided over a court in the Ram Bagh and people complained bitterly that he did not seem to care whether or not they had committed any offence. Sirdar Atmar Singh, a wine merchant, said he was arrested in front of the General on the 13th; his hands were tied and he was dragged through the streets with others who had been arrested. Most of them were handcuffed and they were locked in a cell without food for two days before being paraded before the General who ordered them to be tied to a tree. They remained there until he had finished lunch; then he meted out his punishment. Sirdar Atmar Singh, who was never charged with anything, thought he got off lightly: he was sentenced to mount guard for eight days, but during his time in the police station he was relieved of a gold ear-ring and a valuable watch.

Unwittingly many people were guilty of committing minor breaches of martial law regulations, and though the General's punishments were not excessive in terms of physical pain or monetary suffering, pride was deeply wounded and that often hurt more.

At the same time, the police seemed to have been given carte blanche in their efforts to round up those suspected of having been involved in the rioting or taking part in protests. And as their superiors seemed to be motivated by the principle of a conviction at any cost, they did not feel at all inhibited in how they went about obtaining evidence. The authorities already seemed to have decided on those who were guilty; all that was required was independent confirmation, so the police embarked on a period of almost uninterrupted harassment, extortion and intimidation. Anyone suspected of being even remotely connected with the Congress Movement was considered fair game for police attention.

Maqbool Mahmood, the High Court lawyer who had risked his life trying to get the mob to disperse near the railway bridge when violence first erupted in Amritsar, was arrested and asked to identify the killers of Robinson and Rowlands; when he said he had already made a written statement saying he was unable to do so, his statement was produced and torn up in front of him. He was then asked to make a fresh one containing the names of people the police would provide. When he declined he was threatened with violence, but released without the threats being carried out. But his ordeal was far from over. When he was cited as a defence witness the police called him in and advised him against such a perilous step and pointed out that many people had refused to speak for the defence and he should do likewise. When he submitted that his conscience would not allow him to do so, he was warned that his pleader's (lawyer's) licence would be withdrawn.

Doctor Kidar Nath Bhandari, the Senior Assistant Surgeon at the hospital from which Mrs Easdon narrowly escaped the fury of the mob, was asked by the police to name her assailants; when he replied that he had not seen any of the attackers he was threatened with arrest. Mr Plomer, who was present at the time, made no attempt to stop his subordinate's intimidation, and the doctor and his assistant were marched off to the Kotwali. There he was told he was suffering for nothing; all he had to do was mention a few names. The doctor claimed that he and his assistant were kept at the police station for a week before being marched through the streets in handcuffs with sixty-two other prisoners to the local jail. The elderly doctor, who suffered from a heart condition, collapsed when he reached the prison. There his clothes became infested with lice, but a request to be allowed to change them was ignored. On 2 May, his story continued, he was seen by Mr Irving and when he asked why he was being detained the Deputy Commissioner replied that, though there was nothing against him, he had not

109

made any effort to help Mrs Easdon when her life was in danger. When he tried to explain that he had not been in a position to help, Irving simply said that he had only to mention a few names and he would be released. He and his assistant were set free a few days later without any charges being preferred.

Mrs Nelly Benjamin, the Sub-Assistant Surgeon, who was a friend of Mrs Easdon and who had deliberately misled the mob in order to facilitate her escape, complained that she was twice taken to the Kotwali and asked to name a certain man as one of the attackers. When she said she was not prepared to lie, Plomer threatened to throw her into jail. Having persistently refused to commit perjury she was then tempted with a reward if she identified the man. Again she declined.

Amritsar was alive with stories of police attempts to fabricate evidence, and a great many complained of being tortured, beaten and humiliated. The Kotwali was said to have resembled a primitive concentration camp; prisoners complained of being handcuffed together in pairs and not even separated when they went to the latrines. They were also deprived of food and kept in indescribably filthy conditions.

There was no love lost between the people of Amritsar and the police, and the opportunity to express their grievances to an Indian deputation investigating the troubles was readily seized upon. What was more impressive was the remarkable consistency of their allegations.

Seth Gul Mohammad, a glassware merchant, was arrested while he was at prayer and taken to the police station where an Inspector asked him to give evidence against Doctors Kitchlew and Satyapal. When he refused, he said, the Inspector pulled his beard and slapped his face before handing him over to some subordinates who placed his hand under the leg of a cot while eight of them sat on top. When the pain became unbearable he agreed to say whatever they asked, but when he was taken back to the Inspector he refused to incriminate the two doctors, whereupon he was beaten and caned on and off for eight days and told he would be hanged. Hans Raj, who was in the Kotwali advised him to do as he was told. When he appeared before the Martial Law Tribunal at Lahore he told the Judges he had been forced to commit perjury.

Person after person came forward with stories of alleged

torture by the police. The police vehemently denied all the allegations and the people who made them were never asked to repeat them before any official investigating body. They were all subsequently published in the Report of the sub-committee appointed by the Indian National Congress to inquire into the disorders. The report was largely ignored by the British authorities.

There was, however, one incident which no one attempted to deny and which aroused Indians to even greater anger than the shooting in the Jallianwala Bagh. It was General Dyer's notorious 'Crawling Order'.

On 19 April Dyer saw the bandage-swathed figure of Miss Sherwood lying on a bed in the Fort. The missionary, who resembled an Egyptian mummy, was in considerable pain and her life still hung in the balance. He was so outraged that he decided a special punishment would have to be devised for the cowardly attack on the woman who had done so much for the local people. As he held all white women to be sacred he ordered that the Kucha Tawarian, the narrow lane in which the attack had taken place, should become hallowed ground. He went to the scene and ordered a tiktiki, or whipping triangle, to be erected in the middle, posted pickets at each end and issued instructions that any Indian who wished to pass along the lane would have to do so on all fours. It was not a rash decision for he had 'searched his brain for a suitable punishment' that would bring home to everyone the enormity of the crime. No one was exempt from the order; it applied to those living in the 150-yard-long lane, those living off it, and anyone else who was forced to visit it for business or other reasons. The lane, of Elizabethan narrowness, was heavily populated with three-storey dwellings with shuttered balconies that jutted out and almost touched; running off it were a series of blind alleys. It did not matter to the General that many of the people living there were entirely innocent and ignorant of the assault, or that some of them had attempted to hide Miss Sherwood.

Although Dyer preferred to describe his order as 'going on all fours', it in fact meant that people had to squirm along on their stomachs because soldiers stood over them and prodded them with rifle butts and bayonets if they lifted their legs or arms. Like most Indian streets, it was filthy and the dust and grit surface was littered with refuse and animal excrement. The

111

ordeal had to be suffered if anyone wanted to purchase a loaf of bread or some vegetables, or worship at the temple or go to work. As the order was a verbal one and had never been promulgated, most people only got to know of it by personal experience.

As the days passed and conditions worsened, the Kucha Tawarian became almost uninhabitable. In normal times it was a squalid, insanitary street, but during the seven days the order was in existence it became a foul-smelling, refuse-strewn sewer. Sweepers refused to carry out their duties and the primitive latrines remained unemptied because the men who drove the carts that carried away the night soil boycotted the area. Water-carriers stayed away, and the residents had to slink out under cover of darkness and fetch their own. The sick remained unattended because doctors had no wish to visit patients and arrive covered in filth and smelling like a dung heap. No one was excused the ordeal; even a man who had been blind for twenty years was made to crawl, and urged on his way by heavy army boots.

Dyer had erected the whipping triangle in the middle of the lane for the express purpose of publicly chastising the people responsible for the attack on Miss Sherwood, and when six youths were arrested on suspicion of having been involved he did not wait for them to be tried. He became a self-appointed judge and jury, reached his verdict and ordered them to be taken to the 'Crawling Lane', tied to the tiktiki and given thirty strokes each. It did not matter to him that they might have been punished unfairly; he had made up his mind that they were responsible, and that was good enough. Officially they were caned for a breach of Fort discipline, but he readily admitted that that was not the real reason.

The blunt and forthright Dyer had no time for legal niceties and could not understand the furore that developed over his act. He could not accept that the inalienable right of every British subject to be assumed innocent until proved guilty applied to Indians. Ironically, he was to protest that, when he was forced to leave the Army, justice had been denied him because he had never been put on trial.

Major Shirley, the Provost-Marshal for the area, was another soldier who could not understand all the fuss:

The fact that the men in question were whipped in this street, although not publicly, undoubtedly brought home to the native imagination that the protection of women was considered of primary importance to the authorities, although it might not be universally accepted by public opinion in the East; more especially was the effect salutary in Amritsar at the time, owing to the presence of large numbers of roughs and vagabonds then infesting the city, and from whom no woman would have been safe.

Dyer's action was also condoned by the Adjutant-General, Lieutenant-General Sir Havelock Hudson, during a debate in the Viceroy's Council:

I feel sure that the Council will agree that it is not surprising that the officer in command took the view that some unusual measures were necessary to bring home to the mob that such acts of violence directed against innocent women could not be tolerated. Something was required to strike the imagination and impress on all the determination of the military authorities to protect European women.

The 'Crawling Order' remained in effect until 24 April when Sir Michael O'Dwyer heard about it and asked the Viceroy to order its withdrawal. For O'Dwyer to have been shocked gives some indication of the deep resentment it caused, for he had seen nothing remiss in asking Lord Chelmsford for permission to erect a public scaffold in Kasur. The Viceroy refused and pointed out, 'We are living in the twentieth century and personally I could not revert to old time methods.'

Dyer was not alone in devising punishments that fitted the crime; what were called 'fancy punishments' were introduced in other parts of the Punjab, but the heavy censorship and closure of newspapers plus the restriction of movement meant it was some time before they became public knowledge.

Among the few voices raised in protest was that of Benjamin Guy Horniman, the outspoken editor of the *Bombay Chronicle* who for some time had been a thorn in the flesh of the Indian Government with his pungent criticisms of British rule. The opportunity to silence him came when he published a report smuggled out from the Punjab. He was deported to England on 26 April for 'acting in a manner prejudicial to public safety' and the publication of his newspaper was suspended. It was a move that boomeranged, for it failed to silence him. What could be done in India with impunity could not be done in England, and Horniman seized his deportation as an opportunity to write an account of events in the Punjab based on his personal experiences and observations:

> One of the greatest counts in the indictment against Sir Michael O'Dwyer, as Lieutenant-Governor of the Punjab, is the policy of concealment which he deliberately pursued. In the first place, from the beginning every newspaper in the Province was placed under pre-censorship by the Government and nothing, either by comment or reports of events, could be published without being submitted for official approval and sanction. In this way the publication of inconvenient exposures of the methods that were being pursued was prevented at one stroke.

To some extent Sir Michael O'Dwyer could claim with justification that the measures taken in the Punjab, no matter how repressive, had the approval of the Government of India, for after the initial rioting a resolution was passed on 14 April which stated:

> It remains for the Governor-General in Council to assert in the clearest manner the intention of the Government to prevent by all means, however drastic, any recurrence of these excesses. He will not hesitate to employ the ample military resources at his disposal to suppress organized outrage, rioting or concerted opposition to the maintenance of law and order.

With that clear direction, Sir Michael may have felt it was not necessary to keep Delhi informed of every decision and order made by the military men on the spot; after all, martial law meant that the civil administration had handed over to the army because it could not cope, and having done that it could hardly start objecting to the way they went about it. In any case, he fervently believed that the Punjab was entirely different to the rest of the country, and exceptional measures were required there to establish law and order.

The 'Crawling Order' clearly went beyond the wide range covered by 'exceptional', but there were other measures which in Indian eyes were just as deplorable but which met with the Lieutenant-Governor's approval.

Colonel Frank Johnson DSO, who was responsible for the administration of martial law in the Lahore area, was one of the officers severely criticized. Public floggings were commonplace until he was ordered to stop them. In the market place where some of the punishments were carried out, Europeans, including a number of women, stood urging the wielders of the cane to strike harder. It explained the mood of the British.

Colonel Johnson commandeered 800 tongas and motor-cars belonging to Indians, restricted rail travel, closed all the free restaurants, and arrested numerous people and held them in custody in abysmal conditions without any charge being made. He forced doctors to name those they had treated and put up martial law notices outside the homes of those he suspected of being disloyal in order that he could punish them if someone else removed them. 'I would do it again,' he said. 'It was one of the few brainwaves I had.' He was particularly harsh with students and some of their professors, forcing them to hold roll calls four times a day, and at one college the students were repeatedly forced to march seventeen miles in the heat of the day.

Colonel Johnson personally tried 277 cases which resulted in 201 convictions, and defendants complained that the trials were a mockery, as they were denied adequate legal representation because lawyers were afraid of being branded as seditionists.

At Kasur Captain Doveton made people skip, write poems and touch the ground with their foreheads, and he ordered a group of men to be flogged in front of an audience of prostitutes because they had visited a brothel during the hours of curfew. Indians were totally bewildered by the Captain's obscure sense of justice, for he often singled out the biggest boys for beatings irrespective of whether or not they were guilty.

In Kasur the population was also made to attend an identity parade and an entire wedding party, including the priest, was flogged for a breach of curfew regulations and for being an illegal gathering, as they numbered more than ten.

'Fancy punishments' were also introduced on the personal whim of officers in other parts of the Province. People protested that a British officer had punished them by covering them with whitewash; his explanation was that they had been unloading lime. Women claimed that their veils had been ripped off by Mr Bosworth Smith, a civil administrator who had then spat on them and called them 'flies, bitches, she-asses and swine'. Shopkeepers alleged that they were flogged when they refused to sell their goods at reduced prices to the army and police. Children were made to salute the Union Jack three times a day, and everywhere the salaam orders were ruthlessly enforced. People had to dismount from their vehicles or horses, lower their umbrellas, and step into the road if a European approached. At Wazirabad, a man who failed to salaam an officer was made to kiss his boots; others were ordered to prostrate themselves, rub their noses in the dust and grovel.

To some observers it seemed a curious coincidence that so many officers and officials should suddenly devise punishments that were not only so alike but so out of character with the British tradition of justice and impartiality. Horniman was one of them. He wrote:

> It seems hardly conceivable that fortuitous circumstances could have produced, at one moment and in one Province of the Empire, a coterie of officials who were capable of the frightful excesses which occurred in the Punjab last year. It is hardly credible that the moment should have found ready to hand the men to commit these excesses directly the opportunity occurred, and to vie with one another in their severity and cruelty. The question must suggest itself to the mind of those who know the British character as it really is, whether it was not by premeditated design that the right men were in their places ready for the job when the moment arrived.

However ugly the facts might appear, it was the duty of the British to investigate them without fear or favour or 'abandon our claim to be a justice-, humanity-loving people'.

Horniman was not a solitary white voice in a black wilderness. There were others who were alarmed at what was going on. Although the gagging of the press was extremely effective it was far from total. Several accounts were smuggled out and printed, and this led to demands for the Viceroy to intervene and curb the actions of O'Dwyer and his subordinates. But

Chelmsford was loath to interfere; the furthest he would go was to warn the Lieutenant-Governor of the perilous path he was treading. The 'Crawling Order' and the indiscriminate whippings particularly worried him:

> I would ask you, does not this particular form of punishment offend against all the canons of wise punishment? It is not a deterrent and it is calculated to leave behind a maximum of bitterness. It will be regarded as intended to aim at racial degradation. It is not imposed on the guilty but on Indians as a race. A punishment of this sort will be remembered with rancour long after the stern lessons of justice will be forgotten.

He went on to add that racial animosity, a big enough problem already, would be intensified a hundredfold as the stories spread. But a written caution was about as far as he was prepared to go, for he knew full well that he could not command the support of the majority of whites. Nevertheless, at the same time he was writing to Edwin Montagu saying, 'If only people would realize that the day has passed when you can keep India down by the sword'.

Lord Chelmsford, mistrusted by many of the British in India and not particularly popular with the Indians, had not stamped his period of office with the personal seal of authority; he would try and run with the hare and hunt with the hounds. He paid lip-service to the desire for widespread reforms while at the same time trying to placate those whites who were vehemently opposed to change of any kind. He tried to retain a foot in each camp by saying one thing in India and another in his confidential despatches to the Secretary of State.

His quandary was painfully evident in his correspondence with Montagu in which he criticized O'Dwyer in one sentence and then sought to justify his action in the next:

> As you may imagine at a time like this the European community is the most difficult. It is, of course, to a man a staunch admirer of O'Dwyer and the stern methods adopted in the Punjab . . . they have been most efficacious, but they would be decidedly out of place in any other Province.

Montagu's patience was being stretched to near breaking-point as more and more disturbing news reached London, and he became increasingly bitter over the way martial law was being applied. The vast distance that separated him from the country whose destiny was, theoretically at least, in his hands made his frustration more acute. It took weeks, often months, for news to reach him, and by the time he had reached a decision the situation had changed once more. Nevertheless he was firmly convinced that the measures taken to deal with sedition were ill-advised and would prove ineffective in the long run:

> It gives me furiously to think that the reasons which lead one to resort to this method in India, intimidation of witnesses, partial justice, exists in Ireland, where not only are judges sometimes partial, but juries may be partial and intimidated too. And yet the hardest-handed controller of law and order in Ireland has never been able to maintain anything comparable to the Rowlatt Act. You may say that Ireland is not in a happy condition to suggest an analogy with. Granted, but many a man has tried comparable action to Rowlatt action and many an Irishman will tell you that the condition of Ireland today is partly due to these efforts.

The prophetic words went unheeded, for as the Viceroy was quick to point out there was a growing demand for the methods adopted by O'Dwyer to be introduced into other parts of the sub-continent.

The rift between Montagu and the Viceroy widened with the exchange of every fresh batch of cables. And when Montagu heard the details of the 'Crawling Order' he gave vent to his anger and nothing that Chelmsford could say about General Dyer's past service could appease his wrath:

> I should not have complained if Dyer had lynched those who attacked the lady missionary. It was the savage and inappropriate folly of the Order which aroused my anger, and I did not communicate with you without taking advice. I cannot admit that any services that Dyer has rendered anywhere can atone for action of this kind. Why, for all that Dyer knew the very Sikh who rescued the missionary would have been subjected to his infamous order.

By now the Secretary of State had more or less made up his mind that there would have to be an inquiry into the 'allegations of needless brutality', but he was still wavering; after consultations with his colleagues he might drop the idea, but he thought that unlikely. What concerned him more than anything else was the fact that all the trouble seemed to have been in the Punjab.

> I am strongly suspicious that our old friend, firm government, the idol of the Club Smoking Room, has produced its invariable and inevitable harvest.

Montagu began to fear that his high ambitions were turning to dust, and he took to expressing his misgivings to the Viceroy and lamenting the fact that he had not been able to command the confidence of the British in India. 'In fact the only confidence that I have achieved is the wavering, flickering, fluctuating support of some Indians.' But what depressed him more was that he seemed to be acquiring a reputation for double dealing, falsification of records and untrustworthiness: an impression that was being carefully nurtured by his political enemies in India and at home. 'This is not any more pleasant because I am confident of its baseness,' he wrote.

*   *   *

Montagu was not alone in being riddled with self-doubts; General Dyer was beginning to have qualms about the wisdom of his action in the Jallianwala Bagh and he confided to a personal friend, 'I haven't had a night's sleep since that happened. I keep on seeing it all over again.' Any misgivings were, however, soon dispelled by the adulation that was heaped upon him. He was hailed not only as the 'Saviour of the Punjab' but the Saviour of India, and in a very short space of time he readily accepted the legend that was being created and convinced himself that his action had saved India from open revolution. He and his Brigade Major, Captain Briggs, were made honorary Sikhs at a ceremony in the Golden Temple. It was an astute political move, for it was seen as conclusive proof that the Sikhs of Amritsar had bestowed the rare honour as a token of their gratitude, and public recognition that the General had saved them from a blood bath.

The actual ceremony was described in the most colourful detail and the light-hearted dialogue that went on between the General and Arur Singh, Manager of the Temple, and several priests, gave a vivid impression of affection and respect.

'Sahib,' said the priests, 'you must become a Sikh even as Nikalseyan Sahib became a Sikh.' (John Nicholson, a British hero of the Mutiny).

The General thanked them for the honour, but he could not, as a British officer, let his hair grow long.

Arur Singh laughed. 'We will let you off the long hair.'

General Dyer offered another objection. 'But I cannot give up smoking.'

The priests conceded. 'We will let you give it up gradually.'

'That I promise you,' said the General, 'at the rate of one cigarette a year.'

The ceremony did in fact take place, but it did not delight the Sikh community; it enraged them. They pointed out that Arur Singh was a mere puppet figure, an official appointed by the Punjab Government, and the incident was dismissed as a blatant example of how the British administration used the Golden Temple for political purposes. As a result there was strong agitation for the ending of Government-appointed managers.

When the story began to circulate in India the authorities at the Golden Temple issued what was described as 'a sensational denial' and the Sikh League followed suit, and when it was repeated in Britain the Sikh community wrote a strongly worded letter to *The Times* which stated that the claim could not go unchallenged:

> General Dyer could not have been made a Sikh as he claims, without abjuring Christianity, which he does not seem to have done . . . The Golden Temple where General Dyer claims to have been so invested, be it remembered, is entirely managed by a nominee of the Punjab Government, and surely no martial law administrator can feel proud of any 'honour' conferred upon him under such auspices while martial law was still supreme. We are in a position to say that no public body of the Sikh community conferred any honour on General Dyer.

Despite the objections, the story was given credence in Britain where a growing body of influential politicians were throwing their weight behind Sir Michael O'Dwyer and propagating the legend that was being built around General Dyer. What was at stake was not just the reputation of a civil administrator and a heroic soldier, but how India was in future to be governed. It was, therefore, important to support the policies of Sir Michael and justify the actions of the soldier who implemented them. At that stage, they had only the haziest idea of what had been done by the two men.

Then, with dramatic suddenness, the events in the Punjab were forced into the background by an unexpected uprising in Afghanistan. It caught the Government of India completely unaware and came, according to Lord Chelmsford, 'like a bolt from the blue'. With the whole of India menaced, it was a time to close ranks. In some respects it was an opportune diversion, for the rising was later to be cited as proof that the disturbances in the Punjab were all part of a much wider plan to overthrow British rule in India.

Apart from serving to show how abysmally informed the Government of India was about what was happening in the country, it revealed the lack of communication which existed between Delhi and Westminster. For there was an air of bewilderment when the War Cabinet met in Downing Street on 6 May to discuss the sudden developments in India. Lord Curzon disclosed that the Secretary of State for India had called on him the previous evening and told him that a disquieting situation had arisen in Afghanistan: the Amir was adopting a most truculent attitude and protesting at the abominable way in which Muslims and Hindus were being treated. He had followed this tirade with what was tantamount to a declaration of independence. The Viceroy, therefore, proposed to close the Khyber Pass, stop the Amir's subsidy and break off relations, if he did not withdraw his proclamation. As there was a risk that the Amir would ignore the threats and risk an attack, the Viceroy was urgently asking the British Government to send reinforcements.

At this stage of the meeting Edwin Montagu walked into the Cabinet Room just in time to hear a bemused Winston Churchill, Secretary of State for War, comment rather irritably that the Commander-in-Chief had only recently turned down an offer for three squadrons of aircraft. Now there was an urgent need for reinforcements.

Montagu had to confess that until he had received the latest telegrams he had no idea that the Indian Government regarded the situation as in any way alarming, and he too was surprised at the request. As far as he knew the recent internal troubles had not spread to the North-West Frontier, and the request for

121

reinforcements surprised him, as he believed the measures proposed by the Viceroy would have been adequate. Nevertheless, he conceded, there *was* some concern among Muhammadans about the measure that the Allies were believed to be about to take over defeated Turkey, and in view of this the C-in-C in India was justified in taking precautions. That note of optimism was immediately expelled when the Chancellor of the Exchequer pointed out that General Sir Charles Monro had in fact asked for reinforcements to be diverted from Mesopotamia. Which in turn provoked the rather pernickety response that in that case why had the Government of India not addressed the request to Montagu directly. The question remained unanswered for rather obvious reasons: until now the Secretary of State for India had been repeatedly assured that everything was under control and the situation in India largely exaggerated.

Winston Churchill revealed that he too had received a telegram from the military authorities in India and the request it contained brought the matter much closer to the arena of domestic politics. The situation was so serious that the Commander-in-Chief proposed to retain British troops in India who the British Government were under a strong obligation to bring home without further delay. While Churchill was prepared to acquiesce, he felt that the men should be assured that reliefs would be sent out very shortly; and he went on to add that, while he would undertake to meet the requirements in India if the emergency proved to be a real one, he would ask the War Cabinet for permission to inform the public of the gravity of the situation as they would not take too kindly to big troop movements when they believed the war was over, and would have to be assured that men would not be kept abroad a minute longer than was necessary.

Curzon, who knew better than anyone else in the Cabinet Room how rapidly events in India inflated and deflated, was optimistic that the whole thing would blow over; in the meantime Montagu 'should exercise a discreet reticence in replying to questions in Parliament'.

Curzon's complacency was ill-judged. Trouble did break out, but at least it diverted attention from the growing discontent of the people in the Punjab. It also gave General Dyer the opportunity to enhance his reputation as a brilliant and courageous soldier and enabled him to claim that he was something of a political visionary: he knew all this was about to break when he marched into the Jallianwala Bagh.

7. The Approver

'It is your opinion that the work of prosecution and securing conviction was greatly simplified by the lower standard of evidence that was required by the military courts?' 'Yes.' — Mr Rehill, Superintendent of Police, during the Hunter Inquiry.

The people of the Punjab were bewildered, confused and disillusioned by what was going on in the courts. The British insisted that one of the great benefits conferred on them by the Raj was the introduction of a system of justice that was unequalled anywhere in the world. The lowly untouchable had the same rights as the most eminent Sahib; the law made no distinction of colour, class or creed. And in the main the Indian accepted that. Whatever his faults the white man was fair and justice impartial, whether administered by a gowned and bewigged judge or a District Officer beneath the shade of a tree in the village square. But, when it came to administering justice in the aftermath of the Punjab disturbances, it was neither seen nor heard to be done. The ordinary civil courts were suspended and Special Commissions appointed to try cases arising from the disorders. As far as the Indians were concerned, revenge again seemed to be the motivating factor.

For less serious offences there were on-the-spot Summary Courts which meted out various punishments of which flogging was the most common. In Lahore eighty people were flogged, in Kasur eighty-five, Chuharkam forty, Gujranwala twenty-four, Amritsar thirty-eight and Gurat two.

The Martial Law Commissions, which mainly sat in Lahore, dealt with the more serious cases which nearly all came under the heading of 'waging war'. The Indian Penal Code under which they were charged laid down the penalties:

Whoever wages war against the King or attempts to wage such war, or abets the waging of such war, shall be punished with death or transportation for life, and shall forfeit all his property.

Of 852 accused 581 were convicted; 108 people were sentenced to death, 264 to transportation for life, and forfeiture of all goods, two to transportation for long periods, five to imprisonment for ten years, eighty-five for seven years, and the remainder for shorter periods. The old and young were treated alike and among those accused of 'waging war against the King' were an 11-year-old boy and a man aged 115.

The trials were held in camera, evidence was not recorded, cross-examinations limited, and only the sentences issued to the newspapers. To the 'educated' Indians who were watching the events very closely the trials were simply a façade: all that mattered were verdicts which would justify the claim by Sir Michael O'Dwyer that an organized rebellion existed which aimed at the overthrow of the British.

The most important trial as far as the Punjab Government was concerned was 'The Amritsar Leaders Case' which would prove beyond all reasonable doubt that a revolutionary plot *did* exist. The two doctors, Satyapal and Kitchlew, had been ear-marked as leaders of the revolt but there was a snag; both were under detention when the mob ran riot in Amritsar, and when the illegal meeting was called in the Jallianwala Bagh three days later. To overcome this O'Dwyer sought permission to backdate the introduction of martial law to 30 March, and on 19 April the Chief Secretary of the Punjab Government sent a telegram to the Secretary of the Government of India explaining why this was necessary:

> His Honour fears that if date 13th is allowed to stand it may be impossible to use the Ordinance against those with whom the real responsibility rests.

Chelmsford was clearly in some doubt as to the wisdom or propriety of this move, for two days later a second and more insistent telegram was despatched:

> His Honour is of opinion strongly that unless organizers can be dealt with under martial law we cannot effectively break up the organization behind the disturbances. Apart from this, fixing the date at 13 April makes it very difficult to deal appropriately with the local leaders whose speeches during the preceding fortnight did so much to inflame classes who have joined the disturbances. It will mean penalizing their tools while favouring the conspirators. His Honour for this

reason ventures to press again very strongly for the earlier date.

As on so many previous occasions Chelmsford, against his better judgement, bowed to the wishes of the 'iron man' of the Punjab and the scales of justice were heavily weighted against the two doctors and the others accused with them.

Instead of appearing before a High Court they could now be tried in camera by one of the four Martial Law Commissioners which were composed of two members sitting with a High Court Judge. No verbatim note was taken of the evidence; in fact they were not obliged to record *any* evidence, and there was no appeal against their decision. As outside lawyers were banned from the Punjab the accused were denied counsel of their choice. The press was excluded and the presiding members were able to conduct the trial in a manner that aroused grave misgivings and resulted in widespread protests that the Law had become a tool of the politicians.

The fifteen men accused in the Amritsar Leaders Case appeared before the Martial Law Commission in Lahore on 19 June and included Kitchlew, Satyapal, Doctor Muhammad Bashir, Dina Nath, editor of *Waqt*, Pandit Kotu Mal, Narain Das, Swami Anubhawan Nand, Gurbakash Rai, Ghulam Muhammad, Muhammad Ismail, Moti Ram Metra and Abdul Ram Metra. They represented a cross-section of Amritsar's native population, ranging from the wealthy Cambridge-educated Kitchlew to doctors, merchants, traders and poets who scraped a living by writing odes for weddings and public meetings.

Mr Justice Broadway presided, assisted by Mr A. H. Brasher and K.B.B. Sheikh Backsh. The case was prepared by the police and submitted for examination to the Legal Remembrancer of the Punjab, Mr J. P. Ellis, in much the same way as papers are sent to the Director of Public Prosecutions in Britain. But Mr Ellis made no attempt to disguise his enmity and lack of impartiality.

His summary stated:

For some time past certain persons in Amritsar, several of whom undoubtedly formed their revolutionary ideas during their visits to Germany and other places in Europe or were members of the notorious defunct Shining Club * have

* A revolutionary movement in the Punjab.

126

cherished hostile intentions against the British, and have sedulously endeavoured to instil the poison of their minds into the hearts of others. These people have never failed to seize every possible occasion to spread the ideas which they fostered among the public.

Together, claimed Mr Ellis, they had formed a criminal conspiracy with others elsewhere to overthrow the Government and secure the abandonment of the Rowlatt Acts. Although the conspiracy existed before 30 March they could not be tried for any offences committed before that date as the Commission was not competent to deal with them, although such evidence would be considered. The vital point was made that although the two doctors had been deported at the time of the outbreak of violence in Amritsar they had started it and incited others to wage war against the King.

The main plank in the prosecution's case against the two doctors was that they had made speeches at various times which dwelt constantly on the tyranny of the Government, and its harsh and repressive measures which favoured the British at the expense of the Indian. Furthermore, said the summary, they had urged Hindus and Muhammadans to unite so as to present a united front against the Government, especially in opposition to the Rowlatt Acts. Whilst there was nothing wrong in the two religions uniting, it was reprehensible to do so against the Government.

When the trial opened Kitchlew's counsel submitted that the court did not have the necessary jurisdiction to try his client. As he had not been taken 'in open rebellion' martial law was not applicable and therefore he was entitled to be tried by the ordinary civil courts which still existed to deal with cases not concerned with the emergency. This was abruptly dismissed along with similar submissions. As the trial progressed the unease of the accused increased over the way in which it was being conducted, and Satyapal's counsel telegraphed the Viceroy requesting that the whole issue should be examined independently by a Crown Law Officer and eminent counsel in England. He further objected that his client being tried with others who were charged with committing offences whilst he was under detention plainly prejudiced any chance of a fair trial. He submitted that evidence was being presented without the

127

accused knowing in advance what was alleged against them; yet they were expected to answer it immediately. Furthermore, martial law had not been proclaimed until 14 April by which time the disturbances were over and it was improper to backdate it to 30 March.

The Viceroy saw no reason to interfere.

An ingenious line of defence was presented by the barrister, Mr Hassan Iman, who read out long speeches made by non-official members in the Imperial Legislative Council. None of the speeches by the accused, he said, approached the invective and virulence the Indian politicians had used to condemn the Rowlatt Acts, yet the Viceroy had not censured them or ruled them out of order. If what the men in the dock had said was a crime, then the politicians should be standing alongside them.

Despite the tight security, enough leaked out from behind the closed doors to raise the gravest misgivings in the mind of the most independent observer. Some semblance of impartiality was attempted by the preparation of an official file 'containing a full record of all evidence, exhibits, applications, orders and other kindred papers', but it impressed few people for it was marked more by what was omitted than what it contained.

A host of character witnesses were called by the accused but little or no importance was attached to what they said. They simply reiterated that the accused men were law-abiding citizens of impeccable behaviour.

Among the defence witnesses was Mahatma Gandhi who, rather surprisingly he must have felt, was not himself on trial, for, as founder of the Satyagraha Movement, he had been branded as the mastermind behind the alleged rebellion. Even more surprising, if the object was to arrive at the truth, was the bench's ruling that he should not be allowed to answer questions about the aims and purpose of the Movement.

Newspaper reports of some of the defendants' speeches were produced and these were backed by personal reports by police officers who had attended meetings in disguise, most of which were of no value at all. There was, however, some evidence that seemed to favour the accused and one police officer who had called on Kitchlew incognito in order to infiltrate the Satyagraha Movement admitted that he had been told, 'No violence or force should be used'.

The prosecution's trump card was Hans Raj, who had

turned approver (King's evidence) on the guarantee of a free pardon. The uncorroborated testimony of any 'Judas' is always viewed with great suspicion in a British court and the jury is warned to treat it with extreme caution; but in Lahore there was no jury, only the presiding judge and two supporting members. Without his remarkable memory there would have been no case against several of the accused, but Hans Raj was able to recall the most incriminating evidence. Even during the most violent occurrences he had been able to record the part that each individual had played in the rioting, murder, arson and looting. And his power of observation had never deserted him even when bodies were being cremated on bank furniture and buildings razed and looted.

Even more disturbing to some observers was why he had been accepted by the prosecution in the first place, for he had played such a prominent part in the events that led up to the bloodshed on 10 April and the even more bloodthirsty finale in the Jallianwala Bagh. He was a bigger fish than several of the men in the dock.

It was only natural, therefore, that the long and detailed statement he had made was viewed with the greatest suspicion and mistrust by defending counsel and they tried extremely hard, if unsuccessfully, to find out how he had come to make it.

Little help was forthcoming from Inspector Lala Jowahar Lal, the police officer from Lahore responsible for producing the key witness. He was one of the C.I.D. men who had been seen earlier on in the Jallianwala Bagh but who had departed just before the arrival of the soldiers, as if he knew that they would open fire without warning. He was also one of the policemen accused of trying to obtain evidence by torture.

His explanation as to how Hans Raj came to be the official approver sounded plausible until it was subjected to cross-examination; then it sounded extremely unconvincing. The Inspector said that he had first questioned Hans Raj in the Kotwali on 21 April, a surprising delay as he was known to have been one of the men who convened the meeting and was an energetic figure in the Satyagraha Movement. 'I found he was willing to make a clean breast of everything and applied for a magistrate to record his confession.' That in itself was perfectly acceptable, but what baffled the defending counsel was why he should have destroyed the notes of his three-hour interview with Hans Raj. They were not proper notes, he explained, and only intended for his own use. Eyebrows were raised at this remarkable admission for he had conceded that Hans Raj was the most important witness to the whole conspiracy and the only person who could supply the evidence about various vital meetings which were alleged to have taken place. 'My picking the approver,' he said disarmingly, 'was really a chance. No arrested person except Hans Raj has been made a prosecution witness in this case.'

The Bench accepted his explanation without hesitation, as they did that of other police witnesses who, when asked to produce their notes, replied that they had destroyed them.

Inspector Jowahar Lal went on to say that the day after he had interviewed Hans Raj he took him to Mr A. Seymour, a magistrate, who took down his statement. Hans Raj's began in a manner oddly worded for a man who was certain of his own immunity:

> I see that no one is present in this room except myself and the magistrate recording my statement. No promises or threats have been made to me, and I make the statement of my own free will and accord. I am not handcuffed. I am joint secretary of the Satyagraha Sabha at Amritsar. Doctor Bashir is the secretary.

He declined, however, to make it under oath. There had been no coercion, he said; he had been in the Fort four days before being taken to the Kotwali, and during those four days he had not been questioned or threatened with shooting.

From then on the carefully worded statement, remarkably lucid and well worded for a man of his class, went on to incriminate everyone in the dock while at the same time making it manifestly clear that he had not indulged in any violence himself nor taken part in any of the looting. Although he had joined the mob at the National Bank he had not gone in or armed himself with a stick, but he had witnessed the murder of the manager. Thanks to his phenomenal memory he was able to recall all those who had taken the Satyagraha vow, which was of incalculable help to the prosecution as his mother had destroyed the actual register containing the names, which meant none of the accused was able to refute his allegation.

When it came to the Ram Naumi celebrations at which Hindus and Muslims had united, he said that the purely religious festival had been turned into a political demonstration. It supported another important plank in the Crown's case.

But the most devastating blow to the hopes of Kitchlew and Satyapal came when he stated, 'The Satyagraha Movement as far as we were concerned was a mere *bahana*, a cloak for our active work.' It made nonsense of Kitchlew's claim that non-violence was the keystone of the movement. Although no minutes had been kept of the meetings, Hans Raj was able to recall with astonishing accuracy details of what took place and the wording of the numerous resolutions passed. It was a remarkable achievement, thought the defence, for a man who at the time could not have known he would be called upon to give evidence about them. He hammered another big nail in the coffin of the two doctors by effectively demolishing their argument that they could not be held guilty of any of the excesses of 10 April as they were under arrest at the time. On their deportation, he said, they told him to incite the crowd to take revenge. The telegram he had sent to Gandhi was also submitted as proof that the conspiracy existed beyond Amritsar.

His own role, however, he consistently underplayed. Although others used the Satyagraha vow as a cloak for seditious activities, he adhered to it. He was against all violence and believed 'it was the duty of the Satyagrahas that if bullets were fired to receive them on their breasts'. Despite the chaotic conditions that prevailed during the rioting he was able to name all those he had seen carrying staves, while carefully pointing out that he was unarmed. And he was able to quote a number of very damaging remarks he had overheard. His statement also identified those who were involved in the attack on the National Bank and the murder of Mr Stewart, the assault on Mr Scott, the looting of the Chartered Bank, and gave names of those who had destroyed the Post Office. Although he had not actually witnessed the sacking of the Alliance Bank and the murder of Mr Thompson, he had been told things by those who had been there and could name them.

At 5.35 p.m. Mr Seymour had halted him as he was getting confused. He had resumed at eleven the next morning and, refreshed after a night's sleep, had been able to supply a fresh list of names and a lot more damaging evidence. Although he

131

had not been present at the assault on Mrs Easdon, he knew who was responsible and he could also provide evidence about the attack on Miss Sherwood.

When Hans Raj went into the witness box attempts were made to get him to admit that he had committed perjury in return for a pardon, but he was unshakeable.

When it came to cross-examining the key prosecution witness the defence were at a distinct disadvantage, as they had no idea beforehand what he was going to allege and they had to question him immediately. A unanimous petition from all the defence lawyers was submitted to the court and rejected. Undaunted, a long telegram was sent to the Viceroy in Simla pointing out the irregularities and asking him to intervene:

> Seriously handicapped in being required by Government to cross-examine the approver there and then without accused being supplied with his previous statement, nor with the copy of the approver's examination in chief (which lasted for a day and a half). Counsel expressly forbidden by court to take detailed notes of the witness's statements and to rely solely on the printed copy supplied by the court which had not yet been supplied.

The lawyers also protested that they had had to cross-examine Inspector Jowahar Lal immediately he had completed his evidence, again not knowing what he was going to allege, and pleas for further time to consider it had been refused.

Lord Chelmsford saw no reason to involve himself.

And so the lawyers entrusted with the daunting duty of saving their clients from the gallows were faced with an almost impossible task. The only way in which they could destroy the approver's evidence was to expose his criminal record and other aspects of his life which revealed him as an unreliable witness. Apart from his unsavoury background his own militant role made him particularly vulnerable and he was closely cross-examined about it, but he skilfully avoided incriminating himself. Not that it really mattered; he had been assured of immunity from prosecution. The remarkably accurate memory which had served him so well when it came to naming others deserted him when he was questioned about his attempt to join the police in Amritsar, for by now the suspicion had taken root that all along he had been a police informer.

As for his alleged criminal activities, he simply denied them; he had never stolen or lived off his mother's immoral earnings. More important to the men standing in the dock was his insistence that he had not fabricated evidence. In the face of that all the accused could do was make a complete denial of the charges and try to prove that they were elsewhere at the time.

There was corroboration in the case against Abdul Aziz. Brij Lal, a twelve-year-old Amritsar boy, gave evidence, and a statement he had made to the police was produced in court. Quite apart from his age, its value was questionable, for later the boy was to claim that he had been held in the Kotwali for six days and regularly beaten before being handed over to Hans Raj, who had tried to get him to swear a false statement. However, he had refused and was again beaten. 'Then when I could bear it no longer I made a statement to Inspector Jowahar Lal according to the way Hans Raj taught me.'

He further claimed that when he gave evidence at Lahore his statement was handed to him every day and he was told to memorize it and repeat it when he gave evidence.

The trial dragged on for twenty days in the oppressive heat of the Punjab summer, and the Government was quick to point out to hostile critics that the long time involved hardly suggested that the case was rushed. The actual record of the proceedings might be scant but the trial had been fair and scrupulously conducted.

The accused, on the other hand, were all agreed on one thing — they had been 'framed' by Hans Raj.

Kitchlew, himself a lawyer, said the court was prejudiced and the references to Germany were unfair as he had never stayed in that country more than two months at a stretch. Pleading not guilty to all the charges, he insisted that all the meetings had been constitutional and the speeches moderate and sober. He was not responsible for any of the acts of violence and he strongly denied that he had ever given Hans Raj instructions to seek revenge for his arrest. There had never been a criminal conspiracy and the violence, when it did erupt, had been the direct result of the shooting at the railway bridge.

Satyapal adopted a similar line of defence and drew the court's attention to the fact that he had rigidly observed the order preventing him from speaking in public which had been imposed long before the rioting began. As for Hans Raj, he

133

insisted that he only knew him by sight and had never associated with him; and, rather surprisingly for a man who advocated unity, he added contemptuously, 'I regard him as too far beneath me in the social scale to be a friend or an enemy'. He was equally scornful of Hans Raj's claim that he had urged him to seek revenge: 'He was not a man of power to be asked to take revenge'. And to emphasize his unquestionable loyalty to the Crown he reminded the bench that he had been a Lieutenant in the Indian Medical Service, served in Aden and worked through the 'flu and malaria epidemics.

Doctor Bashir, who had been singled out as one of the principal conspirators, emphatically denied giving Hans Raj instructions to call the meeting at the Jallianwala Bagh, and said the approver had implicated him through sheer enmity. He had not even attended the meeting; it was his accuser who had spurred the mob to violence.

There was a marked, almost monotonous, consistency in the statements of the other defendants and their brevity smacked of resignation.

Mill owner Pandit Koto Mal: 'I don't know Hans Raj. Never saw him until he gave his evidence in court. I do not know why he should speak falsely against me.'

The merchant Narain Das: 'I never saw Hans Raj before 9 April. I cannot say why he should depose against me falsely.'

Swami Andhawan Nand: 'I repudiate whatever he has said concerning me.'

Gurbukash Rai, a homeopathic doctor, said the allegation that he was involved in the plundering of the Chartered Bank was 'pure invention'.

Ghulam Nabe: 'I don't know why he should name me. Have not signed Satyagraha vow, don't know what Satyagraha is.'

The poet Ghulam Muhammad: 'I don't know Hans Raj, I am surprised at his giving evidence against me.'

Abdul Aziz protested that he could not have done any of the things alleged against him as he was seriously ill in bed at the time. 'Case trumped up against me by Hans Raj and the police.'

On 5 July Mr Justice Broadway delivered his judgement which confirmed all that Sir Michael O'Dwyer claimed. The Punjab had been on the brink of revolt. The court pronounced that a criminal conspiracy had existed in Amritsar and elsewhere on 30 March for the purpose of overawing the Government and securing the abandonment of the Rowlatt Acts and had culminated on 10 April in acts of war being waged. People had continued to join the conspiracy until 13 April. The Indian community greeted the latter observation with open scepticism. It was too pat.

Of the riots the Judge said:

> That these acts constituted a deliberate and most determined waging of war cannot be disputed. Indeed, the learned counsel for the accused made no attempt at urging that war was not waged, and we have no hesitation in holding that war was waged on 10 April.

Apart from feeling that the observation was a travesty of what they had said, the stunned defence counsel felt that they had failed in their duty, for they had pressed the point that the speeches of their clients were all moderate in tone and perfectly legitimate. Furthermore, they had repeatedly argued that the court had no jurisdiction to try them under the Indian Penal Code in which nearly every form of agitation was interpreted as 'waging war'.

The joint submission that the accused had not made any speeches that approached the virulence and invective with which the non-official members of the Imperial Legislative Council had attacked the Rowlatt proposals was brusquely dealt with.

The politicians were not on trial and the court was not concerned with what they said. In any case, arguments by gentlemen of high intellectual ability could not be compared with speeches, even if more moderate in tone, made at meetings attended by persons of little or no education, and appeals not to minds but to passions.

The observation brought a smile of wry amusement to the faces of the 'gentlemen of high intellectual ability', for the debates on the Rowlatt Acts had often been marked by rancour, rudeness and bitterness and there had been little evidence that the European members had paid much attention to what they had said.

Hans Raj was not around to hear the high opinion that was expressed of his evidence; he had been rewarded with a pardon, paid a large sum of money and moved to Mesopotamia where he was beyond the reach of any possible revenge.

We have arrived at the conclusion that Hans Raj has endeavoured to tell his story as fully as he was capable of doing and has not deliberately made any false statements. That he has been occasionally confused is apparent, but that is not surprising considering the numbers of persons he had to deal with (a good deal more than the accused in this case) and we have given the accused concerned the fullest benefit of any such confusion of ideas, dates and names.

His story was 'worthy of credence'.

'Not a single one of the accused,' said Mr Justice Broadway, 'has been able to show any valid reason why Hans Raj should falsely implicate him and we have no hesitation in holding that attempts made to prove him a misappropriator of money, a drunkard and debaucher have signally failed.'

It was an observation that was not shared by the men who had been found guilty on his testimony: the mere fact that Hans Raj had saved his own skin seemed a very valid reason. Furthermore, his evidence was pretty well worthless without corroboration. Yet he alone had managed to produce the necessary evidence that confirmed every aspect of the indictment, even the vital words that the two doctors had urged him to incite the mob to seek revenge.

Kitchlew was sentenced to transportation for life with forfeiture of all property. Satyapal suffered the same fate. Muhammad Bashir, who had not attended the meeting at the Jallianwala Bagh but had treated some of the wounded, was sentenced to death on the testimony of Hans Raj that he was involved in the National Bank incident, and Dina Nath, editor of *Waqt*, was sentenced to transportation for life. Abdul Aziz was also sentenced to death.

Five of the accused were acquitted while others accused of lesser offences received prison sentences of varying length.

Earlier Rattan Chand and Chaudri Bugga Mal, who were described as the lieutenants of the two doctors, had been tried with eighteen others for 'waging war', murder, arson and the looting and sacking of the banks. Hans Raj had again been the principal witness for the prosecution. It was almost a carbon copy of the 'Leaders' trial for the accused all pleaded not guilty and claimed they were the victims of fabricated evidence. It was an extremely short case, lasting only three days, and all but one were sentenced to death and forfeiture of all property.

❖ ❖ ❖

The severe punishments inflicted by the Martial Law Commissions had the reverse effect to what was intended; instead of cowing and silencing the critics of the Government, agitation increased and there was a mounting demand for an inquiry into the way in which justice had been administered. Gandhi wanted a public inquiry to restore the confidence of the people in the Punjab, and he cabled Chelmsford, 'The heavy sentences passed against the accused persons have filled the public mind with consternation'.

Lord Chelmsford could afford to ignore the protestations of the man who many saw as the real culprit. But what could not be ignored were the legal moves being set in motion to right what many considered to be a travesty of justice.

In July the wife of Bugga Mal travelled to Allahabad where she urged Pandit Moti Lal Nehru to help the condemned men. He immediately contacted Lord Chelmsford asking for a stay of execution as he was briefing the eminent British lawyer, Sir John Simon, to appeal to the Privy Council. The Viceroy declined to intervene on the grounds that he had no jurisdiction over military courts, but that was of no avail for by now Edwin Montagu had been drawn into the controversy. He sent an urgent telegram to the Viceroy expressing grave doubts as to whether the trials and sentences under martial law ordinance were wholly legal, and he had therefore been instructed to appeal to the Privy Council. He was also perturbed at the Viceroy's refusal to delay the executions:

> In view of the statement that these sentences were inflicted by court martial I feel it is my duty to communicate by telegram to you and to ask you before execution of the sentences to consider and place me in possession of the facts of the case.

It was just another example of how much of what was happening in India failed to reach him.

The Viceroy's reply was that the men had been tried by Martial Law Commissions, not court martial, which was perfectly legal. The fact that the procedure was almost identical to a court martial was neither here nor there. Nevertheless, the executions were stayed, pending the result of the appeal.

Kitchlew, Satyapal and the others convicted with them also decided to appeal through the King Emperor to the Privy Council, and a long-drawn-out legal wrangle developed. Numerous grounds were submitted for overturning the verdicts, but the main ones were that the Special Commissioners had no jurisdiction to try them as there was no state of open rebellion in Amritsar as defined by the regulations. None of the accused had been arrested while committing the offences; the ordinary courts were still in existence and administering justice, and were the only ones which had the necessary jurisdiction. Martial law could not be made retrospective and there was no evidence to justify their conviction of sedition and waging war.

The bitterness which existed in India was even allowed to spill over into the proceedings of the Privy Council, for there were protests that the Government of India was being very dilatory in providing the necessary papers so essential for the appeals of the men under sentence of death. The London solicitors Barrow, Rogers & Nevill were prompted to complain that:

> Little or no attempt has been made by the authorities in India to comply with the terms of His Majesty's Order in Council of 20 October 1919 which directs that an authenticated copy, under seal, of the record proper to be laid before his Majesty on hearing of the Appeal should be transmitted to the Registrar of the Privy Council without delay. If these directions are not carried out we do not see how we can attempt to approve the record in this country.

In addition to this strongly worded letter there were criticisms that the Legal Adviser to the Indian Office had provided incomplete statements in which whole pages were missing.

Not that it mattered much; so violent was the agitation over the sentences imposed that the Government of the Punjab was instructed to review all the sentences, and two High Court Judges, one European and one Indian, were appointed to review the cases which had caused so much anxiety. Sir Edward Maclagan, who had succeeded Sir Michael O'Dwyer as Lieutenant-Governor, was also reviewing the cases and 'tempering mercy with justice'.

But Westminster was desperately anxious that the bitterness between the native population and the Government should be ended, a view which was entirely shared by King George V who issued a Royal Proclamation of Amnesty on 23 December:

> I therefore direct my Viceroy to exercise in my name and on my behalf my Royal Clemency to political offenders in the fullest measure which in his judgement is compatible with the public safety.

Kitchlew and Satyapal together with others whose sentences had already been drastically reduced were released almost immediately, and no one was more incensed than Mr J. P. Ellis, the Legal Remembrancer to the Punjab Government who was in England at the time. He expressed his misgivings to Sir Edward des Chamier, Solicitor to the India Office, and wrote that he supposed the appeals would be withdrawn 'now all the convicts have been amnestied'.

That was far from true, for the appeals of Rattan Chand and Bugga Mal had been dismissed, although the sentence of death had been commuted to transportation for life and they were sent to the Andaman Islands. Kitchlew and Satyapal continued with their appeal; although they were free, they had still been convicted, and they wanted an unqualified 'not guilty' verdict. But in the end, as the months dragged on, they abandoned the appeal.

Ellis's wrath continued to spill out on paper:

> What a prospect there is in the East for the future now all the blackguards are out again. If I have to return again, as I suppose I shall have to, nothing in the world will induce me to take my wife and daughter out, as I do not think we can possibly escape a general massacre of whites in the next few years . . . Six months nominal captivity to be released in a halo of glory is all that the organizers of wholesale murder need fear — it is pitiful.

It was not the isolated view; it was shared by the majority of British in the Punjab, and they did not hesitate to say so. Montagu was most dismayed when he read a Reuters' communiqué which stated that official opinion in India was wholly opposed to the King's proclamation. 'This astonished me and I would like your confirmation,' he telegraphed Chelmsford.

The Viceroy replied that this was not the case. But it was only half the truth; there were members of his Council who were violently opposed to the leniency which had been shown, while nearly all the members of the Punjab Government were bitter and disillusioned.

Lord Chelmsford's lack of candour was understandable for he was in a most unenviable position: he was the spokesman for the British Government whose views commanded scant respect in India. Personally he did not agree with a lot that had been done in the Punjab, but for fear of offending the Europeans he had often supported the local government against his better instincts and he spelled this out to Sir Edward Maclagan.

If the reviews infuriated the white population they delighted the Indians; the reductions were seen as conclusive proof that justice had for a time ceased to exist in the Punjab. Although the commendable objective was to end the bitterness, some of the reviews were astonishing in their leniency. Nothing had done more to embitter the Europeans than the cowardly assault on the woman missionary Miss Sherwood, yet one of the culprits, sentenced to transportation for life, had been released. In other cases the sentence of death had been reduced to jail sentences that ranged from seven years to one. A man sentenced to transportation for life for his part in the attack on Mrs Easdon was released in August. To the Europeans who had suffered many privations during the disturbances and gone in fear of their lives it was all mercy and no justice.

Their resentment further increased when the reviewing Judges also confirmed what many Indian critics had claimed. The two Judges, Mr Justice Mullick and Mr Justice Chevis, the former an Indian and the latter a European, were openly critical of the way in which some of the trials had been conducted. Inevitably there was slight difference of opinion between the two men — the Indian tended to be more critical than the Britisher — but their views were courageous and remarkably impartial, and their report to the Secretary of the Indian Government's Home Department provided little solace for those who had dismissed the criticisms as the irresponsible clamour of people trying to make political capital.

The two Judges began their report by stating that their task had been made very difficult in many cases because of the scant records that had been kept of the evidence, and the unreliability of some of the witnesses, and it was therefore possible that injustices had been done. Bosworth Smith was singled out for special criticism: not only were his records inadequate, they were often indecipherable. He had also quite improperly taken part in the police investigations of cases which he later tried. Furthermore he had ordered people to be whipped for offences not punishable by whipping.

The most important trial they had to review, from the political and legal point of view, was the Amritsar Leaders Case, for it was upon Mr Justice Broadway's judgement that the Government of the Punjab relied for the vindication of the measures it had taken. It was a case that many sincerely believed should have been left well alone; there was nothing to be gained from airing in public what had taken place in private. In any case, and this point had been made by the two Judges, nearly all the accused had now been released or had completed their sentences. Doctor Muhammad Bashir was one of the exceptions: he had been sentenced to death but this had been commuted to six years' imprisonment. The doctor was alleged to have taken part in the attack on the National Bank in which two Europeans died and to have incited the mob to seek revenge for the arrest of Kitchlew and Satyapal. 'The Judges point out that this part of the case against Muhammad Bashir rests on the uncorroborated testimony of the approver.'

Mr Justice Mullick also expressed the view that the agitation against the Rowlatt Acts did not amount to waging war, an opinion that was of vital importance not only to those who had been convicted but to the Government of the Punjab.

Mr Justice Mullick dismissed the evidence of Hans Raj as worthless:

> He certainly is not the type of approver on whose uncor-roborated testimony a conviction can be based. I do not think that Bashir can be convicted in respect of any of the offences committed on 10 April. As for the 11th and 12th, the evidence, even if we place implicit reliance on the approver, does not show that Bashir committed any offence on these days.

Referring to the meeting in the Jallianwala Bagh the Judge emphasized that the doctor was not even there:

So far as I can see there is no clear evidence that the meeting was an unlawful assembly within the meaning of the Penal Code and even if it was Bashir cannot be held guilty of any offence committed by it.

He recommended that the doctor be released.

Mr Justice Mullick also recommended that Abdul Aziz should be pardoned for he could not accept the evidence of the boy Brij Lal as corroboration of what Hans Raj had alleged. Mr Justice Chevis disagreed with him, but the outcome was that the Indian Government agreed to his release.

The balance in the scales of justice had been righted, but it had all taken too long and the belated measures did nothing to appease the resentment and anger of the Indian politicians or the men who felt they had been unjustly punished.

Neither of the two Amritsar doctors, having been given their freedom, felt the slightest need to be grateful or constrained to keep silent, and they were outspokenly scathing in their condemnation of the trial procedure which had so nearly resulted in them spending the rest of their natural life on the Andaman Islands.

Kitchlew said:

The trial was a huge farce. The attitude of the presiding judge was obviously hostile to the accused persons. Prosecution witnesses who deposed in our favour were bullied by the court . . . Counsel were treated not only with scant courtesy but were not even allowed to cross-examine witnesses at length.

And he enlarged on his previous allegations that witnesses had been maltreated, evidence not properly recorded, while he himself had been kept in a locked room day and night and not allowed to see anyone. 'In short, Mr Broadway behaved not as a judge but as a prosecutor.'

Satyapal described the trial as a mockery and dismissed the idea of an organized rebellion as 'absolutely chimerical — an apparition without reality'. His main target for criticism was, however, Sir Michael O'Dwyer:

He was the most repressive and reactionary governor in whose hands the destiny of the Punjab has ever been placed. Reaction, repression, coercion, suppression by force of any public opinion unpalatable to him, however legitimate and fair, were his chief characteristics.

It had all been said before and it was to be repeated again by many influential Indians, and it was secretly believed by Lord Chelmsford and Edwin Montagu, although both shrank from expressing their views publicly.

Unfortunately for the two Englishmen, events were snow-balling and building up into an avalanche. India's foremost poet, Nobel Prize Winner Sir Rabindranath Tagore, wrote to the Viceroy relinquishing his knighthood a letter that was to be quoted throughout India:

> The enormity of the measures taken by the Government in the Punjab for quelling some local disturbances has, with acute shock, revealed to our minds the helplessness of our position as British subjects in India.

More with an eye to a wider public than the Viceroy's personal ear he wrote:

> The accounts of insults and sufferings undergone by our brothers in the Punjab have trickled through the gagged silence, reaching every corner of India, and the universal agony of indignation roused in the hearts of our people has been ignored by our rulers — possibly congratulating themselves for what they imagine as salutary lessons.

The spate of invective increased as the words flowed.

> The time has come when badges of honour make our shame glaring in their incongruous context of humiliation, and I for my part wish to stand shorn of all special distinctions by the side of those of my countrymen who, for their so-called insignificance are liable to suffer a degradation not fit for human beings.

It was all heady stuff which the Indian population loved. Chelmsford passed the letter on to Edwin Montagu who tactfully decided that nothing should be done and the Viceroy replied, 'His Excellency is unable to relieve you of your knighthood, and in the circumstances of the case, he does not propose to make any recommendations on the subject to his Majesty the King Emperor.'

Gandhi also returned the medals he had received in honour

of his services to the British.

Months had passed since the first shots were fired and Gandhi had forecast the demise of the British Raj, but the events had aroused little interest among the general public in Britain, who were blissfully ignorant of what was going on six thousand miles away. In normal circumstances a major disaster in which thousands of Indians died often merited no more than a paragraph in the stop press, and there was certainly no space available for the complicated legal issues that were being aired in the Privy Council or the Indian Courts.

In any case, the Indian situation was a never-ending saga that would have been impossible to recount in any coherent manner. None of the events took place in a chronological order; they overlapped or got bogged down in interminable wrangling, and there were long periods when nothing happened. Decisions were made which on reflection were regretted; instead of soothing they inflamed, instead of being interpreted as conciliatory gestures they were seen as admissions of guilt.

The rapidly deteriorating situation might have been avoided if communications between Delhi and Westminster had been speedier and more efficient. Urgent telegrams had to be drafted and then transmitted, and if they were confidential there were further delays as they were coded and then decoded. Longer communiqués went by sea which took several weeks, for on arrival there was a lengthy rail journey. At times information was withheld from the Viceroy and incidents toned down. And this was reflected in some of the despatches to Edwin Montagu. The system meant that effective liaison between the two capitals was almost impossible.

The outlook would not have been quite so gloomy if only time and distance were involved, but it was more than physical miles which separated Delhi from London. Chelmsford and Montagu were finding it increasingly difficult to see eye to eye. They were like two doctors who agreed in their diagnosis but could not agree on the course of treatment to be adopted.

8. The Hunter Committee

'I seem to be everlastingly making suggestions to you which you cannot accept, and finding that I cannot accept your suggestions.' — *Montagu to Chelmsford.*

When Edwin Montagu, under severe pressure in the House of Commons to shed more light on what was going on in the Punjab, first mentioned the possibility of an inquiry, he was firmly of the opinion that it would result in stirring tales of heroism and a complete vindication of the men who had put down a dangerous rising. In his Budget speech on 22 May he announced in solemn tones, 'The danger is not passed; it exists. It is not something that is finished. It threatens. There has been the loss of much property and of many innocent lives.' He was anxious, however, not to rush things. 'Let us talk of an inquiry when we have put the fire out. The only message we send from this House today is one of sympathy with those upon whom the great responsibility has fallen to restore the situation.' When the time was ripe for an inquiry he was quite sure it would not only help to remove the causes of the disorder but would dispose once and for all of the libellous charges that had been levelled at British soldiers and the men who had been entrusted with the extremely difficult task of dealing with the riots.

It did not occur to him then that there had been a deliberate suppression of news or that he only had the flimsiest idea of what had happened in the Jallianwala Bagh. A seditious meeting had been put down with regrettable but unavoidable loss of life, and Lord Chelmsford after some initial wavering had finally got around to telling him that India had been teetering on the brink of another Mutiny.

Within a week of making his speech the war in Afghanistan

was over and the Punjab was peaceful once more; there was no valid reason for delaying the inquiry any longer. He asked Lord Chelmsford to submit his proposals about the form the inquiry should take and added, 'It must be relentless in coming to the truth'. He also took the opportunity to congratulate the Viceroy over the action he had taken to stop public floggings:

> If that sort of thing is condemned by the Commission, action must follow, and if the Commission decides that there have been events in the Punjab in the past or at the moment which justify the view that O'Dwyerism is not suited to that Province, it will only accord with my view that this method of Government always brings sooner or later its reward.

When he was dictating that, he confidently felt that the Viceroy fully shared his views. Nothing could have been further from the truth. The suggestion appalled Lord Chelmsford. There must be no victimization. Politically he was in a cleft stick, for although he had often assured Montagu in his private despatches that they shared the same targets and ideals, he had already aligned himself with the action taken by the Lieutenant-Governor. The day before Montagu had addressed the House of Commons, Chelmsford had written to King George V, 'Sir Michael O'Dwyer has acted with his accustomed courage and promptness, and we must be grateful for the fact that we had him at the head of affairs in the Punjab when this outbreak took place.' He could hardly be expected to renege on that.

The reaction in India to the proposed inquiry was understandably unresponsive; both the civil and military authorities were firmly opposed to any investigation and every possible objection was raised in an effort to stop it. General Sir Charles Monro, the Commander-in-Chief, was outspoken in his objections: it would only serve to call into question the authority of the army and its officers, and have a discouraging effect on all ranks.

Some Provincial Governments, including Bombay and Bengal, feared it would only provide an opportunity for extremists to fan the flames of discontent. Sir Harcourt Butler, the Governor of the United Provinces, told the

Viceroy, 'I dread this inquiry into the causes, course and consequences of the recent disturbances. My own province is excluded from the inquiry, but it will be deeply stirred by it. I can see scarcely any limits to racial feeling already high which will be let loose by it.' His advice was that it should be dropped altogether.

The Indian Government also expressed the view that it would be extremely difficult to get men of sufficient calibre from Great Britain to sit in judgement, with the result that they would be in danger of being judged by second-rate politicians of little independence. Once again Montagu was faced with the often-repeated claim that the men who governed India on the spot were the only ones who really understood the sub-continent.

Foremost in the Viceroy's mind was the explosive situation that would arise if Sir Michael O'Dwyer was censured. Therefore he warned Montagu that the demand by Indian extremists for a much wider inquiry into the causes of the disturbances would be resisted, for it was their sole aim to discredit the whole course of British administration in the country, and in particular to blacken the name of the retired Lieutenant-Governor.

'This extension of the inquiry,' he warned, 'we are bound to resist.' After paying tribute to all that Sir Michael had done for the war effort, he insisted that he could not be party to any attack on him. And to leave the Secretary of State for India in no doubt that it was no idle threat, he said, 'His decisive action in the late emergency is strongly supported by European opinion, and any attempt to make his administration responsible for the disorder is certain to arouse the keenest bitterness in the European community, private and official.'

Having got that off his chest the Viceroy then got down to brass tacks and began to submit proposals for the inquiry. Its scope, he suggested, should be limited to finding out how the disorders originated, who organized them, and for what purpose. The extent and character of the various incidents should be investigated, along with the steps taken to deal with them.

We cannot of course contemplate inclusion of any extremists known to be hostile to the Government or Sir Michael O'Dwyer personally, such as some Indian press suggest. We consider that status of inquiry should be that of a Committee appointed by the Government of India.

Evidence should not be given on oath and counsel should not appear, and only members of the Committee should be permitted to examine witnesses. Finally the Committee would report to the Government of India which in turn would make recommendations to the Secretary of State for India in Council.

Lord Chelmsford also informed him that it was proposed to pass a Bill of Indemnity, as information had been received that steps were being taken to bring civil actions against officers and officials over incidents arising from the administration of martial law.

While all this was taking place, Gandhi and other leading figures in the Indian National Congress had become convinced that there was little or no possibiity of an impartial inquiry. Gandhi in particular felt that there was little chance of the Committee including 'such official and non-official members as to inspire full confidence'. Therefore, they would go ahead with their own investigation, and it would not be confined to the disturbances but would embrace the whole of Sir Michael O'Dwyer's period of office.

At the same time that Lord Chelmsford was submitting his proposals, Montagu was asking him for more information about what had been happening in the Punjab. He was aware of the tightrope the Viceroy was having to walk, and he made his request as tactful as possible: he did not want to publish anything he wished to withhold or had not been authenticated, but he would appreciate anything that would help him to reply to the press which was upbraiding him over the lack of news.

The Viceroy denied withholding anything and in turn criticized Montagu for not giving him the backing he was entitled to, and Montagu was forced to reply that, whilst he was always open to appeal, he could not go against the views of the Home Government.

As summer passed into autumn Montagu became more and more fretful over his inability to get the inquiry off the ground. The business of getting a chairman was maddening. He was determined to get the best man but, 'doubtless for the most admirable reasons in the world', he found himself balked whichever way he turned.

On top of these frustrations, he was at last receiving detailed news of what had happened in the Punjab, even if it was not from the source he had requested it, and it only served to deepen his depression and apprehension. In the communiqué in which he had spoken of his problem in finding a chairman, his anger got the better of him and the impartiality his position demanded completely deserted him. Having ordered an inquiry he set about doing its job.

In a long and bitter postscript he unburdened himself to the Viceroy:

If you want a frank expression from me about affairs in the Punjab, I will give it to you. This is on the evidence before me, which is not complete and provisional:

1 I believe that O'Dwyer's enthusiasm permitted of abuses of recruitment and in getting subscriptions to War Loans which provoked unrest directly and indirectly through the increase of the economic factors.

2 I believe that, as is always the case, long suppression of political activities has left the Punjab more excitable and less informed as to the value of public speeches than it should have been.

3 I believe that the wrong Section of the Indian Penal Code was used to deal with offenders, and the Section about waging war against the King was never meant for this kind of offence. That I am justified in thinking this is shown by the fact that in order to meet the needs of the case you have had to reduce the stringent punishments which were compulsory under that Section.

4 I believe that at Amritsar there is at least ground for supposing that deportation, which is not a punishment, but only a deterrent, and is only therefore a matter of expediency, was unsuccessful because it did fan the flame.

5 I believe it was a profound mistake not to allow counsel from the outset from other Provinces.

6 I further believe that your difficulties are increased by the fact that you feel the Government depends upon your

supporting officials, provincial and central, whether they are right or wrong. I do not dissent from this view. It's the one which I should have expected from you. But I've only got to enunciate two general principles. First, that you must govern India in all respects as a country on its way to self-government, and not as a dependency unless all the work you and I are doing is to be a sham, and secondly, that heads of government, including Viceroys, will soon have to make many appeals and public speeches in explanation of their policy.

Seldom if ever had a Viceroy been subjected to such an unrestrained reminder of what his duties entailed, but Lord Chelmsford was unabashed and unrepentant, and within a matter of days he was confiding to the King that the criticisms that had been voiced over the steps taken to quell the disturbances and the punishments imposed would be answered by the inquiry:

> There are those who think it is a mistake to have constituted any such inquiry, but for myself I feel strongly that it would have been most inadvisable for the Government to burke an enquiry with disturbances of such magnitude. I am convinced that the case which we shall be able to put forward in support of our action is a strong one and I am not afraid of the verdict which may be found.

Montagu did not share his optimism. More 'unpleasant rumours' were reaching him that public meetings were still being banned, newspapers suppressed and punitive measures introduced. This was at the end of August, and the Secretary of State's objections were not entirely fair. The martial law regulations had all been lifted. But it reflected once again how the abysmal communications system prevented a true appraisal of the situation. Montagu thought he was expressing views on the current position when he telegraphed:

> Now what is the use of all this if it be true? Is it defensible in the first place, and if it is defensible, is it any use? If you prohibit public meetings, if men have something to say to one another, they will say worse things at private meetings …Now if it had not been for the promised inquiry I should have passed orders on my views long after expressing them

officially to you.

He went on to add that he was not suggesting that the Viceroy was wrong to back the Punjab Government or the military when they were faced with such enormous problems, but when the troubles were over he should be firm in his denunciation of some of the things which had happened:

> I state emphatically once again that there is no defence in my opinion either for the prohibition of lawyers from other Provinces to defend people on trial for serious crimes, or for whipping in the case of people not guilty of crimes of violence, and it ought to be known publicly that your Government does not countenance such things.

He pleaded with Chelmsford not to adopt the view that the Government of India had to defend everything that had been done or that the inquiry should whitewash everything. 'In that case we shall have achieved nothing and we shall have done more to embitter feelings than anything.' The inquiry must be totally fearless, and he said he had stated this in a letter to Lord Hunter, former Solicitor-General for Scotland, who had been appointed to preside over the inquiry.

The exchanges between the two men did little to lessen the growing mistrust, and while Lord Chelmsford was prepared to admit that neither of them was blind to the fact that O'Dwyer was not sympathetic to the political aspirations of the educated Indians he was not prepared to condemn him out of hand as Edwin Montagu was. There was ample justification for the action that had been taken, while at the same time he conceded that he had not overpainted the situation in India in order to avoid panic among people in Britain who had relations there. Possibly as a result of this the seriousness of the position had not been made apparent.

Montagu was not appeased and he could not restrain himself from saying that he was upset that the Viceroy had not taken him into his confidence and informed him that the situation was worse than he had admitted. By which time the Secretary of State for India was beginning to have doubts himself about the wisdom of having an inquiry, but it was far too late now to draw back.

The two men were now perilously close to open animosity — Lord Chelmsford threatened to express their differences in public and Montagu was forced to rebuke him:

> It is against all the traditions of your office and mine, and it
> does not make for the prestige of either part of the Indian
> Government... It is one of the most unpleasant duties that
> you have to carry out orders from home and conceal the fact
> that you dislike them extremely. That has always been the
> trouble with occupants of your position. I do not think I can
> claim to have been loyal to you in this respect.

That was as far as Montagu was prepared to go to heal the rift.
Whatever the Viceroy might say or think, the inquiry would be
absolutely fearless.

The two men were still poles apart when Lord Hunter sailed
for India with a letter from Montagu telling him that he had
nothing to fear from a searching inquiry.

By then the relationship between the Viceroy and Montagu
had reached its lowest ebb. 'I seem to be everlastingly making
suggestions to you which you cannot accept, and finding that I
cannot accept your suggestions,' lamented Montagu. 'I feel
very uncomfortable. I wish that you had not left so much to
O'Dwyer. I wish O'Dwyer had not left so much to the
Military.'

Once more doubts about the wisdom of an inquiry assailed
him, but Lord Hunter was beyond recall.

9. Dyer Explains

'No more distasteful or responsible duty falls to the lot of the soldier than that which he is sometimes required to discharge in aid of the civil power. If his measures are too mild he fails in his duty. If they are deemed to be excessive he is liable to be attacked as a cold-blooded murderer.'— Lieutenant-General Sir Havelock Hudson.

The Afghanistan rising was quickly suppressed and no one played a more heroic part than General Dyer. The Amir had grossly miscalculated. He had timed his invasion to coincide with what he had been led to believe would be a widespread revolt in India, but when Dyer set off it was so quiet in the Punjab that only eight British soldiers remained in Lahore. And there was little doubt in the minds of the Europeans that the peaceful conditions that now existed were due entirely to Dyer's firm action in the Jallianwala Bagh.

Within a short time the skilled frontier soldier had added fresh laurels to his crown, for his defeat of the Afghan Commander-in-Chief, Nadir Khan, during the siege of Thal had been the decisive battle. But the General had paid a high price: his health had been far from good when the campaign began, but fighting in that rugged terrain where rain was a rarity, and the eyes were scorched by the stinging salt that blew off the treeless desert-like soil, had placed almost impossible strains on his already overtaxed system. During the advance on Thal his bearer had continually to drape cold towels round his head to relieve the intense pain that was nearly always with him. While he was actually dictating his orders for the final assault on the heights above the city he had collapsed in agony and had only been revived by the aspirin and brandy which, on his doctor's orders, Captain Briggs, his Brigade Major, always had at hand.

Even so, the Jallianwala Bagh was never far from his thoughts, and he confided to Lieutenant-Colonel Morgan, 'I hear they want my blood for Amritsar.' Morgan told him not to worry as General Beynon had approved his action and Sir Michael O'Dwyer had endorsed it. Admittedly, Beynon had said, when they met in Lahore, 'But what I could not understand is why you shot so many.' But if Dyer had any doubts they were soon dispelled. General Sir Arthur Barrett, commanding at Peshawar, told him: 'That's all right, you would have heard about it long before this if your action had not been approved.'

Broken in health but not in spirit, he bade farewell to Briggs and both men were visibly moved at the parting, for an almost father-son relationship existed between them.

General Dyer was sent to the hill station of Dalhousie on sick leave and there he began to prepare his official report to the General Staff, 16th Indian Division. It was completed on 25 August. Arrogantly confident that his act would not be questioned, he wrote a long account, marked in parts by odd personal phraseology, that went well beyond the requirements necessary to account for his action. It was an error he was to regret. If he had confined himself to talking as a soldier all would have been well, but he committed the cardinal error of seeing his duty as something far greater and more important than dispersing a seditious meeting.

In a long preamble — 'in order to show why I considered it my bounden duty to disperse by rifle fire the unlawful assembly in the Jallianwala Bagh on 13 April 1919' — he recalled that he had previously often restored law and order without resorting to violence.

I mention the above incidents merely to show that when possible I use my best endeavour to suppress riotous crowds without the use of unnecessary force. At Amritsar the case was different.

The crowd, in complete defiance of his orders, had forced his hand and he had had no alternative; the city was in a state of complete lawlessness and from the military point of view he had every reason to open fire. He recounted his proclamation which was deliberately flouted:

The gathering in the Jallianwala Bagh must have received ample warning of my coming and I personally had ample time to consider the nature of the painful duty I might be faced with.

The scene was still vividly fresh in his mind and came alive as he described it.

> I was faced with a dense mass of men evidently holding a seditious meeting. In the centre of the square was a raised platform and a man on it was gesticulating and addressing the crowd. The crowd appeared to be a mixed one, consisting of city people and outsiders. I did not see a single woman or child in the assembly. Many villagers were, I understand, induced to come to the Bagh by a promise that their taxes and land revenues would be abolished as the British 'Raj' was at an end. Evidently those who came believing the British 'Raj' was at an end were themselves not very innocent.

The General was writing with hindsight, and this became all too apparent when his report was being read. But so far he had not written anything to which his superiors could seriously object. Then the warning lights began to flash.

> There was no reason to further parley with the mob; evidently they were there to defy the arm of the law. The responsibility was very great. If I fired I must fire with good effect, a small amount of firing would be a criminal act of folly. I had the choice of carrying out a very distasteful and horrible duty or of neglecting to do my duty, of suppressing disorder or of becoming responsible for all future bloodshed. We cannot be brave unless we be possessed of a greater fear. I had considered the matter from every point of view. My duty and my military instincts told me to fire. My conscience was also clear on that point. What faced me was what on the morrow would be the Danda Fauj (Rebel Army). I fired and continued to fire until the crowd dispersed and I consider this the least amount of firing which would produce the necessary moral and widespread effect it was my duty to produce, if I was to justify my action. If more troops had been at hand the casualties would have been greater in proportion. It was no longer a question of merely dispersing the crowd, but one of producing a sufficient moral effect, from a military point of view, not only on those who were present but more specially throughout the Punjab. There could be no question of undue severity.

Blissfully unaware of the political significance that would later be attached to his words, Dyer went on to state in a matter-of-fact fashion that the troops had then returned to the Ram Bagh where their ammunition pouches were examined and it was recorded that 1650 rounds of .303 Mark VI ammunition had been fired.

Open rebellion existed in Amritsar and he had suppressed it, and of the 25,000 to 30,000 who had assembled there, 'every man who escaped from the Jallianwala Bagh was a messenger to tell that law and order had been restored in Amritsar'.

The General went on to explain why he had turned his back on the wounded:

I did not offer help because the military situation had to be considered throughout the incident. The crowd was so dense that if a determined rush had been made at any time, arms or no arms, my small force must instantly have been overpowered and consequently I was very careful of not giving the mob a chance of organizing. I sometimes ceased fire and redirected my fire where the crowd was collected more thickly. By the time I had completely dispersed the crowd my ammunition was running short. I returned to the Ram Bagh without counting or inspecting the casualties. The crowd was free now to ask for medical aid, but this they avoided doing lest they themselves be proved to have attended the assembly. They asked me if they might bury their dead, and to this I consented.

His report gave the impression that this permission was given that evening and not the next, but this was a point that escaped attention at the time. What did not was his apparent indifference, or blindness, to the fact that he had acted with incredible callousness. Furthermore, he had not answered the question, he had evaded it. He had only withdrawn when the meeting had been dispersed and there was no possible danger of attack.

The report then went on to deal with the 'Crawling Order' and the whipping in the Kucha Tawarian.

Six persons were whipped in the street where Miss Sherwood fell but as both ends of this street were closed to the public, it can hardly be looked upon as a public thoroughfare.

The General then explained how this came about. After seeing Miss Sherwood swathed in bandages he had personally inspected the spot where she was assaulted and ordered a triangle to be erected there, and issued orders that anyone who wished to leave or enter the street would have to do so on all fours. It never entered his mind that anyone would do it voluntarily, and he could only conclude that they did it to make martyrs of themselves.

The youths had been flogged there as he considered it a suitable punishment for the attack on the missionary. He did not mention that they had not been tried or found guilty of the assault.

And there the General hoped the matter would be allowed to rest. He had stated as openly and as frankly as possible why he had acted as he did and he could not see anything in his report that would not command approval from his military superiors; all he had done was to remind everyone, as if they needed reminding, that he had saved India for the Empire. In any case, it was widely known, if not officially announced, that the Government of India was to pass a Bill of Indemnity which would ensure that no officer would suffer for carrying out his duty during the martial law period, provided he had acted in good faith. And that, General Dyer was convinced, he had done.

        ✻   ✻   ✻

When the Government of India announced that it proposed to introduce an Act of Indemnity the news did nothing to improve the rapidly worsening air of mistrust among a large number of Indians. They felt it was being done with unseemly haste and saw it as a deliberate attempt to forestall the actions of the Hunter Committee, and nothing the Government said could dispel the suspicion that something underhand was going on.

When the Bill was debated in the Imperial Legislative Council, great pains were taken to explain why it was necessary and Members were told that by English constitutional law any servant of the Crown, even in times of grave disorder, who infringed the law was liable to face the legal consequences, no matter whether his action was correct or he was merely obeying orders.

'Thus if an Indian soldier is ordered to fire on a dangerous mob and kills a man he is liable to be hanged for murder. If he refuses to obey the order he is liable to be shot for disobedience'.

Therefore it was essential to protect those officers who had acted in good faith in suppressing the disorders. If this was not done then the State quite clearly could not in times of trouble rely on the troops to restore law and order.

The Bill would simply protect from legal action those who had acted in *good faith* and in the belief that their actions were necessary. It still left it open for the courts to decide whether or not the action was *bona fide*, and if they found the action was indefensible the officer concerned would have to face the legal consequences.

It did not protect any officer from departmental punishment, reprimand, degradation or dismissal if the Committee of Inquiry found his actions unjustifiable.

Neither did it commit the Indian Legislative Council to approving the actions of the Punjab Government; an assurance which would have sounded empty if critics had known of the assurances the Viceroy had demanded from Mr Montagu.

The Bill was debated in September and it was a foregone conclusion that it would be passed. Even so several non-official Members tried hard to scotch or delay it. The most forceful critic of the measure, and also the spokesman for the Indian National Congress which was wholly opposed to it, was Pandit Madan Mohan Malaviya. He had already been appointed by the Congress to sit on its own committee of inquiry into the disturbances and had made a personal tour of the disaffected areas and spoken to many people who had been personally involved. He was armed for the debate with a mass of material which he unhesitatingly used with all the fervour of prosecuting counsel. For to him it was not merely an occasion to debate the rights or wrongs of the proposed Bill but an opportunity to attack everything that had been done in the Punjab past and present.

Like many of his political colleagues he had little faith in the Hunter Committee and would have preferred a more wide-ranging investigation in the form of a Royal Commission. He was a brilliant but loquacious orator, who, like so many Indian politicians, did not know when to sit down; his own words mesmerised him. During a speech that lasted four and a half hours he expounded on all the grievances of the people of the Punjab, berated Sir Michael O'Dwyer's rule, attacked General Dyer's callousness and condemned out of hand the shooting in the Jallianwala Bagh; and he accused the Government of the Punjab of withholding information and the Indian Government of a cover-up.

But as in all debates which develop into head-on political clashes the real issues became blurred as points were scored. It was only natural that the less committed Indian Members should have become confused over some of the things that were said.

As the debate dragged on it revealed the open hostility that existed between some non-official Members and the Europeans, for the verbal exchanges were often marked by personal abuse. Most Indians felt that the Bill was being introduced simply because the Government was determined to see that Dyer and other officers and officials were not punished for what they had done.

Sir William Vincent, the Home Department Member who introduced the measure, patiently explained the Act clause by clause, but he only seemed to confirm the suspicions and fears of some of its critics; he seemed to be saying that it could do all the things they had been assured it could not. Especially worrying was the clause which said that any officer was immune from legal action if he had acted in 'good faith'. It was so difficult to define 'good faith'. It was in the same category as 'minimum force'.

Sardar Sundar Singh Majithia, one of the Punjab Members, said he would only give his assent to the Bill if those who had broken the law were liable to punishment. '. . . I want to be assured fully that Government has no intention to afford protection to those who have acted against the strictest sense of justice and against good faith'.

Sir William assured Members that the Bill would in no way forestall the coming inquiry, and he added that it would have no effect on the report of the Committee, neither would it hamper its work.

This Bill simply deals with suits and legal proceedings, and really all that it seeks to do is to protect from legal proceedings *bona fide* action taken with a reasonable belief that it was necessary to suppress disorder, and not any action taken *mala fide* or without good reason.

Sir William said he would be surprised and disappointed if the

Council did not give the protection to officers for actions which were morally right though possibly not legally right.

> How can any Member of this Council expect an officer to act confidently, firmly and decisively if he knows that this Legislative Council and the Government will repudiate his action at the first opportunity?

Mr J. P. Thompson, Chief Secretary to the Government of the Punjab, was as bad as Pandit Malaviya when it came to discussing everything but the Bill that was being proposed. He took the debate as an opportunity to denounce all that Pandit Malaviya had said. When it came to the number of people killed in the Jallianwala Bagh he became quite incensed at the Pandit's estimate that more than five hundred had died. British inquiries showed the figures to be two hundred and ninety-one and anything beyond that had to be viewed with the 'gravest suspicion'.

Inevitably, in a debate that was essentially legal, precedents were produced to justify the action proposed, and there were references to Wat Tyler, Pitt, George III, Jack Cade and Charles Dickens.

Sir George Lowndes, the Law Member, skilfully steered the debate away from personal attacks and got back to the business in hand. 'After the disturbances have been put down we do not want the battles fought all over again in the Courts; what we want is peace and quiet.'

But one particular observation of Sir George's lacked the ring of truth as far as Pandit Malaviya and his supporters were concerned.

> When we talk of indemnifying officers, it is not the high officers of Government you are asked to indemnify. It is the Gurkha soldiers who fired on the mob and, maybe, killed people; it is the Indian soldiers and Indian officers whom you are asked to indemnify just as much as the British officers. Every soldier who fires according to orders and, maybe, kills a person, may be liable under common law of the country to be indicted for murder.

This observation reeked of hypocrisy for not even the staunchest supporter of the Government would claim that the Bill was being introduced to protect the fifty nameless soldiers who had marched off into total anonymity.

But the speech which aroused most indignation and prompted a furious reaction from Montagu was the one made by Sir Havelock Hudson, the Adjutant-General, who, in what was described as the 'Soldiers' View', seemed to approve Dyer's action and condone the 'Crawling Order'. Recalling all the events which had led to the shooting in the Jallianwala Bagh he said:

> It was clearly the duty of the officer in command to disperse this unlawful assembly. Realizing the danger to his small force, unless he took immediate action, and being well aware of the inadequacy of the measures taken to restore order on 10 April, he ordered fire to be opened. The crowd was dispersed and the force was withdrawn. I have given the Council this narrative to show how the situation would be viewed by the soldier, and will content myself with saying that from the military point of view the sequence of events justified the exercise of military force, and that the subject of its exercise was fully attained.

As for the 'Crawling Order', he felt sure that Members would agree that in view of the attack on Miss Sherwood 'some unusual measures were necessary to bring home to the mob that such acts of violence directed against defenceless women would not be tolerated.'

However, Dyer was not the sole object of his comments, for it was known that other officers had been severely criticized, among them the pilots of aeroplanes which had been used to quell riots:

> It may, of course, be argued that a bomb cannot be dropped nor a machine gun fired from an aeroplane with any great degree of accuracy. This may be true, but when the mark aimed at is an unlawful assembly it is not very material whether those in front or behind are made to suffer.

The most important thing to bear in mind was that the man on the spot was the only one who could decide on the amount of force necessary.

Finally Sir William Vincent pointed out that only the officers of the Crown would be protected by the Bill, the Government itself was not.

We leave any remedy there may be against the Government entirely open. If there is any complaint to be made in a civil action, any claim to damages open, let the man who complains sue Government, let him take his chances in the courts; we all know how Government is sued — in the name of the Secretary of State. Have we attempted by this Bill to preclude actions against the Secretary of State? Are we not responsible? Have we not from the very first as a Government taken responsibility for what we have thought to be necessary?

The Bill was passed, as everyone knew it would be, but it had at least provided a platform for the Indian viewpoint to be expressed, the Punjab Government to refute it, and the Government of India to honour its pledge to the men who had been called in to restore law and order.

On 11 October the lengthy and long-awaited statement from the Punjab Government was submitted to the Government of India. After careful study it was then sent to the Hunter Committee which was due to begin its sittings in Delhi on 29 October. A copy was also sent to Westminster, but it did not arrive until 18 December; not that the delay mattered a great deal for Edwin Montagu had committed himself to waiting for Lord Hunter's findings, and therefore any expression of his personal opinion would have been out of place. Needless to say, it did not impress him.

Understandably for a Government under such fierce attack and one that saw itself unfairly cast as the prisoner in the dock, it was more of an apologia than a strictly factual account, which made its worth somewhat debatable in the eyes of the Members of the Committee. It admitted few errors, sought justification of its actions on the flimsiest and often most unreliable evidence, dismissed criticisms with a curtness that smacked of arrogance, and skirted controversial issues. In short, its contents did not measure up to its bulk.

The most important task facing the Government of the Punjab was to establish without fear of contradiction that a conspiracy to create widespread revolt did exist, and this the report set about achieving with considerable confidence. Page after page were devoted to extracts from speeches and newspaper articles to support the contention that sedition was widespread, and details were included of the fines imposed on editors and the number of newspapers which had been closed. Unfortunately, some of the extracts tended to confirm the suspicion that anything and everything was considered seditious.

But the Government did not rely solely on the extracts. Conclusive proof that there *was* a conspiracy was contained in the independent judgement of Mr Justice Broadway in the Amritsar Leaders Case, and others in which it had been found that the accused had waged war against the Crown. The widespread riots in the city which the civil authorities had been unable to cope with were ample justification for the introduction of martial law.

In answer to criticisms that it had been harshly administered the report reiterated that martial law cannot be administered with kid gloves. It had been necessary, in order to restore law and order and create the required change of morale among the people, to introduce an entirely new type of administration:

> It was necessary that it should be in a position to secure unquestioning obedience to its orders; and it was inevitable that it should be given summary powers of a type which would be impossible in ordinary circumstances. That the administration of martial law should cause inconvenience to many who were not directly concerned, and did not even sympathize with disorder, was inevitable; but it is equally clear that it succeeded, and with a speed that must be its best justification, in restoring an atmosphere of law and order in the proclaimed districts.

It was an honest opinion that could have been expressed a little more tactfully, for it implied that there was no distinction between the law-abiding citizen and the rebel.

The allegation that certain officers had deliberately flouted instructions was dismissed with the bland observation:

> It is possible that in isolated cases officers may have exercised their discretion improperly; one case at least has been mentioned in the Lahore District Report. The stories of promiscuous whipping under martial law, without discretion of age or social position, are of course without foundation.

The report, moreover, made it abundantly clear that the Government did not accept that any of the trials, whether by

Special Commissioners or Summary Courts, had been improperly conducted or that there had been any miscarriages of justice.

The widespread allegations of police brutality and coercion merited the complacent reply, 'That cases could altogether be avoided, in regard to the police, was impossible'. No attempt was made to explain why, and it seemed as if the Government which demanded unquestioning obedience to its orders also anticipated unquestioning acceptance of its report.

Graphic and often harrowing accounts were given of the rioting and looting that took place in Amritsar on 10 April, and there were particularly vivid descriptions of the attack on Miss Sherwood, the sacking and burning of the banks and the cremation of the innocent bank employees. Undoubtedly the detail was intended to arouse emotion, but they were extremely factual accounts and represented an accurate picture of the dangers confronting the small and isolated white community, and the fears that consumed them. The impression was given that, rightly or wrongly, they feared a second Mutiny which would dwarf the still remembered slaughter of 1857.

Little attempt was made to add to what was known of the Jallianwala Bagh incident. It was a seditious meeting called in open defiance of the General's proclamation and he had had no alternative but to disperse it by gunfire. While admitting that there were a number of peasants present who had not attended the meeting for any political purpose, it did not elaborate. It also dismissed the claim that there were large numbers of children killed.

Aware that the loyalty of the Indian troops was always a constant source of anxiety, the report set out to expose widespread discontent in the Indian Army which had been insidiously fanned by extremists. At times, however, the report seemed to be clutching at straws to stress the dangers that existed, for some of the examples quoted were remarkably trivial. In any event, it had to concede that the troops had remained remarkably loyal: in the whole of the Punjab only eighteen Sepoys had been convicted of offences arising from the disturbances. Furthermore, the evidence tended to show that what discontent there was had little or nothing to do with politics. It was largely over pay and conditions and the way the Indian soldier was being treated in the aftermath of the war. An added weakness to the argument was that many of the statements referred to incidents which occurred *after* the rebellion had been suppressed, so could not have been taken into consideration by the Government when it was drawing up its plans to cope with the emergency. Apart from anything else, there was similar unrest among a large number of British soldiers in India.

The report went on to try and establish a connection between the disturbances and the war with Afghanistan. It was true that the Amir of Afghanistan had not made his move without being informed that India was on the brink of a revolution, and there was evidence to support that. But in its efforts to make political mountains where only molehills existed, the Government of the Punjab often stretched credulity to breaking point. Apart from Russia's involvement in Afghanistan and other Islamic countries, large amounts of roubles were being smuggled into India to foment revolt. Furthermore, there was a three-way link-up between the Russians, Indian extremists and the Independent Labour Party, 'definitely Bolshevik in all but name only'. Regular contact was maintained between some Indians and George Lansbury, and Indian money had been sent to England to finance the *Daily Herald*, 'the chief Bolshevik newspaper in England'.

Another sinister portent was that Indian railway workers had been in touch with the Railway Workers Union in Britain with the object of forming their own union, while the Government clerks in Lahore had tried to do the same thing. But again the Government undermined its own case by admitting economic conditions were the main cause of industrial unrest.

Such tenuous arguments undoubtedly appealed to people who had spent most of their lives in India where social progress moved at a snail's pace, but to those with some knowledge of the political scene in England they seemed naive to say the least. The observations of the Punjab Government merely confirmed the suspicion that the men who ruled the Province were political dinosaurs in their concept of how to govern and ostriches when it came to recognizing legitimate political demands.

10. Damning Evidence

'It was a merciful act but at the same time it was a horrible act, and it took a lot of doing.' — General Dyer.

Lahore, the capital of the Punjab, sprawled along the left bank of the River Ravi. The summer of 1919 had been the hottest in living memory with the temperature soaring above 115 and the city had lived up to its unenviable reputation of being one of the most unbearable places on earth. But by November the agonies of the last few months had been forgotten; the cold season was well advanced, and although the sun still shone with incandescent brightness it was benevolent and there was often a cool breeze fanning the leaves of the trees.

In many respects Lahore was a microcosm of the British Raj at its zenith. High above the surrounding countryside stood the Old City where the vast majority of the Indian population lived in a bustling, congested network of tortuous lanes. In prosaic contrast was the European quarter dominated by the majestic tree-lined Mall with its impressive but unimaginative buildings. The civil lines were comprised of neat bungalows surrounded by gardens in which their British owners tried desperately hard to grow flowers from seeds imported from England, and create lawns that were lush and true enough for tennis and croquet.

On 11 November the mood of the city underwent a dramatic yet indefinable change. There was an air of expectancy abroad in which tension, exhilaration and a sense of foreboding and optimism shared equal parts. Lord Hunter and the members of his Committee had arrived in the city.

No one was more aware than Lord Hunter that his Committee did not command the absolute support and respect of the British or Indians. Although its members had been chosen after a lot of careful thought and deliberation and with a genuine desire to create a well-balanced and impartial team, it inspired little confidence. It was widely known that Lord Hunter had not been the automatic choice for President, and there was a feeling among the British that they had been fobbed off with second-best, despite the fact that he was a lawyer of outstanding ability and integrity. But that prejudice should have been countered by the other appointments. The Hon Mr Justice G.C. Rankin was a distinguished judge of the Calcutta High Court and a man who knew India intimately. The Hon Mr F. W. Rice was Additional Secretary to the Government of India, Home Department, and the Hon Mr Thomas Smith was a Member of the Legislative Council of the Lieutenant-Governor of the United Provinces. The Army was ably represented by Major-General Sir George Barrow, Commanding the Peshawar Division, and the Indian side by the Hon Pandit Jagat Narayan, B.A., a Member of the United Provinces Legislative Council, and Sir Chimanlal Harila Setalvad, an Advocate of the High Court of Bombay, and Sardar Sahibzada Sultan Ahmed Khan, Muntazim-Ud-Doula, M.A., LL.M. (Cantab) and a Member for Appeals in Gwalior State.

It had already got off to a bad start. The Indians thought it was a case of the Indian Government sitting in judgement on itself, for all the Members bar Lord Hunter had been appointed by the Government. Sir Michael O'Dwyer had been incensed at the inclusion of Pandit Narayan and the Punjab Government had vigorously opposed his appointment. The Indians further objected that only official witnesses were to be heard. The vanquished had as much right to speak as the victors. On 12 November there was another setback for the already harassed Lord Hunter when the President of the Indian National Congress informed him that as the Punjab Government refused to release the imprisoned leaders on the guarantee of adequate securities in order to give evidence, the Congress would not appear before the Inquiry to give evidence on behalf of the people.

The boycott was not as high-principled as it appeared, for the independent inquiry set up by the National Congress was well under way and many of the prisoners and eye-witnesses to events had already been interviewed. This meant that the Indian Inquiry would be able to hear much of the evidence presented to Lord Hunter without having to reveal any of the material it had collected itself or subject it to open scrutiny.

The first session of the Inquiry had all the elements of a First Night about it. Queues formed outside the impressive white-walled building and Indians jostled and pushed each other in an effort to grab the seats which had been set aside for the public. The gallery was crowded with Europeans. As witnesses arrived they were booed or cheered and derisive cries of '*Government ka mama*' (Government's uncle) greeted the appearance of the Hon Major Malik Sir Umar Hayat Khan, a staunch supporter of Sir Michael O'Dwyer and the Punjab Government.

The Indian journalists were also having a field day. For the first time in months they could freely report what was about to be revealed without having their copy censored or their newspapers threatened with closure. Unfortunately their impartiality was suspect, and not without reason, for some of them saw it as an occasion for reprisals.

The evidence was submitted to the Committee in the form of a prepared written statement, followed by verbal evidence on which the witness could be questioned. Miles Irving appeared and gave a detailed account of the build-up to the disturbances and the period of Martial Law. He was followed by various other officials, police officers and soldiers. Inspector Jowahar Lal had a particularly torrid time at the hands of Pandit Narayan who questioned him closely and at length about the statement of Hans Raj and his own reasons for destroying the notes he had made during their interview. But apart from the damaging admission that he had left the meeting in order to save his own skin because the Army would soon be arriving, he survived the interrogation reasonably well.

The reporters took desultory notes as witness after witness gave evidence. They were waiting, as everyone else was, for the appearance of the one man who was largely responsible for the atmosphere that pervaded the city: Brigadier-General Reginald Edward Harry Dyer.

Dyer was not short of friends and supporters, and those closest to him were extremely worried. They were well aware of his temperamental excitability in moments of stress and knew he was quite capable of losing his composure under cross-examination, especially from the Indian members. The Indian Government, contrary to its original decision, had urged him to avail himself of Counsel, and this advice had been pressed by friends, including General Sir William Beynon who knew him well and liked him very much. But he obstinately refused and insisted that he would conduct his own case.

There was a burst of applause from the British members of the public as he strode in and gave Lord Hunter a parade-ground salute. The President quietly invited him to sit down. Lord Hunter opened the questioning and the General answered in an outspoken manner without pausing to search for words, at no time showing the slightest hesitation. He called Lord Hunter *Sir* and never became ruffled, but later it was noticed that he did not accord the Indian members the same courtesy and at times was brusque to the point of rudeness.

Lord Hunter's questioning seemed gentle enough to start with, but the line began to harden when the General was asked why he had not tried to stop the meeting assembling in the Jallianwala Bagh. Dyer replied that he thought he had done enough to deter them. When he heard the meeting was being held in defiance of his orders, he took a small force there, marched in and opened fire immediately. At no time did it occur to him to order the crowd to disperse. No, he had not consulted the Deputy Commissioner about his intentions for he had made up his mind that if he did not fire immediately he would be failing in his duty.

'My mind was made up as I came along in my motor car — if my orders were not obeyed, I would fire immediately.'

As soon as the soldiers opened fire the crowd began to disperse.

Lord Hunter said quietly, 'If the crowd was going to disperse, why did you not stop firing?'

Dyer seemed to have misunderstood the question for he explained that it was his duty to fire until the meeting dispersed and if he had limited his fire the effect would not have been sufficient and he would not have been justified in firing at all. But then he undid his somewhat turgid explanation by admitting that he could have dispersed the meeting without firing at all.

'Why did you not adopt that course?' asked the President.

'I could not disperse them for some time; then they would come back and laugh at me and I consider I would be making myself a fool.'

It seemed a perfectly rational answer to a man who had been born in the country and spent the bulk of his service life there. One had to command respect if one was to govern.

He went on to say that everything pointed to the existence of a widespread revolt which was not confined to Amritsar. The crowd before him were rebels who were trying to isolate his forces and sever them from outside supplies. 'Therefore I considered it my duty to fire on them and to fire well. I looked upon it as my duty, a very horrible duty.'

As for the number of casualties he could only estimate those, and this he had done by dividing the number of rounds fired by five or six — he wasn't sure of the exact number — and calculated the dead at 300. The wounded would be considerably higher. When his estimate was queried by one of the Indian members he became rather irritable. 'Had I not been a musketry instructor?' he retorted.

The questioning followed no chronological order; it moved from one subject to another, then returned to something he thought he had adequately answered a few minutes earlier. It was confusing and irritating. Dyer was not a sophisticated man and he only knew one way in which to answer questions: with total honesty. When he gave as his reason for not attending the wounded that it was not a military matter, he was stating a fact. He was not concerned with the impression his answer created. And he was as forthright about the President's observation that martial law had not been proclaimed at the time of the shooting. It existed *ipso facto* when Miles Irving asked him to take over.

Hunter then asked him about attempts to undermine the loyalty of his soldiers.

'There were a good many rumours, and I was informed that the citizens of Amritsar had been giving my Sepoys sweets and so on with a view to getting at them. Beyond that I did not see anything wrong among the troops,' he replied.

When it came to the subject of whippings his candour began to arouse concern among his friends. He thought it would make a good impression. 'I do not think I have whipped anyone in public,' and added unnecessarily, 'It was not due to me that I did not, but I was ordered not to. So I took down what I looked upon as a platform for public lashings. I never lashed anybody on it.'

Unfortunately for the General, the President was not satisfied with the answer and he continued to pursue it. What about the people who had been whipped in the Kucha Tawarian? He did not consider that a public place. Neither was he concerned that innocent bystanders had been forced to watch. 'Unfortunately for them, owing to the wicked acts of others, they came under martial law; and if they had to look at things like that, it may have been unfortunate, but under martial law it could not be helped.'

From now on he began to make some very rash observations. Perhaps he was tired, or in pain, or perhaps his confidence had outgrown his sense of discretion, but his replies to persistent questions about the 'Crawling Order' suggested that he had let his emotions overrule his sense of balance.

'I felt a woman had been beaten. We look upon woman as sacred or ought to. I was searching my brain for a suitable punishment to meet this awful case. I did not know how to meet it in a suitable manner. There was a bit of an accident in that. When I posted the pickets I went down and ordered a triangle to be erected. I felt the street ought to be looked upon as sacred. Therefore I posted a couple of pickets and told them no Indians were to pass, they must go on all fours. It never entered my brain that any sensible or sane man under those conditions would intentionally go through that street.'

But how else could people living there go about their normal business? It seemed an unnecessary quibble to the soldier. They could leave when the pickets had been removed. He had forgotten the curfew. In his mind it was no great inconvenience if they had to suffer a little for all that Amritsar had done. Although there were no back entrances they could easily go out over the roof tops.

Even those staunchly behind the General found his answers perplexing and at times almost unintelligible. When it was pointed out that the street was not one frequented by the missionary's attackers he said, 'No, I had erected a platform in the middle of the street and when I got those men who had beaten Miss Sherwood, I wanted to lash them there. I wanted also to keep the street what I call sacred. Therefore I did not want anybody to pass through it. It was an accident that these men had to crawl there.'

The General was gradually losing his veneer of total self-confidence. Yet he seemed unaware that some of his answers appeared nonsensical. If he had not wanted anybody to pass through, why had a party of prisoners been escorted there?

'I did not hear of that. If they took anybody deliberately, even those were not sent there deliberately. It was a pure accident that they got there. My orders were published and therefore when the Sergeant saw them, he made them do what I had ordered; but I never judged that any sane man would go there voluntarily.' It seemed pointless to remind him that prisoners did not go anywhere voluntarily.

Lord Hunter was still far from satisfied that he knew *why* Dyer had whipped the six men in the street; he had told him that although he knew they were the men who had attacked Miss Sherwood they had not been whipped for that. It was self-contradictory.

Lord Hunter was patience personified.

'Lashing was not given in respect of the assault on Miss Sherwood. Therefore I do not see that the punishment that was meted out in consequence of that could have any effect as a lesson to others. Were the punishments meted out in respect of some breach of fort discipline or order?'

'It was a coincidence, I suppose, when I found that these were the men who had beaten Miss Sherwood. That was the place to lash them.'

It was all too much for Lord Hunter who observed, 'I can quite understand that if they had been lashed at the time, but in consequence of their having beaten Miss Sherwood they were not lashed. Except for a different offence. I do not quite see how you achieve anything by having them lashed in the street.'

The questioning was then taken over by Mr Justice Rankin who returned once again to the Jallianwala Bagh. He wanted to know why the General had not issued any warning for the gathering to disperse. Had he thought that his small force might be attacked?

'No. The situation was very serious. I had made up my mind that I would do all men to death if they were going to continue the meeting.'

The melodramatic phrasing surprised General Barrow and he made a mental note of it.

Unaware of the impression his words had created in the mind of a fellow officer, he blithely continued to answer the

Judge who asked if he had resorted to what had been called 'frightfulness' for the benefit of the Punjab as a whole. Dyer pondered the question. 'No. I don't think so. I think it was a horrible duty for me to perform. It was a merciful act that I had given them the chance to disperse. The responsibility was very great. I had made up my mind that if I fired I must fire well and strong so that it would have a full effect. I had decided if I fired one round I must shoot a lot of rounds, or I must not shoot at all. My logical conclusion was that I must disperse the crowd which had defied the arm of the law. I fired and continued to fire until the crowd dispersed.'

'From time to time you changed your firing and directed it to places where the crowd was getting thicker than other places?'

'That is so.'

When the Judge reverted to the whipping in the Kucha Tawarian, General Dyer became hopelessly muddled. The men, he insisted, had not been flogged for the assault. But everyone knew they were guilty. They were punished later for that offence.

'You said everybody knew they were guilty of this offence against Miss Sherwood, but how did that come about? How did everybody know?'

'I did not mean to convey that these particular men had really committed that offence,' he commented weakly.

Question followed question with great rapidity, and still the real purpose behind the General's decision remained blurred.

'The chances were from what I had heard and been told that these men were the particular men. If they were not the particular men and another man was beaten, still it did not matter very much whether he was beaten there or somewhere else, if he was convicted. I did not wish to run the risk, if he had committed the offence against Miss Sherwood, of his being beaten somewhere else. Therefore when I heard that these were the men, I had them beaten in the same street.'

It all seemed a fuss over nothing to Dyer. The men had only received thirty lashes.

'In the old days it used to be hundreds of lashes. Nowadays I look upon it as a not very severe sentence.'

If the General had thought the Judge had been pugnacious in his probing he soon realized it had been quite gentle in comparison to the interrogation he suffered at the hands of the

Indian members. Sir Chimanlal Setalvad began innocuously enough by asking him if he thought himself competent to take over from Miles Irving.

'Oh yes, rather,' said Dyer confidently.

The Indian led him gently through the events leading to the shootings in the Jallianwala Bagh, and, lulled into a false sense of security, Dyer readily admitted that when he first heard of the meeting he had already made up his mind to fire.

Blind to the trap into which he was being led, he rashly answered hypothetical questions rather than decline to give an opinion on something that had not happened.

'Supposing the passage was sufficient to allow the armoured cars to go in, would you have opened fire with the machine guns?'

'I think probably yes.'

Naturally the casualties would then have been much higher. Sir Chimanlal then turned to the General's written report and casually inquired if his idea had been to strike terror and produce a wide moral effect throughout the Province rather than just dispersing the assembly.

'If they disobeyed my orders it showed there was a complete defiance of law, that there was something much more serious behind it than I imagined, that therefore these were rebels and I must not treat them with gloves on. They had come out to fight if they defied me, and I was going to give them a lesson.'

'I take it that your idea in taking that action was to strike terror?'

'Call it what you like. I was going to punish them. My idea from the military point of view was to make a wide impression.'

Dyer elaborated: Not only in Amritsar but throughout the Punjab.

'You thought that by striking terror in that manner you would save the British Raj? You thought the British Raj was in danger?'

'No, the British Raj is a mighty thing. It would not be in great danger but it might bring about more bloodshed, more looting, more lost lives.'

He had taken the action to save life and property and prevent a mutiny. 'It was a merciful act but at the same time it was a horrible act and it took a lot of doing.'

The Indian pressed him further. Did it not strike him that the frightfulness was doing the Raj a disservice?

'I did not like the idea of doing it, but I also realized that it was the only means of saving life and that any reasonable man with justice in his mind would realize that I had done the right thing; it was a merciful though horrible act and they ought to be thankful to me for doing it. I thought it would be doing a jolly lot of good and they would realize that they were not to be wicked,' he added in words that would have been more applicable to a schoolmaster admonishing a naughty pupil.

The General seemed to be going out of his way to antagonize his questioner with answers that were deliberately callous and offensive to Indian sentiments. That was clearly Sir Chimanlal's intention and, seeing how obliging the General was, he began to bait his questions with less subtlety. Had he fired on people who were lying down?

'I probably selected another target. There might have been firing on the people who were still lying down though I think there were better targets than that.'

Did he take any measure to help the wounded?

'No, certainly not. It was not my job. But the hospitals were open and the medical officers were there. The wounded only had to apply for help. But they did not do this because they themselves would be taken in custody for being in the assembly. I was ready to help them if they applied.'

As for the salaaming order, he saw nothing wrong with it at all. During martial law everyone was bound to salute him.

General Sir George Barrow had been getting more and more apprehensive at the reckless way in which his comrade-in-arms was walking into trap after trap and steered the questioning to less emotional matters. He began asking about martial law. First he set out to establish that Dyer sincerely believed that although martial law had not been officially proclaimed he was entitled to anticipate it as war was being waged against the Crown.

'I think you referred in your statement that expressions of special satisfaction were conveyed to you by a good many people, Indians, on your prompt action?'

'Yes, sir.' The tributes came from many quarters. 'They all said that I had saved the situation; I had saved the Punjab, and all kinds of praise were showered on me which I did not mention.'

175

It was a short-lived diversion for the interrogation was immediately taken up by Pandit Narayan. If Setalvad had wielded a rapier Narayan used a bludgeon. And a rattled Dyer foolishly committed himself to answers that on reflection he regretted.

Given the opportunity of correcting the impression that justice did not enter into his consideration when he had the six men whipped, he recklessly threw it aside and revealed himself to be totally incapable of recognizing the fact that the more he talked the more he appeared a fanatical bigot who quite happily punished people not for what they had done but for the impression it would create. The only time he displayed any hesitation was when he was questioned about certain orders he had issued and replied that Captain Briggs, his Brigade Major, was in a better position to answer. But Briggs, unknown to him, was seriously ill with appendicitis and was soon to die on the operating table. Such was the atmosphere of racial tension at the time that the story circulated among the Europeans that he had been poisoned with powdered glass.

Narayan was like a terrier with a bone. Few observers could have believed it possible that there was any more to be said over the 'Crawling Order', but he managed to produce a string of questions that shed no fresh light on the episode but clearly indicated the open hostility that now existed between the two men. When he referred to Dyer's report the General snapped, 'Read according to my words, not yours.'

There was also back-stage tension that few people were aware of. At one stage during the Inquiry the President and Sir Chimanlal Setalvad clashed, with the result that the Indian and European members drifted apart. During a discussion Lord Hunter lost his temper and retorted, 'You people want to drive the British out of the country.'

Setalvad became equally incensed and replied, 'It is perfectly legitimate for Indians to be free of foreign rule and Independence can be accomplished by mutual understanding and good will. The driving-out process will only become necessary if the British are represented in this country by people as short-sighted and intolerant as yourself.'

It was the parting of the ways, for, although they continued to work together, the Indian members did not speak to Hunter once the day's hearing was over.

General Dyer had been answering questions almost non-stop for several hours, and still there seemed no end to his ordeal. Narayan hammered away about the Jallianwala Bagh, clearly in the hope that the General would provide him with some more indiscreet observations. And he readily obliged.

'I directed the fire personally,' he said. 'I can tell you if you want what orders I gave. I never gave an order for firing overhead. Absolutely none.' Neither would he speculate on what might have happened if he had chosen a different course of action. 'I am not going to pass an opinion as to what would have happened if I had done something else.'

Narayan quietly asked him what he meant by saying his action had had a salutary effect.

'It is difficult to say. I want to punish the naughty boy: it would be difficult to say what would be the effect of punishment on a boy who is not naughty.'

'You never gave a moment's thought as to what would happen to the four hundred or five hundred persons that were killed inside the Jallianwala Bagh, as to how they would be attended to, as to how their relatives would come and take them away, as to how any water would be administered to them, as to how any medicine would be administered to them? It never occurred to you as to how it would be possible after 8 o'clock to remove the dead bodies?'

'They asked if they might remove them, and I allowed them to remove them; they could bring them what they liked,' said Dyer curtly.

Narayan was relentless. He knew he had exposed a raw nerve edge and persistent probing would produce a violent reaction. Had there been a modification to the curfew regulations? Had there been a proclamation to that effect?

'I allowed them to go. That is quite enough,' snapped Dyer.

'You had already made up your mind at the Ram Bagh that you had a very unpleasant duty to perform and that you had to do it?'

'Yes.'

'Did you make any ambulance arrangements?'

'I had no time for that.'

177

When General Dyer finished his evidence on 19 November he was visibly tired; he had been under an immense strain for hours on end, but he was confident that he had answered all the questions honestly and fearlessly. It was not in his nature to be evasive. He rose, put on his cap, saluted smartly, turned about and strode out; a ripple of applause greeted his departure.

When Dyer read through the newspaper reports of his evidence, he expressed surprise when he saw some of his replies in cold print. He could not recall making them, and he complained that words had been put into his mouth by some babu. He was particularly incensed about replies attributed to him when dealing with the 'Crawling Order' and the flogging in the Kucha Tawarian. And he strenuously denied ever saying he would do all men to death. When he had completed his evidence he was invited to tea with the new Lieutenant-Governor, Sir Edward Maclagan, who congratulated him on his testimony and said he wished all Englishmen would stand up for women as he had done. It was an opinion that was endorsed by the European community.

With his evidence completed, Dyer was free to leave Lahore. He decided to return to Jullundur via Delhi, and he and a party of fellow officers boarded the night train and crowded into a sleeping compartment. Unbeknown to the General, the top berth was occupied by a young Indian named Jawaharlal Nehru who was returning from Amritsar where he had been assisting the Congress sub-committee looking into the Punjab troubles. The fortuitous encounter was to have a traumatic effect on the Harrow-and-Cambridge-educated barrister. Next morning the British officers began to talk freely about the Jallianwala Bagh: it 'would teach the bloody browns a lesson'. If they were aware that an Indian was in the top bunk, they did not reveal it or curb their words. One of them, in pyjamas with bright pink stripes and dressing gown, was expounding at great length and in an agressive and triumphant manner of his accomplishments in Amritsar. In a short time Nehru realized that it was General Dyer. He boasted that he had held Amritsar at his mercy and felt like reducing the rebellious city to ashes, but had taken pity on it and refrained. The Indian was appalled at his callousness, and by the time the train reached Delhi Nehru was smouldering with hatred and resentment. The lawyer who had been a great admirer of Britain became, almost overnight, their implacable enemy.

11. In Camera

*'The idea which pervades everyone in India is that
the Army is intended to hold India against the
Indians'— Lord Curzon*

The Hunter Committee held twenty-nine sessions in Lahore
spread over a six-week period, and as the days passed interest began to wane. It was not that the disturbances were
no longer a topic of conversation. The drop in interest was
due entirely to the fact that the remaining important
witnesses were to be allowed to give their evidence in
camera. Guards were posted at the main entrance to keep
out unwelcome intruders; the Press was excluded and the
gallery closed. But the decision to hear the evidence behind
closed doors of the three men who between them knew a
vast amount about the cause and effect of the troubles was
not just a clumsy attempt to suppress unpalatable facts and
escape criticism. The Government of India believed that if
the men were to be of real value to the Committee they must
be free to reveal *all* the information they had at their
disposal. And much of it was of a highly confidential and
inflammatory nature. Publication of their evidence would be
prejudicial to the interests of the State and public safety
would be endangered, for some of it would deal with
military intelligence and strategy.

There was another factor that had to be borne in mind if
harmonious relations were to be restored between the two
communities: a lot of what they had to say concerned
Indians who commanded considerable public support, and
some of the observations were highly critical and unflatter-
ing. The same problem existed over references to the role
played by several of the larger political movements. If the

considered opinions of the witnesses were made public their lives could be in jeopardy.

The three men in question were the Hon Mr J. P. Thompson, Chief Secretary of the Punjab Government, General Sir Havelock Hudson, the Adjutant-General, and the Hon Major Malik Sir Umar Hayat Khan. Sir Umar was despised by a great many Indians for his open and unswerving support and loyalty to the British. He was, they said, always shouting wolf and being listened to.

Sir Umar treated their derision with contempt. No one could accuse him of paying lip service to the British — he backed his words with deeds; and no one could question his personal courage, for he had served with distinction in France and Mesopotamia. Although himself a wealthy landowner, he honestly believed that the millions of underprivileged peasants received a better deal from the British than they would if governed by educated Indians. He quite frankly admitted to the Committee that he was referred to as 'Uncle of the Government', an intended insult which he took as a tribute.

There was no doubt in his own mind that the Government of the Punjab placed a great deal of reliance on the information he provided about who was fomenting rebellion. It was also abundantly clear to the Members that, in his zeal to be of assistance, Sir Umar claimed to know far more than he did. And like Sir Michael O'Dwyer, whom he respected and admired, he had a built-in antipathy to Indian lawyers and politicians.

During his long evidence he said that he was convinced that an organized conspiracy *did* exist and that the Afghanistan rising was carefully timed for the hot weather when the British soldiers would not be able to operate efficiently in the oppressive heat of the Frontier.

He informed the Committee that he had been in Lahore on 6 April when the hartal was declared. Prompt action then, he insisted, would have prevented further outbreaks. Furthermore, there would have been no riots in Amritsar on the 10th. Being an Indian, he explained, he was better able to read the thoughts of his countrymen and earlier on he had led a deputation which had warned the Government of the dangers of Muslim-Hindu unity, which was a cloak for political agitation.

The trouble with all his evidence was that it was mainly opinion, for he seemed to have few facts with which to support his sweeping conclusions, a point made by one of the Indian members.

When violence did erupt, Sir Umar said that he personally drew up a list of what action should be taken to end the disturbances: these included the forcible opening of shops and bazaars with armed guards mounted outside to ensure that their owners were not intimidated. Steps should also be taken to see that tonga and carriage owners were not molested at their stands. Known trouble makers should be arrested. Telegrams and mail should be censored and the railways controlled to limit the movement of agitators. Professors and students suspected of stirring up trouble should be dismissed.

When the news of the Amritsar shooting became known, it definitely had a quietening effect; even so, he formed his own information network. Men were sent off to pick up any news while others were told to act as detectives. Soldiers were instructed to move among their comrades to gather any evidence of possible disloyalty.

They had, he claimed, provided him with a great deal of evidence about attempts to seduce the Sepoys from their loyalty although he was not prepared to name regiments. On the whole the troops had remained steady in their allegiance although he had heard of men eating dhobi nuts to make them sick rather than go to the front in Afghanistan. He had gone to Peshawar to serve as a Special Service Officer.

If the Government had acted more forcefully on his information and not settled for half-measures, he was sure the violence could have been avoided. He was particularly scathing about Mr Gandhi and his followers.

'If Government is firm with those who are teaching these things and hang them or at any rate send them to the Andamans or somewhere, that would stop it. That is the best way.'

It was left to General Sir Havelock Hudson to put Sir Umar's opinions in perspective and this he did with remarkable candour: it was based too much on hearsay evidence and unsupported statements to be reliable.

The Adjutant-General for the troops in India, who had incurred Mr Montagu's displeasure for what appeared to be his unqualified approval of the 'Crawling Order', continued to speak his mind when he gave evidence and the longer he spoke the more obvious it became why the Government of India was so anxious that some evidence should be given in camera. For the picture he painted revealed a situation that would have caused considerable alarm and despondency at home and grim satisfaction to those nations which did not like the British or agree to their continued presence in India. The British Army in India was grossly undermanned, ill-equipped, poorly trained, riddled with illness and bloody-mindedness — a lamentable state of affairs in a country whose Government was trying so hard to convince Lord Hunter that they had known for some considerable time that a revolution was in the offing.

Sir Havelock spoke bluntly about the problems. When the Afghan war broke out, he said candidly, it became imperative to detain a large number of British soldiers who were awaiting demobilization, and this created a great deal of bitterness and resentment. With the war in Europe over, the overriding need was to get Britain's industry back on a peace-time footing, and so men were demobbed according to their trade and not the amount of time they had served. So great was the discontent this aroused that it had to be revised. Unfortunately, it took some time for the decision to reach India.

When the riots broke out and Europeans were killed in the Punjab, many men who were due to go home were asked to remain and this they did willingly. The manpower crisis increased when the Afghan War broke out and the War Office issued an order compulsorily detaining a large number of soldiers.

'They said they did not mind remaining in India to help their fellow-countrymen, but a war with Afganistan was not their business, but the business of the Indian Government and they ought to keep enough men in India to do it. They were not at all in a contented frame of mind.'

The Committee, which had heard so much about the danger of disloyalty among the Sepoys, was left with the uncomfortable thought that there was perhaps more trouble

183

with the British Tommy.

The military situation as outlined by the General was certainly disquieting. Before the war there had been fifty-two regular battalions of infantry, but at the time of the Punjab disturbances they had been reduced to eight. In addition, there were fifteen territorial battalions of good and reliable soldiers.

Before the war there had been 77,200 British soldiers in the country, but by the spring of 1919 the number had dwindled to 60,000, 3,000 of whom were employed as clerks. The number of horse batteries had dropped from eleven to two, and instead of forty-five field batteries there were nineteen.

The weak link was the garrison battalions, and the General gave details which would have evoked a howl of protest in England if they had been known. Some of the men had been wounded as many as four times, and many were over fifty-five.

'These men are all right to show white faces, but not for utilization for the purposes for which a soldier is utilized,' he said.

In the Rawalpindi Division only fifty-one of the 1,348 men were fit for service. The garrison artillery company of 140 men could only boast six fit men. In the Lahore Division only thirty-eight of the 249 men in the two artillery companies could be called upon. Only half the territorial battalion was fit for duty, and of the garrison battalion only five of 539 men were available. A similar situation existed in almost every other division, he said.

The desperate situation, he explained, had to be taken into consideration when martial law was considered, for it meant if the Army was given overall authority it was the equivalent to increasing its efficiency by one hundred per cent. Hudson admitted that martial law was kept on longer than necessary. 'As a matter of fact, it could have been withdrawn a fortnight earlier, but there was an unfortunate misunderstanding between the Home Department and the Army Department. It is due to the present system of circulating files, by which very often they are being hung up.'

He was equally frank when it came to the extremely sensitive subject of the loyalty of Indian soldiers. Although there was a lot of evidence, it related to very small and unimportant things, and personally he did not think there was any organized or serious attempt to undermine their loyalty.

When it came to expressing an opinion on the Jallianwala Bagh shooting, he was reluctant to commit himself beyond saying the incident should be judged by the results — and there had been an immediate halt to the trouble. It had a tremendous effect throughout the country and showed that the Government was prepared to act firmly.

Pandit Narayan was not going to let the matter rest there. 'You say you judge a man by the results? Supposing I take this particular instance: supposing instead of firing upon this mob and killing about 200 or 300 persons, Dyer had bombarded the city of Amritsar and killed 10,000, would not the same results have followed? Simply because there were no further disturbances you conclude that the act was justified? I say there must be a limit somewhere. So far as the superior military authorities are concerned, they must come to a conclusion whether a certain action was justified or not?'

General Hudson had seen how Dyer had become his own executioner by answering hypothetical questions and he was not going to fall into the same trap.

'You must not ask me to make the definition.'

The Pandit persisted: 'Under military law, may I understand, the end justifies the means?'

'That is the position, and I am afraid it is the position all the world over.'

It was an answer that was more than acceptable to the Pandit and he immediately switched tack. How could the news of the shooting have had a widespread effect throughout India when no telegrams were allowed to be sent from Amritsar on 14, 15, 16 and 17 April? Again it was more an observation than a question.

Narayan then turned his attention to the question of martial law and the Adjutant-General was forced to admit that he knew very little about it as there were no precedents in India for him to follow. For as the witness patiently explained, 'There is no authority for anything to do with martial law, there is not such a thing in the world.'

When Sultan Ahmed Khan took over, he managed to elicit

that when Dyer assumed control in Amritsar he exercised a quasi-civil authority.

Sultan Ahmed Khan asked: 'Therefore he was half a civilian and half a military man. How can he be?'

'Of course he cannot be, but that is the only way of expressing it. We will drop the word out altogether and call it all military.'

'You might be able to explain it to me?'

'That is the only explanation I can give, that he was really acting half as a Commissioner, because he was administering the law of the district.'

'Could he do it legally?'

'No.'

'That part of his action was illegal?'

'Absolutely, but it was legal to this extent that he was responsible for keeping law and order and he did it under martial law.'

'Is it not a contradiction in terms?'

'Yes.'

The interrogation came to an end when the Adjutant-General reiterated that nothing was legal under martial law. That was why it had been necessary to introduce a Bill of Indemnity.

When Mr J. P. Thompson gave evidence on Tuesday, 9 December, the tortuous ritual began all over again. He could only confirm what the Members had already heard a score of times. Yes, there was an organized plot. Yes, there was an attempt to seduce the troops. Yes, Dyer's action had ended all further trouble. When the Indian Members did not get the answer they wanted, they rang the changes until they extracted some kind of concession. Occasionally it was significant, sometimes it amounted to very little. But it was all grist to the mill.

As far as Thompson was concerned, it was the political scene which was uppermost in their minds and they worked, sometimes subtly, sometimes crudely, to establish that the aim of the Punjab Government was to divide and rule. The witness would not agree, although he confessed to mistrusting educated Indians, and he did not disguise his dislike, which led to questions about what he meant by 'double-facey'. Was it something he attributed to all Indians?

'No, I do not attribute it to all Indians, but I think it is probably the outcome of historical circumstances. People have acquired a very great power of concealing their feelings.'

Sir Chimanlal Setalvad: 'Because they are afraid of the authorities?'

'Probably.'

'They have to say things to please them although they may not express their correct feelings?'

'Yes, that is the explanation of it.'

Having committed himself to those somewhat indiscreet observations, Mr Thompson loyally supported Sir Michael O'Dwyer and protested that the criticisms levelled at him were unjustified. 'He wanted the atmosphere of the place as calm as possible during the war, and all those measures taken by the late Lieutenant-Governor in regard to the Press and political agitation must be regarded as war measures and judged as such.'

Thompson was blunt and certainly no one could accuse him of being 'double-facey', particularly when it came to giving his opinion of Gandhi and the Satyagraha Movement: 'One really doubts whether the man is sane, judged by ordinary standards.' The Indian leader was a complete enigma to him and passive resistance beyond his comprehension. It did not occur to him that much of it echoed what Christians accepted without question. 'The whole of the disorders had their direct origin in the action of Mr Gandhi.'

Although he approved of Dyer's action he was less positive about the number of casualties: 'I think that when the question was put to the Punjab Government no amount of disapproval could have brought the dead back to life. There was a great deal to be gained by not weakening our forces by any declaration of disunion between the Civil and Military authorities. I think you have got to remember that.'

'If you ask me whether 379 deaths were too many, I think they probably were,' he added.

He also disclosed how out of touch his Government was during martial law. 'So far as I remember flogging in public did not come to our notice till practically after it ceased.'

It was some time before the questioning got back to General Dyer and the Jallianwala Bagh. Then Mr Thompson provided a vital piece of extra evidence. Soon after the shooting he had seen the General who had told him that he feared his small force was about to be attacked, and so he opened fire. Would he have done the same?

'Probably not. I should not have had the pluck.' And he added, 'Possibly I should not have gone on firing as long as General Dyer.'

When the session ended the Committee of Inquiry moved to Bombay for its final sitting.

*   *   *

Sir Michael O'Dwyer had meantime returned to India and was staying at Maiden's Hotel in Delhi not far from the ridge marked by the Mutiny Memorial. It was from there that O'Dwyer wrote to the Viceroy offering to give evidence. In a rather cheerful note he wrote: 'I helped to set the military machine in motion, and when the soldiers have been called upon to justify their actions it would not look well if the Arch-fiend (!) stood aside.' Apart from that he was anxious to appear before the Committee as he had evidence that would reveal a plot of long standing.

But it was to be another month before it happened. In the meantime, something occurred that took the tragedy of the Jallianwala Bagh into nearly every home in England and jolted the people into an awareness of what had been going on in India.

On Saturday, 13 December, the *Daily Express* carried a story headlined '2,000 INDIANS SHOT DOWN', and below in smaller but still bold type, 'General's Terrible Remedy to Curb Rebellion', and 'I Looked on it as a Horrible Duty'.

Incredibly it was datelined Allahabad, 20 November. It had taken a month for the copy of the *Express*'s Indian correspondent to reach Fleet Street. Above his despatch were four introductory paragraphs outlining 'the dramatic and terrible story'.

The actual report said that General Dyer's evidence at Lahore had aroused intense interest in India:

Responsible people have said that General Dyer's prompt and salutary action, in conjunction with that of Sir Michael O'Dwyer, saved India from a widespread conflagration.

It then went on to recount the rioting and murder in Amritsar and the assault on Miss Sherwood. Unless one looked at the small print giving the date, the impression gained was that it was a recent event.

The report quoted large extracts from Dyer's evidence and commented that at times his answers were terse. It was obvious that the reporter had selected those quotes which would have the biggest impact on the newspaper's readers. He could have dispersed the crowd without firing but he feared they would come back and laugh at him and he would have made a fool of himself.

On Monday morning the paper followed up its scoop with more details from Dyer's evidence including his failure to treat the wounded and his testimony about the 'Crawling Order'.

Edwin Montagu was appalled when he read the reports, and immediately sent off a blistering telegram to the Viceroy. 'I am bound to tell you that they have created a very strong and very painful impression here ... The *Daily Express* was the first paper to call attention to the evidence on Saturday morning; the evening papers took it up as a sensation and people were made to believe that the affair had happened within the last few days.' He knew that he was in for a rough time in the House of Commons and two days later he faced a barrage of questions over what the *Daily Telegraph* described as the 'remarkable evidence given at Lahore'. As he had feared, Members wanted to know when the Hunter Report would be published and why they had been kept in the dark about the true nature of events. He had to assure them that he had not known the details until he read the newspaper accounts of Dyer's evidence.

'That is not an official communication,' he said, rather lamely, 'and I do not know whether the evidence is actually as reported.'

He could not, he snapped, expect the Committee to report bits of the evidence; its task was to investigate all aspects of the disturbances. Against a background chorus of 'Hear, Hear', Sir Donald Maclean, the Liberal Member for Peebles, enquired with marked asperity if it was the practice for the Secretary of State not to hear of an occurrence of this nature until eight months later.

Montagu insisted that he had not been guilty of deception: he had published the communiqués as he had received them and they contained all he knew. The newspaper reports *had* been profoundly disturbing and he assured the House that the findings of the Hunter Committee would be published without delay. Meantime, it would be wrong to prejudge the issue.

Members were not satisfied. Why had it taken the best part of a year for them to hear the details? Was the Government of India still imposing a strict censorship of cables, as the *Daily Express* report had been sent by ordinary mail? Montagu's answer, which convinced no one, was that the lines had been congested.

Montagu managed to stave off further attacks by appealing to the House to wait for Lord Hunter's report.

Then more details began arriving from India and he was driven to the depths of despair. On the first day of the New Year he was in touch with the Viceroy:

> Cages for prisoners, the whipping of selected schoolboys, the punishments devised by Captain Doveton, and so on. I must again remind you that throughout the long months until the District Reports arrived, I had no news from you as to what occurred at Amritsar other than your contemporaneous telegrams, and the District Reports added little to my knowledge.

He now suspected that there was a deliberate plot in India to drive a wedge between him and the Viceroy.

> I have seen private telegrams to the editor of one of the smaller daily newspapers which support this view, and I have heard rumours that members of your Government are associated with it.

Lord Chelmsford indignantly denied the existence of such a plot. There were differences of opinion, that was all.

If the Secretary of State was prepared to await the findings of Lord Hunter, there were many Indians who wanted immediate action. *The Tribune* demanded that Dyer should be relieved at once and attacked the Viceroy for deliberately withholding the truth about events in the Punjab. At the same time it was announced that the Jallianwala Bagh was to be purchased by public subscription and made into a national memorial.

On 23 December the Royal Proclamation giving amnesty to political offenders was issued, and although the released prisoners could not give evidence to Lord Hunter as he had finished his session in Lahore, it did not prevent them from continuing where they had left off. At a Congress Meeting in Amritsar, Doctor Kitchlew called for the recall of Chelmsford.

The wheel had turned full circle.

12. O'Dwyer and the Indian Lawyers

'I have no hesitation in saying that General Dyer's action that day was the decisive factor in crushing the rebellion, the seriousness of which is only now being generally realised' — Sir Michael O'Dwyer to the Hunter Committee.

Sir Michael O'Dwyer appeared before the Hunter Committee in Bombay on 15 January, confident that he could convince the European Members that everything that had been done in the Punjab was justified. He had prepared a long statement in which he stated that he was aware six months prior to the disturbances that serious trouble was in the offing, but owing to the victory over Germany and the easing of many wartime measures he was unwilling to bring in special legislation to deal with the threatened dangers. He preferred to rely on persuasion. Like Mr Thompson, he believed the recent disorders could all be blamed on Gandhi who had been exploited by various leading political parties. Satyagraha was bound to end in violence and rebellion.

He was under no illusion about the Indian Members. Two of them, Sir Chimanlal Setalvad and Pandit Narayan, he considered incapable of being impartial. They would act as prosecution counsel as soon as they were given the opportunity to question him. He had very good grounds for his fears. Setalvad was one of the lawyers who had been refused permission to enter the Punjab to defend one of the leading political agitators; Narayan was an old political foe. As soon as O'Dwyer read of the latter's appointment he had protested that the past precluded him from being dispassionate. In 1918 Narayan had been forced to make a public apology and withdraw remarks he had made about O'Dwyer's administration. A formal objection to his selection had also been made by the new Lieutenant-Governor of the Punjab, Sir Edward Maclagan. But the appointment had been agreed to by the Indian and British Governments and there was no way of rescinding it.

When it came to O'Dwyer's verbal evidence, it soon became clear that Lord Hunter and the other Members were far from satisfied that he had made out a convincing case. Lord Hunter expressed the view that political protest and revolution were not synonymous: 'Why do you jump to the conclusion that there was a revolutionary movement for overthrowing the Government by violence?' He went on to add that he thought it was surprising that the organizers of the alleged rebellion had made no attempt to arm themselves with weapons.

'Of course', said Sir Michael, 'these people do not always reason far ahead. I think their first object was undoubtedly to paralyse government by following the method of so-called passive resistance, that is to say, to refuse supplies, to boycott Europeans and their servants, to paralyse communications by railway and telegraph strikes, to immobilize troops, to create strikes of Government servants and perhaps to refuse payments of taxes.' Lord Hunter remained unconvinced: to him paralysing the Government by civil disobedience was quite different from overthrowing it by violent means.

The former Lieutenant-Governor was adamant that there *were* people in the Punjab who were prepared for, and did resort to, violence. In his own mind Satyagraha must lead to absolute anarchy. 'If Gandhi's doctrine is taken on here, the intelligentsia will disappear and Government will disappear with it,' he warned Lord Hunter. 'Of course this doctrine of Mr Gandhi's may appeal to very highly educated and spiritually minded people, but the question is not how it appeals to the professor, but how it appeals to the man in the street.'

It was a line of discussion that was obviously not going to lead anywhere and the President steered it back to the Amritsar shooting. What evidence did he have when he expressed his approval?

'I am quite prepared to give you my reasons. Amritsar was in a state of open rebellion. Nay, not only Amritsar, but the surrounding countryside was being affected by Amritsar.

The civil authorities had informed General Dyer that it was impossible for them to restore and maintain order.'

Dyer took over and, having issued a warning about illegal assemblies, was not only entitled but bound to disperse it.

'I may say, as head of the Government of the Punjab at the time, that if General Dyer had not dispersed that crowd by force, we should have had an infinitely more serious state of rebellion.'

When Sir Michael had written to the Viceroy he indicated that he possessed evidence of a plot that was not available to anybody else. But the claim dwindled under the questioning of Sir Chimanlal Setalvad.

'I have no proofs of it,' admitted Sir Michael, 'but I am strongly inclined to believe that it did exist. There was some organization.'

Assuming that there was such a plot, wasn't it ridiculous that no attempt was made to secure arms?

'Possibly ridiculous. I think they were counting on other factors. They were counting on the spread of disorder, on getting the Indian troops on their side, on getting demobilized men on their side, and perhaps also on getting the emigrants on their side. That is why from the very beginning attempts to seduce the troops were made and even attempts to seduce the police were made.'

Setalvad promptly reminded him that the Adjutant-General had said there was no serious attempt to tamper with the troops, but Sir Michael could not agree.

Sir Chimanlal showed no sign of flagging even after weeks of asking the same questions of countless witnesses. Could Sir Michael elaborate on the General's action:

'We have it in evidence that General Dyer himself said that he could have dispersed it without firing?'

'General Dyer must be a very sanguine man.'

Whatever his critics may have said about him, none could question his loyalty to the men called upon to administer martial law, and, despite intense pressure, he refused to criticize, admonish or pass judgement on their actions. In Dyer's case he mentioned mitigating circumstances which the General had not referred to in his own evidence. Recalling his meeting with him soon after the shooting Sir Michael said: 'I think I ought to mention this in justice to

General Dyer. He was aware that his retreat might be cut off. I think he said, after he had fired the first volley, the crowd made a rush. He thought that this was intended to intercept his retreat and he went on firing, but he thought afterwards (he was very frank about it) that that was not their intention, after seeing the place more fully, and that this was one of the methods of egress so as to escape from the Jallianwala Bagh.'

When Pandit Narayan took over, it was obvious that he was going to attack the former Lieutenant-Governor, criticize his whole period of office and reveal that he had ruled with a rod of iron and suppressed all political aspirations of the people. He had been forced to apologize for his earlier attack on O'Dwyer's administration, but now he was protected by privilege and he took full advantage of the situation by expressing his opinions in a whole string of rhetorical questions.

Sir Michael remained commendably unruffled even when Narayan tried to make him look foolish. Recounting the build-up to the rioting in Amritsar O'Dwyer made a passing reference to the cricket match which had been interrupted. Narayan remarked caustically: 'Because certain people who wanted to play were asked to stop on the day of the hartal, therefore they showed they were the head of a dangerous conspiracy.'

In the end it was the Indian who lost his temper. 'You make a statement and you do not give me a chance of eliciting anything from you, and to everything I ask you the answer is either "I do not know" or "I cannot say".' It was an unfair observation; O'Dwyer *had* answered nearly every question promptly and frankly and not always to his own advantage.

At the end of the second day O'Dwyer began to display signs of irritation at the blatant hostility and the transparent tactics to try and blame him for everything. And when he was questioned about another witness's evidence he snapped, 'I had no time to read the evidence fully. I had but little time to prepare my own.'

The tenacious Narayan began once more to go over the whole period of martial law during which he compared O'Dwyer to Nadir Shah, who had sacked Delhi in 1793 and slaughtered thousands of innocent people, and whose name was still mentioned with horror.

'Having regard to all these facts, would they be very far wrong if they compared your administration to that of Nadir Shah's?'

Patiently but without any visible effect, Sir Michael pointed out that he was not responsible for what had been done by the administrators of martial law. Finally, stung to resentment, he reminded his interrogator that 120,000 people had been massacred in Delhi during Nadir Shah's three-day reign of terror.

With the completion of his evidence, the Committee retired to Agra and there, within sight of the majestic onion domes of the Taj Mahal they began to work on the report.

13. The Indian View

'It is not possible for us to condense into the compass of a brief review the story of persecution, corruption and disregard of human feelings, that is revealed in the evidence we are presenting to the public.' — Report of the Commissioners appointed by the Punjab Sub-Committee of the Indian National Congress.

When Dyer returned to duty at Jullundur he appeared to have made a remarkable recovery. Furthermore, his future seemed assured for he had been told that he had been appointed to command the Northern Division which meant promotion to Major-General and a possible knighthood. Then in January he was laid low with jaundice, but under the care of his devoted wife he began to get better, and as soon as he was able to leave his bed he decided to go for a short walk. When he arrived home he complained of agonizing pains in his head and severe cramps which racked his body. In the evening he became delirious and the doctor who was called in said his heart was affected. He was immediately taken to the British hospital.

Dyer was fifty-five but looked considerably older; thirty-five years of active service had taken their toll. Clearly unfit for duty, he applied for six months' sick leave in England, but this the Commander-in-Chief refused; if he wished to return home he would have to vacate his appointment. It was a bitter blow for a man who was under the impression that he had been promoted. The knife was twisted when he received another telegram informing him that the appointment had been withdrawn. This was immediately interpreted by his supporters as a blatant betrayal. Sir Charles Monro was punishing him before the Hunter Committee had even finished their deliberations in Agra, or was seeking an easy way out of an embarrassing situation should the Report be critical of his conduct.

It was a suspicion that was not without foundation for it would have made things much easier for everybody if he had

197

resigned. That, however, was not the sole motive behind Monro's action. Dyer was obviously not fit for any more active soldiering, but, apart from his physical condition, in the eyes of the Army Selection Board in India, he had reached the peak of his military career. Although a good soldier, he was only of average ability and on his record did not come up to standard for promotion to Major-General. Amritsar or not, he would never have received further employment or advancement in the Army. The appointment which had been withdrawn was only of a temporary nature until a permanent commander was appointed. This explanation, when given much later, did nothing to convince his supporters that he had not been made a scapegoat. Whatever the reasoning, Dyer's health began to deteriorate further.

*　　　*　　　*

Meanwhile, in Agra the Members of the Hunter Committee were busy sifting through the millions of written and spoken words that had been submitted in evidence during their marathon Inquiry. The task confronting them was daunting; they had to reach decisions and pass judgement on the numerous incidents which had marked the disturbances. And they just could not agree. The open breach that existed between the European and Indian Members was a constant headache for Lord Hunter who knew that no matter how fearless the final Report was, it would not satisfy anybody. If it was too harsh it would alienate the Anglo-Indians; if it seemed too lenient it would antagonize the Indians. As the days passed Hunter realized that his hopes for a unanimous Report were rapidly fading.

The same thoughts were occupying Edwin Montagu's mind. He considered it essential that the British and Indian Governments should show a united front when the Report was submitted: it would be disastrous if they should appear to be at loggerheads. Once again the telegrams began to flow from Westminster. While the Secretary of State was anxious to assure Chelmsford that there would be no 'head-hunting', he hoped they would be able to reach unanimous agreement, and in order to do that he felt it was necessary that they should know each other's views in advance. He sought assurance from the Viceroy that Dyer's evidence had come as a complete shock, and this Chelmsford readily gave. A whole string of questions followed, to which Chelmsford replied that he could not possibly anticipate the Report.

On 8 March Lord Hunter submitted the Report of his Committee to the Government of India. It was a bulky tome, but because the whole of it had to be telegraphed to London and then held up while the two Governments exchanged their views on its contents and recommendations, it was not published until late May.

*   *   *

Unfettered by the cumbersome procedure that bedevilled the British and Indian Governments and with no vast ocean acting as a barrier to their deliberations, the Inquiry set up by the Punjab Sub-Committee of the Indian National Congress was able to forestall Hunter by completing its Report on 20 February.

Its Members consisted of the Hon Pandit Madan Malaviya, four barristers, Mr Gandhi, Mr C. R. Das, Mr M. R. Jayakar, Mr K. Santanam, Secretary, and Mr Abbas Tayabji, a retired judge of the Supreme Court of Baroda.

The Members stated that since they began work in November they had examined 1,700 witnesses in all the areas affected, and selected for publication 650 statements, all of which had been checked and verified and the witnesses cross-examined.

They had also freely availed themselves of the evidence given to the Hunter Committee.

It was a blockbuster of a Report, for, despite its claims to have been as relentless as possible in the pursuit of the truth, it amounted to a savage indictment of the Governments of India and the Punjab, and the photographs included were clearly intended to arouse deep feelings of anger and resentment among the Indian population.

Its chief weakness in the eyes of the British was the inclusion of Mr Gandhi in the investigating team. How could it possibly be impartial if the one man so many claimed was responsible for the outbreaks of violence played such an important part in its preparation and presentation? If the National Congress had seen the Hunter Committee as the Government of India sitting in judgement on itself, then this was a perfect case of the pot calling the kettle black.

Page after page was filled with extracts from speeches made by Sir Michael O'Dwyer to underline his dislike of educated Indians and to expose what the Members claimed was his repressive rule:

> He scented danger in every honest speech made by the leaders and he detected conspiracy in every combination, and thus forgetting himself issued his orders against Dr Satyapal and Dr Kitchlew and Mr Gandhi. He must have known that this could only end in exasperating a people who had already been incensed against his rule. We feel tempted to say that he invited violence from the people, so that he could crush them.

Having damned O'Dwyer, they wished to emphasize that the people of the Punjab nevertheless remained loyal:

> We wish here to draw a broad distinction between loyalty to the British Constitution and the King, and the indiscriminate support of a tyrannical deputy who disgraces a high office to which he may be called.

Long extracts were quoted from the verbal evidence of General Dyer, all of which were carefully selected to show him in the worst possible light. If, they submitted, the British Raj was to be purged of the inexcusable wrong he had committed, he should be immediately relieved of his command and brought to justice. Nothing could condone the violent excesses of the mobs who had looted, plundered and murdered Europeans; such acts were indefensible, 'but no deeds, however dastardly, of an enraged mob can warrant a slaughter of innocent people, such as General Dyer was guilty of.' The death roll in the Jallianwala Bagh was estimated to be a staggering one thousand people.

The words of condemnation scorched through the printed pages:

> We have been obliged in places to use strong language, but we have used every adjective with due deliberation. If anything, we have understated the case against the Punjab Government.

Whereupon the Inquiry turned its attention to the Indian Government, and the Viceroy in particular was subjected to a ferocious personal onslaught.

> His Excellency the Viceroy never took the trouble of examining the people's case. He ignored telegrams and letters from individuals and public bodies. He endorsed the action of the Punjab Government without enquiry. He clothed the officials with indemnity in indecent haste. He never went to the Punjab to make a personal inquiry, even after the occurences. He ought to have known, at least in May, everything that the various official witnesses have admitted, and yet he failed to inform the public or the Imperial Government of the full nature of the Jallianwala Bagh massacre, or the subsequent acts done under martial law.

If the proposed reforms were to succeed, those officials who had erred should be brought to justice in order that the administration of the country should be freed of corruption and injustice. Indictment followed indictment, and it was only through a sense of public duty that the Inquiry felt compelled to say:

> His Excellency Lord Chelmsford proved himself incapable of holding the high office to which he was called, and we are of the opinion that His Excellency should be recalled.

Before coming to a detailed list of conclusions, the Members of the unanimous Report declared that in their opinion a number of men, including O'Dwyer, Dyer, Colonel Johnson, Colonel O'Brien and Mr Bosworth Smith, deserved to be impeached, but they purposely refrained from advising such a course as they believed India could only gain by waiving such a demand. Their dismissal, however, was essential.

Their findings and recommendations were:

> The people of the Punjab were incensed against Sir Michael O'Dwyer's administration by reason of his studied contempt and distrust of the educated classes, and by reason of the cruel and compulsory methods adopted during the war, for obtaining recruits and monetary contributions and his

suppression of public opinion by gagging the local press and shutting out nationalist newspapers from outside the Punjab.

The Rowlatt agitation disturbed the public mind and shook public confidence in the Government...It should be repealed.

There was no conspiracy to overthrow the Government of the Punjab.

The arrest and deportation of the three Indian leaders was the direct cause of the hysteria in Amritsar. . .

Nothing could justify the introduction of martial law for it was introduced when order had been restored. . . Furthermore, it was continued far longer than necessary. . .

The Martial Law Tribunals and the Summary Courts were used to harass innocent people and had resulted in abortion of justice on a wide scale.

The 'Crawling Order' and other 'fancy punishments' were unworthy of a civilized administration and were symptomatic of the moral degradation of their inventors.

The Jallianwala Bagh massacre was a calculated piece of inhumanity towards utterly innocent and unarmed men, including children and unparalleled for its ferocity in the history of modern British administration.

The language may have been intemperate at times, but the findings contained nothing that Mr Montagu had not himself expressed in private. However, he realized as soon as he heard the details that they were totally unacceptable to the Indian Government and the Anglo-Indians. Therefore, he was greatly relieved when he was able to inform Lord Chelmsford that the Report had been virtually ignored by the newspapers in England.

Sweeping as it was in its censure, the Inquiry would have wished to have gone further. What the Members would have liked to say but could not, for lack of proof, was that the shooting at Jallianwala Bagh was a carefully prepared trap. In a private note Mr Jayakar wrote:

On all the facts it is suggested that the meeting had been planned by Hans Raj and his associates with a view to making a large number of people gather at the Bagh. Whether the authorities at Amritsar were parties to this plan and yielded to it in their desire for revenge, we are unable to say, as we have not enough evidence before us to support a definite finding. But it is any rate perfectly clear that Dyer took the fullest advantage of the meeting in effecting on the inhabitants of Amritsar as condign and complete a punishment as was needed to satisfy their lust for revenge.

There were many, however, who did not share Mr Jayakar's caution. They firmly believed there *was* a plot and with the passing of time it was publicly stated. The *Bombay Chronicle*, in an article headed 'The Issue', claimed that Hans Raj was a lure and quoted Pandit Mohan Malaviya as saying, 'The man who was instrumental in holding the meeting was in communication with the police the whole day'. And the newspaper went on to say that the Indian Inquiry had seen documents which supported the idea of a plot but the owners had refused to part with them for fear of the authorities. The article went on to assert that the documents had raised grave doubts in the minds of the Members as to whether a death trap had not been prepared in order to teach the people of Amritsar a lesson.

Some claimed that the plot had been hatched at the meeting in Lahore attended by Lieutenant-Colonel Smith and other leading European and Indian personalities at which they had urged Sir Michael O'Dwyer to take strong and forceful action.

From his exile in London Guy Horniman added his voice to those who supported the idea of a carefully hatched plot. The accusations were considered so outrageous that they did not merit an official denial. They were dismissed as just another attempt to undermine public confidence in the British Raj. In pursuit of that objective the extremists were able to interpret something devious in everything the British did.

Before departing for India Lord Hunter had been briefed to conduct a fearless Inquiry in order to restore good relations between the British and Indians. He was convinced he had done so when he signed his official Report. On 28 March it was handed to the Viceroy. It was one of the most momentous documents in the entire history of the British Empire and millions awaited its publication with anxiety and apprehension. Had a jewel been thrown away, or had it been firmly cemented in the crown?

14. Dyer Disgraced

'I think he should be relieved of his command and called upon to retire or be compelled to do so if he declines. I cannot contemplate the retention of a man of his mentality and with his record in a position of responsibility.' — Chelmsford to Montagu.

Simla was thronged with people escaping the heat of the plains. But there was an air of constraint abroad, while the Viceroy, the hub of the social scene, and his Executive Council pored over the Report of the Hunter Committee. More than a year had passed since the disturbances and the day of reckoning was imminent.

As every Member of the Council anticipated, the Report was not unanimous: there was a Majority Report signed by the Europeans and a Minority Report signed by the Indians. The two Reports, in fact, had a great deal in common, although the language of the Indian Members was far harsher and the criticisms and conclusions more stringent. It was what they had feared, so it came as no great surprise. The Majority Report did; it was a severe indictment of many of the things that had happened in the Punjab.

The Government accepted without reserve the Majority Report. It was hard-hitting and a blow to their hopes, but it was far more acceptable than the Minority Report which was similar in tone to the independent Inquiry set up by the National Congress.

The Government would have liked to deal with it there and then. But that course was not open to them. The Cabinet Committee which had been set up in London to deal with the Report had to know the details of what they proposed to do. The idea was that the two Governments would then be able to exchange views and present to the waiting world a statement that showed total agreement. It was not to be. Simla and

Westminster were not just separated by distance, they were poles apart when it came to implementing the findings of the Committee.

Disappointingly for the Indian Government, Edwin Montagu and his colleagues seemed to find more in common with the Minority Report than with the views of the European Members. In a secret memo to the Cabinet dated 6 May, Montagu said he was disappointed with the Indian Government's Draft Resolution: 'In our opinion it is not, as a whole, a very satisfactory document'. He and his colleagues were, however, hopeful that their own recommendations could be incorporated in a revised Resolution. But many of the suggestions from London were unacceptable: the criticisms were too strong and relations between the two Governments became very strained. A proposal that the British Government should send its own proposals which would precede those of the Indian Government was rejected. There was no precedent, protested Chelmsford, for Westminster to dictate to the local Government. In any case, their positions were wholly different. London, he stressed, did not have to worry about the civil and military opinion in India which, irrespective of what Lord Hunter might say, still adhered to the view that Dyer had saved India. Neither would they accept any criticism of the former Lieutenant-Governor:

> We should definitely exonerate O'Dwyer from any censure, and state that he acted with decision and vigour in a time of great difficulty, crushing a dangerous rising which might have had widespread and dangerous results in the whole of India.

He intimated that his Government would refuse to publish the views of the Home Government as part of their own Resolution and insist instead that Westminster made its own pronouncements.

Chelmsford wanted to avoid a head-on collision if at all possible, but rather than give in on what he considered to be points of grave importance he would stick to his guns and let the world know that Simla and Westminster were at loggerheads. And he reminded Montagu that it was in order to obtain unanimity that the Draft Resolution had been sent.

While the wrangling went on General Monro took a vital

decision that virtually scotched any plans Montagu had for dealing with General Dyer. He was relieved of his command and sent home on sick leave.

The first Montagu knew about Dyer being on the high seas was a secret cable from Lieutenant-Colonel A. S. Cobbe dated 21 April informing him that Dyer was aboard a hospital ship. The secret communiqué went on to say that, assuming he had not vacated his command, an order removing him from his appointment would result in him becoming unemployed and only entitled to unemployment pay for his rank. Presumably he would then elect to retire on a pension or be compulsorily retired. Dismissal from the service, he added, would mean forfeiture of his pension and the possible forfeiture of his medals and decorations.

Montagu was naturally annoyed; he thought Dyer had been treated too lightly. Chelmsford promptly informed him that the Commander-in-Chief's action was as far as he could go. 'He has no authority to order Dyer to retire except under your instructions conveyed through the Government of India.' As Dyer was on the way home it would be more correct if that decision was given to him by the Military Secretary responsible for disciplinary matters concerning Indian Army officers in England. And he reminded him that Dyer had the right to appeal to the Army Council.

Winston Churchill, the Secretary of State for War, did not need reminding that the retirement of General Dyer did not rest with the Commander-in-Chief. He was anxious to know why Monro had acted as he had. Lord Chelmsford immediately 'cleared the line' for an apologetic reply. There was no desire, he explained, to rush a decision but General Monro knew that Dyer was very ill and about to be invalided home, and he also thought it expedient to get him out of India as soon as possible:

> He now realizes that the course he adopted was precipitate and that this action should have been deferred until your approval of our Resolution had been received. He regrets the embarrassment he has caused you.

At the same time, the Viceroy said, he felt he was to blame for not making it clear to the Commander-in-Chief that nothing should have been done without the Secretary of State's consent.

There was still, however, the Hunter Report to deal with.

The Majority Report had severely criticized Dyer over his action at the Jallianwala Bagh. He was censured for firing without warning, and continuing to fire until his ammunition was almost expended. Neither could his act be justified because of the effect it might have in other places. 'The employment of excessive measures is as likely as not to produce the opposite result to that desired.'

The Majority Report also made the important observation that when Dyer's proclamation was interpreted into the vernacular, the vital words 'if necessary' were left out when reference was made to opening fire. And, referring to his own statement, they pointed out that he never mentioned that he feared his small force was going to be attacked. In fact he had admitted that his mind was made up before he left his headquarters.

> The action taken by General Dyer has been described by others as having saved the situation in the Punjab and having averted a rebellion on a scale similar to the Mutiny. It does not, however, appear to us possible to draw this conclusion, particularly in view of the fact that it is not proved that a conspiracy to overthrow the British power had been formed prior to the outbreak.

Jallianwala Bagh was the only occasion on which the use of firearms to disperse a crowd was criticized. Every other instance was approved.

The Indian Members were far more severe. They compared his action with the atrocities committed by some German officers in France and Belgium in 1914 and they branded him as inhuman for leaving the wounded untended and for saying that he would have used machine guns if he had been able to get the armoured cars into the Bagh. The majority condemned the 'Crawling Order', the 'fancy punishments' and the salaaming orders. Neither could there be any defence for the dropping of bombs on two outlying villages and the Khalsa High School, or the excessive use of machine guns.

The Government examined Hunter chapter by chapter, and at the end of each suggested what action should be taken. Bearing in mind the hostile reaction their Resolution was bound to provoke among Anglo-Indians, it was an honest and fearless document which did not attempt to evade the serious issues raised.

The events in Amritsar, they conceded, had tended to obscure what had occurred elsewhere; nevertheless, they regretted the complete abdication of civil authority when the city was handed over to General Dyer. They considered his proclamation should have been more widely promulgated and notices posted in the Bagh and at the Baisakhi Fair. Before opening fire he should have given a warning which would have enabled those who were ignorant of his orders to leave. At the same time they believed that he had acted in good faith although with a misconceived sense of duty.

> Nevertheless after carefully weighing all these factors, we can arrive at no other conclusion than that at Jallianwala Bagh General Dyer acted beyond the necessity of the case, beyond what any reasonable man could have thought to be necessary, and that he did not act with as much humanity as the case permitted. It is with pain that we arrive at this conclusion, for we are not forgetful of General Dyer's distinguished record as a soldier or of his gallant relief of the garrison at Thal during the recent Afghan war. We must direct that the judgement above pronounced be communicated to His Excellency the Commander-in-Chief with the request that he will take appropriate action.

In a private note to Montagu, the Viceroy said that in accepting the Committee's findings it was not incumbent on them to prosecute Dyer:

> I cannot help thinking that in his evidence he did himself scant justice. In his desire to be honest he would excuse or mitigate nothing, and he made unnecessarily exaggerated statements.

Before leaving the tragic events of the Jallianwala Bagh, the Report vehemently denied that there was any conspiracy of silence between the Government of India and the Secretary of State to conceal what had happened, but regretted details had only become known as a result of the revelations made before the Hunter Committee.

The Government also accepted many of the strictures Hunter had made on the administration of Martial Law. In some instances the police had been guilty of unnecessary severity, and the number of people arrested and not brought to trial had been regrettably large, and the period of detention unusually long. Many of the sentences were too severe, and certain people, among them Kitchlew and Satyapal, should have been tried by the civil courts.

Praise for O'Dwyer, on the other hand, was unqualified:

It was fortunate that, when the disturbances broke out in April 1919, the Punjab was in charge of a Lieutenant-Governor of great experience and courage. The Government of India consider that Sir Michael O'Dwyer acted with great decision and vigour in a time of great danger and that he was largely responsible for quelling a dangerous rising which might have had a widespread and disastrous effect on the rest of India.

The Report also contained a long communiqué from Edwin Montagu which stated that the British Government had studied the Report and been informed of the conclusions of the Indian Government. He stressed that the Hunter Committee findings would be of little value if they were not put to practical use: the most important thing was not to apportion blame but to prevent a recurrence of the troubles.

Of General Dyer he said that he had violated the principle of minimum force to which the Government was committed. Montagu's views on Dyer unfortunately made the Indian Government's observations sound like a mild rebuke, particularly over the 'Crawling Order':

Had the order been carried out as a punishment upon persons actually guilty of the crime which it was intended to stigmatize, it would have been difficult to defend; inflicted as it was upon persons who had no connection with that crime, with the object of impressing upon the public of Amritsar through the humiliation of those persons the enormity of the crime committed by certain individuals of that public, the order offended against every canon of civilized Government.

There were certain standards of conduct which no civilized Government could neglect and Dyer's conception of his duty was so at variance with the British Government's, 'that it is impossible to regard him as fitted to remain entrusted with the responsibilities which his rank and position impose upon him.'

He approved the decision of the Commander-in-Chief and the case had been referred to the Army Council.

He was also firmly opposed to the backdating of Martial Law although he accepted that the Judicial Committee of the Privy Council had announced the Government of India was empowered to do so.

Neither did Montagu feel that Lord Hunter had gone far enough in his strictures about the administration of martial law. H. M. Government expressed strong disapproval of some orders and punishments,

> and ask me to leave to you the duty of seeing that this disapproval shall be unmistakably marked by censure or other action which seems to you necessary upon those who were responsible for them.

Sir Michael O'Dwyer suffered the mildest of rebukes, although His Majesty's Government did not consider him immune from criticism. Before giving unqualified approval to General Dyer's action he should have found out more about it.

There were tributes to the officers and men, both civil and military, Indian and British, who had responded so well during the emergency. And finally there was a fulsome tribute to Lord Chelmsford.

The people of India and Great Britain and the rest of the Empire had been assured that the two Governments were almost as one in their beliefs and convictions.

The solidarity was a shallow façade. Concealed from the public were the secret letters and telegrams between the Viceroy and Montagu and the Cabinet deliberations which revealed a wide disagreement on many points. But they were pigeon-holed and protected from public disclosure by the 50-year rule.

Montagu had wilted under the stubborn resistance of the Indian Government and watered down his opinions. He had wanted to say that in his opinion those who devised 'fancy punishments' were to be condemned more than Dyer for they could not claim in their defence that they were trying to suppress a rebellion. And it was a matter of deep regret to him that some of them had administered martial law not as men compelled to act sternly against those owing allegiance to the King Emperor, 'but in the spirit of an Army of Occupation in a hostile country'. The Government also wanted to insert a passage which repudiated 'the doctrine of frightfulness' on which Dyer based his action. Neither was the Government happy about the unqualified approval given to O'Dwyer. Without expressing any firm opinion on the merits or demerits of his period of office, the Government wanted to leave it open by saying, 'History alone can pronounce verdicts on those views.' Furthermore, Montagu had hoped that he would have the support of his colleagues in 'condemning more strongly than Lord Hunter's Committee have seen fit' the Punjab Government's decision to try people by Commission for offences committed before any trouble broke out.

But Lord Chelmsford insisted that the strictures should be eliminated. He would not, he said, accept the use of the word 'frightfulness'. The inclusion of the word would be seized upon by the extremist press with disastrous effects. Neither would he entertain any reference to an Army of Occupation.

> Lastly, we venture a respectful protest against the language used regarding Sir Michael O'Dwyer, and ask for its reconsideration. We have expressed our views in our Resolution and we adhere to them. In any case, it is, in our opinion, the duty of Government to apportion praise and blame in such circumstances, and we cannot think it right that it should be left to history to give the verdict.

O'Dwyer, he urged, should not be denied the credit due to him for quelling a disturbance which, if not stopped, would have spread throughout the country. A verdict as proposed by the Home Government would be a sorry return for all he had done. The Government of India could not incorporate in its own Resolution 'language which censures ourselves, criticizes the Committee and condemns our officers to an extent which we are not prepared to endorse.'

Chelmsford was adamant: although closeness to the events may have clouded their vision they had done their utmost to be impartial and he hoped his Government had not fallen short of what London had required. They had, but Westminster had to concede defeat. There was no alternative. Otherwise the Government of India would, as threatened, publish its own Resolution and leave the Home Government to do the same. The effects of such a course were too disastrous to contemplate.

Inwardly Montagu was deeply resentful. In his long letter to the Viceroy which accepted the recommendations of the Government of India and which was published with the Hunter Report, he went as far as he dared to hint at a disagreement. But in a private letter he was more outspoken:

If I have not succceeded, I can do no more. I foresee the future. I shall be cursed by one section of the public because there is no blood, not even penal servitude, and no impeachments. I shall be cursed by the other for daring to say anything in criticism of Sir Michael O'Dwyer. I have no doubt in my own mind that we have said or done nothing about Sir Michael O'Dwyer that is not justified, but I feel also that he represents a régime that is doomed. Either we must govern India as O'Dwyer governed the Punjab or we can govern it another way. The truth is that I do not believe that you will be able to go on governing it in that way without the most frightful troubles and difficulties.

15. Homecoming

'It was my duty — my horrible, dirty duty'. —
General Dyer on arrival at Southampton.

On 9 March, the day after Lord Hunter submitted his Report
to the Viceroy, General Dyer received an urgent signal order-
ing him to report to Delhi without delay and to be prepared to
be away from his headquarters for some time. He was completely unaware that after only a cursory glance at the Report
the Viceroy and his Executive Committee had realized that a
decision over the future of the man still hailed as the Saviour of
the Punjab could not be deferred. He had to be got out of India
as soon as possible. But Dyer was once again ill in bed and his
doctor replied that he was unfit to travel. A further telegram
arrived informing him that he must report to the Military
Secretary as soon as possible.

Although desperately ill, he left his sick bed and made the
long and exhausting train journey to Delhi. He had in fact
already made up his mind about his future, for a Medical Board
had just recommended six months sick leave in England which
he proposed taking before formally resigning. That face-saving
course was not to be made available to him.

When he arrived in Delhi he reported to the Adjutant-
General, who informed him that the Hunter Committee had
censured him and that the Commander-in-Chief agreed with
them. Consequently he was to be relieved of his command and
no further employment offered to him in India. Dyer indignantly pointed out that as he had never been tried he should not
be condemned, and he requested to see General Sir Charles
Monro and put it to him personally. The request was granted,
but there was no comfort forthcoming. Although Monro liked

Dyer and was in fact sympathetic towards him and well aware of the problems that had confronted him in Amritsar, he knew that the members of the Viceroy's Council were unanimous in their opinion that he should go.

Monro spoke briefly to Dyer, and simply endorsed what the Adjutant-General had said. He refrained from expressing his personal view that an officer of Dyer's rank and experience was expected to show a higher degree of self-restraint and a cooler and more reasoned appreciation of a tight situation. Dyer concealed his feelings remarkably well, and he seemed outwardly calm and composed as he listened to the words that had shattered his career. He saluted smartly, turned on his heels and walked out of the room.

On 27 March he sat down and wrote a formal letter to the General Officer Commanding the 2nd Division at Rawalpindi:

> Sir, I have the honour to state that during my recent visit to Delhi the Adjutant-General in India informed me, that owing to the opinion expressed by the Hunter Commission regarding my action at Amritsar during April 1919, it was necessary for me to resign my appointment as Brigadier-General Commanding the 5th Infantry Brigade. Accordingly I hereby ask that I may be relieved of that appointment.

Whereupon he returned to Jullundur to make arrangements for handing over his command and settle his private affairs.

On 6 April the crates containing the Dyers' personal belongings and all they wished to retain as reminders of a lifetime in India were nailed down. They were ready to go home.

In the afternoon a small deputation of women called at Flagstaff House and presented him with an illuminated address designed by 'a local lady artist'. The leader of the deputation said it was being presented on behalf of the ladies of the Punjab.

The beautifully designed address said:

> We the undersigned desire to express our heartfelt gratitude for the firmness you displayed in the crisis which arose in this Province last April. We deplore the loss of life which occurred, but we believe that it was your action which saved the Punjab and thereby preserved the honour and lives of hundreds of women and children. We trust, sir, that you

will understand that we who would have suffered most had the outbreak spread, are not unmindful of what we owe to you.

That evening General Dyer and his wife made a final inspection of the house which had been their home for so long and then slowly descended the front steps where an emotional scene confronted them. The entire garrison had turned out to see them off. Officers, N.C.O.s and Sepoys came to attention and saluted while the ladies applauded. A long procession of officers and their wives, British Other Ranks and Indian soldiers followed them along the flare-illuminated road to the station. As they boarded the mail train for Bombay the vast gathering began to sing, 'For He's a Jolly Good Fellow'. The reporter from the *Pioneer Mail* said they almost lifted the roof off the station and certainly woke up those passengers who were asleep. 'General and Mrs Dyer were visibly affected by the warmth of the send off.'

At Bombay they boarded the hospital ship *Assaye*, and when it sailed Dyer was on deck to acknowledge the waves and cheers of the large crowd which had gathered to wish them *bon voyage*, and to take a final look at the India he loved.

It was during the long voyage home that Lord Chelmsford informed Edwin Montagu that the Hunter Report was on its way and should arrive about the same time as the General. 'He is in a very bad way, and his condition is such that the doctors fear that any prolonged excitement may cause haemorrhage of the brain,' the Viceroy warned.

Monro had been proved right in one respect. The warmth of the farewells was ample proof that it would have been unwise for Dyer to have been in India when the results of the Hunter Committee were published.

On 3 May the *Assaye* berthed in Southampton. No sooner were the mooring lines secured to the bollards and the gangway in position than a reporter from the *Daily Mail* was sprinting aboard. The next day was the newspaper's 24th birthday and a headline-making scoop was necessary to mark the occasion. Somehow or other the *Daily Mail* had received a '*tip off*' about the General's arrival.

The reporter described their meeting and gave a sympathetic portrait of the man whose name was now a byword:

The General, burnt brick-red by thirty-five years' service in India, is thick set and fairly tall, with greying hair and kindly blue eyes. His attitude to the Amritsar affair may be judged by the first words he has ever uttered in public defence of his action: 'It was my duty — my horrible, dirty duty.'

The long sea voyage had enabled General Dyer to recover some of his former vigour and confidence, and he spoke forcefully in his own defence:

I had to shoot. I had thirty seconds to make up my mind what action to take and I did it. Every Englishman I have met in India has approved my act, horrible as it was. What would have happened if I had not shot? I and my little force would have been swept away like chaff and then what would have happened?

He answered his own rhetorical question: there were thousands of natives marching on the city at the time. The civil authority had handed over control to him and he had carried out his horrible, dirty duty. No one in authority had condemned him for it. On the contrary, he had been given command of another operation and congratulated by the General Officer Commanding.

But now I have been told to go. I have not been asked to resign my commission, but I was requested to resign my appointment, and being a soldier, there was nothing for me to do but to obey.

He reiterated that the right course would be to court martial him. 'I have never been heard in my own defence.'

He was particularly contemptuous of the Hunter Committee: he had been judged by a Committee which included an Englishman who did not understand India and three Indians who were biased. He was not a lawyer, simply a soldier who had served a lifetime abroad, but he should have been given the opportunity of defending himself.

The next day the Socialist *Daily Herald* retaliated by inviting Miss Helena Normanton, the editor of *India* (the organ of the Indian National Congress), to comment on the *Mail*'s scoop, and this she did with alacrity. Dyer should be tried, but not by court martial:

The whole of India is very anxious that the British authorities should not conclude that by merely making a scapegoat of General Dyer they can reconcile India. The real responsibility rests upon those who placed him in power and condoned his deeds so long, especially Sir Michael O'Dwyer, the then Lieutenant-Governor of the Punjab, and above all the Viceroy, Lord Chelmsford. Nothing would placate India more than the removal of the Viceroy.

Reaction to the *Daily Mail* story was also immediate in India and once again revealed the deep division that existed. *The Times of India* rejected Dyer's claim that every Englishman approved of his action:

On the contrary, wherever the tragedy is discussed there is heard nothing but loathing of the horrible circumstances which linked the slaughter at Jallianwala Bagh with the name of an Englishman.

Reuter's correspondent cabled from Simla that the *Pioneer* took an entirely opposite view, and several letters to the editor supported a proposal to set up a fund to present Sir Michael O'Dwyer and the General with swords of honour, 'for their services in saving India from the horrors of another 1857'.

There was, however, total agreement on one thing: the public demand for the immediate publication of the Report was growing.

There was a further complication in Britain. Some Members of Mr Montagu's Committee believed that Dyer had been treated too leniently and wanted some guidance as to what further action could be taken against him. Sir Edward des Chamier, the Legal Adviser at the India Office, had, therefore, been asked to submit a note outlining what exactly the legal position was. On 23 April he submitted a secret note several pages long which did nothing to solve Montagu's problems, for its contents presented an immovable object confronted by an irresistible force. Basing his opinions on the Majority and Minority Reports, he said it was clear that Dyer had intended to cause death or bodily injury likely to cause death, and under the Indian Penal Code he had committed culpable homicide not amounting to murder, the punishment for which was anything from a nominal sentence to transportation for life, or in the case of a European, penal servitude.

He could also be prosecuted in India by the Government in which case he would not be protected by the Indemnity Bill. If on the other hand a private prosecution was mounted he could claim that no court could take action against an officer who was acting under martial law, provided, of course, that he could show he had acted in good faith. It would be up to a jury to decide that point.

Dyer, however, could not be tried by court martial for murder or manslaughter as Amritsar was less than a hundred miles from Lahore where there was a High Court competent to deal with him.

On the other hand, he could be tried in England if he was apprehended or arrested there. He could be detained under the Fugitive of Offenders Act, but as Sir Edward pointed out, this was impractical as all the evidence was in India.

Having outlined all the courses open, Sir Edward then pointed out the pitfalls. It would be extremely difficult to obtain a conviction, for a jury, whether in England or India, would probably take the view that he was right in what he did, and acquit him.

There were many other opinions expressed by the Legal Adviser, all fraught with disaster:

I believe that a prosecution of General Dyer in India, and still more so in England, would be bitterly resented in India, not only by the British but by a considerable number of Indians, and I doubt whether any good would result from such a prosecution.

At the same time, it was doubtful whether a prosecution could be avoided if it was brought by an individual or a relative of one of the victims. A District Magistrate could not ignore it, and if he did the High Court, or as a last resort the Privy Council, could compel him to take action.

But that was still not the end of his legal opinion.

A Public Prosecutor appointed by the Government could still withdraw the prosecution before the jury was asked to return a verdict, in which case he would have to be acquitted.

It was cold comfort for Mr Montagu, for Sir Edward had exposed a legal minefield where one false step could detonate an explosion that would make a mockery of the Hunter

Committee. Whatever course was taken it would in his opinion result in acquittal. Dyer would then have a very strong case for demanding his reinstatement.

Understandably the Cabinet Committee recommended that the Government should not institute any criminal proceedings but on the contrary take every possible step (short of ad hoc legislation) to frustrate any legal action in India or Britain. Nothing, however, could be done to stop a private prosecution. Although such a move would inevitably result in financial ruin for Dyer and his family, the Committee could not recommend that the Government should assist him in defending it.

Mr J. P. Ellis, who had earlier warned of a 'downing of tools' in India if Dyer was censured, wrote to Sir Edward:

I am sorry for Dyer — it is better, however, to fall doing one's duty than flourish like a bay-tree yapping after the fashion of a pi-dog. The metaphor is mixed but the application is clear.

Sick as he was, Dyer was not the type of man who would give up without a fight, and while Montagu and Chelmsford were still trying to sort out their differences he called at the India Office and asked for the opportunity to defend himself before the Home authorities. It was agreed that he should be allowed to state his case before the Army Council.

Dyer was encouraged by the knowledge that he was not short of friends and allies. Sir Michael O'Dwyer had been busy behind the scenes drumming up support, and within a short space of time he could count upon the wholehearted backing of a number of powerful politicians and public figures, plus the voice of the influential *Morning Post*. Dyer was also assured of the finest legal advice, for among his champions was the mercurial Sir Edward Carson MP. Neither would he be permitted to suffer any financial hardship, for plans were already in hand to launch a public appeal for funds.

O'Dwyer was determined to make the case of General Dyer a major political issue. At stake was not simply the reputation of one soldier; a far more important issue was involved: the way in which India was to be governed in the future.

The King was extremely worried about the explosive situation that was developing. Rather surprisingly, Chelmsford

219

chose it as the moment for an indiscreet attack on Dyer. He wrote to the King — fortunately for Dyer's supporters, it was a personal and private letter — and confided how he had been close to taking disciplinary action against him during the Sar-had campaign:

> . . . I found that he was annexing large chunks of Persia — neutral country — and as no remonstrance seemed to have any effect, I had to tell Sir Beauchamp Duff — the then Commander-in-Chief — that I could not tolerate this, and that I should have to recall General Dyer. Fortunately, ill health on General Dyer's part saved me from having to take this extreme step, and he came back to India on leave . . . But there is no mistaking the impression he made on those out of the way places of the world, and the story goes that to this day women hush their crying children with the name of General Dyer much as the Saracenic women used to frighten their crying babes with the name of Richard Coeur de Lion . . . I am afraid that we shall be told that we have sacrificed a very gallant officer, yet I would respectfully submit that if we are to wipe out the sad memories of last year, we can only do so by dealing out absolute justice in the case of officers who have exceeded their duty.

Judgement in Britain was deeply divided. As Lord Stamfordham, replying on behalf of the King, wrote in a letter to Chelmsford:

> On one side he [Dyer] is condemned for what is regarded as heartlessness, callousness and indifference to the value of human life; on the other side there are those who sum up their position in the words 'Dyer saved India'. This latter view is strongly held by the Military Members of the Army Council, and I have heard it repeated by thoughtful men who have lately returned from India.

It was a disturbing appraisal and one which had occurred to Edwin Montagu. What would happen if the Army Council took a different line to Lord Hunter, the Viceroy and the British Government?

16. The Army Council

*'What a disgraceful rush the whole thing is, and
purely political' — Field Marshal Sir Henry Wilson,
C.I.G.S.*

Montagu's fears were not imaginary, as he and the members of
his Cabinet Committee were soon to find out. Winston
Churchill, the Secretary of State for War, had a meeting with
Field-Marshal Sir Henry Wilson, the Chief of the Imperial
General Staff, and told him that the Cabinet's decision regard-
ing Dyer was final and reference to the Army Council was a
formality. The military members were expected to endorse it
without dissent. But Wilson had no intention of being a rubber
stamp to Cabinet decisions and told Churchill so in no uncertain manner. Furthermore, he had the backing of several
senior officers who insisted that Dyer had the right to reply and
they would not be bulldozed into a decision. They would
judge it on its merits. Churchill, anxious to avoid a head-on
collision, said he would refer the matter to the law members.
   Churchill, always headstrong, did not like his decisions
questioned by soldiers and he had another private meeting with
Wilson at which tempers became very frayed. Churchill said he
very much objected to having a pistol placed at his head or
being ambushed by the military members. Wilson told him
rather brusquely, 'You have only yourself to thank'. Churchill
tried to convince the C.I.G.S. of the rightness of his action, but
Wilson would not budge. The politician finally gave way to the
soldier and said he would consult the Cabinet and then call
another meeting of the Army Council. Wilson reminded
Churchill that nothing should be decided behind his back.
   Wilson confided in his diary:

It appeared to me, listening, that the story was a very simple one. The Frocks [politicians] have got India (as they have Ireland) into a filthy mess. On that the soldiers are called in to act. This is disapproved of by all the disloyal elements and the soldier is thrown to the winds.

It was his firmly held view that Dyer was entitled to the support of his fellow officers until proved wrong by a Court of Inquiry. It was an opinion heartily endorsed by most of his colleagues. If Dyer was not given a fair hearing military morale would be deeply affected. General Rawlinson, who was due to go to India as the new Commander-in-Chief, assured Wilson of his wholehearted support. If Dyer was not given the opportunity to state his case he would refuse to take up his appointment.

Montagu and Bonar Law sided with Churchill and tried to dissuade the military members from taking such an unequivocal stand, but they would not budge and the deadlock was only ended when it was agreed that Dyer should have the right of reply and full access to the Hunter Report. But almost a month elapsed before Dyer was told of the decision. The time lapse was inexcusable and the suspicion grew that the delaying tactics were deliberate: Wilson was due to go to Germany and it would be extremely advantageous if Dyer's case was considered in his absence.

Dyer was not going to make the mistake of preparing his own defence; he had learned to his cost how dangerous that course was. So he contacted solicitors, Sharpe, Pritchard & Company, who briefed Mr Reginald Hill and Mr Austin Jones, two leading Counsel, to draw up his statement.

The split between the politicians and the military members of the Army Council was not allowed to remain a secret. News of the wrangling was 'leaked' to pro-Dyer supporters, and at a Cabinet Meeting on 8 June attention was drawn to a question to be asked in the House by Mr Rupert Gwynne who planned to ask Churchill if the question of Dyer's conduct had been referred to the Army Council, and if it had what was the result.

It was agreed that Churchill would simply confirm that the Army Council would consider it and that Dyer had been asked to submit a detailed statement.

Meanwhile, Sir Michael O'Dwyer had returned from India

and seen a copy of the Hunter Report, and he realized that Dyer would be handicapped by not having access to the evidence given in camera. It was vital to the vindication of the General. While some of it had been published, most of it had been suppressed. It would, he believed, reveal the existence of a deep-rooted plot to overthrow the British.

O'Dwyer wrote to Montagu asking for permission to submit a statement, not on his own behalf but to explain the true situation which existed in Amritsar. This was turned down and he promptly asked to be allowed to appear in front of the Army Council before Dyer was dealt with. But his request was not even passed on to the Council.

The newspapers were filled with speculative reports that the military members had fallen out with the politicians. The *Sunday Express* was the first to headline the 'Dramatic Decision by the Army Council' not to accept the Hunter Committee findings, and on 20 June it disclosed that the Army Council proposed to restore General Dyer to the Army. It was, the paper claimed, a decision they had reached despite considerable pressure from the Cabinet.

Winston Churchill was immediately under fire in the House of Commons where he had to assure Members that there was no truth whatsoever in the reports. 'The Army Council is still awaiting the statement which General Dyer is being allowed to submit.'

His denial did little to end the crystal-gazing. Whilst it was within Churchill's power to overrule the soldiers, it was something he dared not do, said the newspapers.

News of the 'split' soon reached India and Chelmsford was quick to remind Montagu that any modification of the punishment would have a disastrous effect on Indian opinion and intensify racial feeling.

Dyer's long-awaited statement was eventually submitted by his legal advisers on 3 July. It was a detailed analysis of events in the Punjab and a point by point rebuttal of the findings of the Hunter Committee. It clearly owed more to the lawyers than it did to Dyer, for it was meticulous in its examination and extremely impressive in its conclusions. It was more concerned with legalities than emotive issues, and presented a completely fresh approach.

Field-Marshal Wilson was informed that the Army Council

would meet the following day; rather testily he pointed out that he was due to go to Germany on an official visit. 'What a terrible rush the whole thing is, and purely political,' he protested.

He was in fact in Germany when the meeting took place and it was Major-General Sir George Barrow, who had sat on the Hunter Committee and was now one of the Military Members, who insisted that the Majority Report and the Cabinet decision should be endorsed. Shortly afterwards Winston Churchill informed the House that the Army Council had decided that in spite of the great difficulties which confronted Dyer in the Jallianwala Bagh he could not be acquitted of an error of judgement. They had considered the decision of the Commander-in-Chief, India, that Dyer should be removed from his command, and no further employment offered to him in India, that he should revert to half-pay, and that he had been passed over for promotion. 'These decisions the Army Council accept.'

He went on to say, 'They have also considered whether any further action of a disciplinary nature is required from the Army Council. In view of all the circumstances, they do not feel called upon from the military point of view with which they are alone concerned to take any further action.'

With this the Cabinet agreed.

But the row was still far from over. On 8 July the House of Commons was due to debate the case of General Dyer. With the clear intention of not providing Dyer's supporters with any ammunition with which to destroy the Government's case, Churchill decided that Dyer's statement should not be released until after the debate. It was a decision that was hard to justify and it smacked too much of Parliamentary tactics.

But the Government had more than enough on its plate already without Dyer's carefully argued defence. Sir Michael O'Dwyer, extremely angry at being snubbed, had thrown the cat among the pigeons by sending to the newspapers a long and detailed criticism of the Hunter Committee and its findings. He considered it was his duty to put before Parliament, 'the final tribunal of the British public', the points he would have submitted to the Cabinet Committee and the Army Council.

The scope of Hunter, he argued, was too limited for a full appreciation of the situation which existed in India, and the six

(*above left*) The Jallianwala Bagh in 1919—the narrow entrance which prevented Dyer from using his armoured cars.

(*above right*) 1919—the point inside the Bagh from which Dyer's men fired. The height of the surrounding walls is clearly shown.

(*below*) 1919—a general view of the Jallianwala Bagh, taken approximately from where Dyer stood. The building on the right, beneath the tree, is the shrine. To the left, just visible beneath the smallest of the three trees, is the well.

(*top*) 1979—the widow of Nanak Chand on the balcony of her home in the 'crawling lane'. Her husband, who died in 1971, survived the shooting after a friend removed a bullet from his leg.

(*bottom*) Mr U. N. Mukerji (*left*), Secretary of the Jallianwala Bagh Trust, who ran away when the troops arrived. With him is Atma Singh Sidhu, who escaped unharmed having been buried under a pile of bodies.

(*above*) The memorial to Dyer's victims in the Jallianwala Bagh today.

(*below right*) The entrance to the Bagh, as narrow as ever, but now marked 'historic'.

(*below left*) Daulat Ram Bhatia on the spot where the soldiers fired. He was wounded in the massacre, which took place on his fifteenth birthday.

NOTICE

THIS PLACE IS SATURATED WITH THE BLOOD OF ABOUT TWO THOUSAND HINDU, SIKH AND MUSLIM PATRIOTS WHO WERE MARTYRED IN A NON-VIOLENT STRUGGLE TO FREE INDIA FROM BRITISH DOMINATION. GENERAL DYER OF THE BRITISH ARMY OPENED FIRE HERE ON UNARMED PEOPLE. JALLIANWALA BAGH IS THUS AN EVERLASTING SYMBOL OF NON-VIOLENT AND PEACEFUL STRUGGLE FOR FREEDOM OF INDIAN PEOPLE AND THE GROSS TYRANNY OF THE BRITISH. INNOCENT, PEACEFUL AND UNARMED PEOPLE WHO WERE PROTESTING AGAINST THE RAWLETTE ACT WERE FIRED UPON ON 13th. APRIL, 1919. UNDER A RESOLUTION OF THE INDIAN NATIONAL CONGRESS THIS LAND WAS PURCHASED FOR rs. 5,65,000 FOR SETTING UP A MEMORIAL TO THOSE PATRIOTS. A TRUST WAS FORMED FOR THIS PURPOSE AND MONEY COLLECTED FROM ALL OVER INDIA AND FOREIGN COUNTRIES. WHEN THIS LAND WAS PURCHASED IT WAS ONLY A VACANT PLOT AND THERE WAS NO GARDEN HERE.

THE TRUST REQUESTS THE PEOPLE TO OBSERVE THE RULES FRAMED BY IT AND THUS SHOW THEIR REVERENCE TO THE MEMORY OF THE MARTYRS.

PEOPLE WERE FIRED AT FROM HERE

(*opposite top left*) A memorial notice giving the Indian view of the massacre.

(*opposite top right*) The shrine inside the Jallianwala Bagh, where many sought refuge from the bullets.

(*opposite bottom*) Dyer's firing point, remembered in several languages.

(*top*) The 'crawling lane' today.

(*bottom*) The magnificent Golden Temple in Amritsar, where Dyer was supposedly made an honorary Sikh.

(*above*) The Dyer case debated in the House of Lords, 24 July 1920.

(*opposite*) Disgraced and ailing, clad in a borrowed coat with a hospital docket still attached, General Dyer lands at Southampton. It is interesting to compare this photograph with that facing page 96.

(*top*) Eight years after the Amritsar massacre, Dyer's body is borne in state past the Guards Division memorial to the Church of St Martin-in-the-Fields, 27 July, 1927.

(*bottom*) Mounted on a 13-pounder field gun of the Royal Horse Artillery and escorted by NCOs of the Irish Guards, Dyer's coffin processes beneath the flag that had flown over his Amritsar headquarters.

months' delay before the Committee began its hearing had seriously prejudiced the findings. Once again he attacked the constitution of the Committee and said it was incapable of being impartial. And he was particularly critical of Lord Hunter's decision not to consider the judicial findings of the Special Tribunals which conclusively revealed details of the widespread rebellion.

> Nothing has done more to prejudice the case of General Dyer and the other officers administering martial law, with the press and public at home, than the suspicion that things had been done by them which would not stand the light of criticism, and were therefore concealed or minimized by them or by the authorities in India. There is absolutely no foundation for such a suspicion.

Montagu, he repeated, had been kept fully informed and he had supplied him with full details of what had happened in the Jallianwala Bagh.

He was being branded in public as a liar. The true facts would reveal that Dyer was perfectly justified in taking the action he did. He and others who had been criticized were entitled to the support that had been promised them. 'In the last resort they look to the Imperial Parliament for the final judgement.'

Even without Sir Michael's support, General Dyer had presented an extremely powerful case. He shirked nothing and even answered the allegations made in the Minority Report; something he had no need to do for no one had ever accepted it. The trouble was that Dyer had shifted his ground and although his arguments were submitted with considerable skill and eloquence, they could not dispel the bad impression his verbal evidence to Hunter had created. It was as if with hindsight he realized the errors he had made during his interrogation in Lahore.

Of the vital issue revolving around his action in the Jallianwala Bagh Dyer insisted that as the man on the spot he was more aware of the critical situation than anyone else. It was *not* just an unlawful assembly but a rebellious gathering which included the people who had looted and murdered in Amritsar.

> I had before me in the Jallianwala Bagh not a fortuitous gathering, which at worst had assembled negligently or even

225

recklessly contrary to a proclamation, but a mob that was there with express intent to challenge Government authority and defy me to take any effective action against it and in particular to defy me to open fire upon it.

The question remained: why had he not told this to Hunter? If he had explained that his force was about to be attacked there would have been no controversy in the first place. Therefore, it raised another question: how much were the words his and how much his lawyer's? Despite his protests, most of his evidence before the Hunter Committee had been voluntarily and readily given. His statement and his evidence seemed irreconcilable.

Dyer was less convincing when it came to explaining the 'Crawling Order'. 'The Order meant that the street should be regarded as holy ground and that, to mark this fact, no one was to traverse it except in a manner in which a place of special sanctity might naturally in the East be traversed.' He closed with a moving passage. 'The charges of inhumanity are, I submit, baseless, and I request that I may receive an explicit assurance that my character is regarded as completely free from stain on this score.'

Churchill's decision to hold back Dyer's statement misfired. Somehow or other supporters of the General managed to see copies before the debate opened. In any case, Sir Michael O'Dwyer's long statement to the press had provided them with a lot of additional ammunition.

Sir Michael had every reason to be satisfied that his slashing attack on the Hunter Committee had reopened the controversy in India. Now he was determined to do the same in England.

17.   The Commons Debate

'It was a Dyer debate pure and simple, and for that reason it will create disappointment and misgiving in India.' — Mr. J. T. Bennet, MP, in a letter to The Times.

A long queue straggled along the pavement outside the House of Commons on the morning of 8 July. Many had been waiting for several hours. Some time during the day the House was to debate the case of General Dyer and everyone was looking forward to the political free-for-all that was confidently predicted. *The Times* that morning had expressed the hope that moderation would prevail, but those who had queued for hours hoped otherwise.

Inside the House, looking down into the Chamber, were Sir Michael O'Dwyer and General Dyer. Dyer sat hunched beside his wife and alongside her was Lady Carson, wife of the distinguished lawyer. Those observers unfamiliar with Parliamentary procedure were baffled at what was taking place below them. Ostensibly members were being called upon to approve a contribution of £53,000 towards the cost of the Department of the Secretary of State for India. The Labour Members had proposed an amendment reducing the sum by £100 on the grounds that the Government had done nothing to remove the conditions which had provoked the disturbances in India. In effect it was a vote of no confidence in the Government's handling of Indian affairs.

Edwin Montagu was the first to speak. He said that he understood the debate was to be confined to events in India and after consideration he had decided that the best course for him to adopt would be to say as little as possible; it would only add to the controversy. He had expressed his views and those of the Government. The despatch by his Committee had been fully

227

approved by the Cabinet and he had no wish to add or withdraw anything. The question, therefore, was whether Members would endorse the views of the Government, the Hunter Committee, the Commander-in-Chief in India, the Government of India and the Army Council, or whether they wanted to censure them. The issue confronting the House was simple:

'If an officer justifies his conduct, no matter how gallant his conduct is — and everybody knows how gallant General Dyer's record is — by saying there was no question of undue severity, that if his means had been greater the casualties would have been greater, and that the motive was to teach a moral lesson to the whole of the Punjab, I say without hesitation, and I would ask the Committee to contradict me if I am wrong, because the whole matter turns on this, that is a doctrine of terrorism.' If Members agreed to that then they justified everything Dyer did. 'Once you are entitled to have regard neither to the intentions nor to the conduct of a particular gathering, but to shoot and to go on shooting with all the horrors that were involved in order to teach somebody else a lesson, you are embarking on terrorism to which there is no end.

'I say further that when you pass an order that all Indians must crawl past a particular place, when you pass an order to say that all Indians must forcibly or voluntarily salaam any officer of His Majesty the King, you are enforcing racial humiliation. I say, thirdly, that when you take selected school-boys from a school, guilty or innocent, and whip them publicly, when you put up a triangle where an outrage, which we all deplore and which all India deplores, has taken place, and whip people before they have been convicted, when you flog a wedding party, you are indulging in frightfulness and there is no other adequate word which could describe it.

'Are you going to keep your hold upon India by terrorism, racial humiliation, and subordination, and frightfulness, or are you going to rest it upon the growing good will of the people of your Indian Empire? I believe that to be the whole question at issue.'

It was no good, he insisted, for Parliament to introduce reforms if the administration on the spot did not recognize them. 'There is the other choice, to hold India by the sword, to recognize terrorism as part of your weapon, as part of your armament, to guard British honour and British life with callousness about Indian honour and Indian life.' He reminded them that there had been thirty-seven instances of firing during the disturbances but only the shooting in the Jallianwala Bagh had been condemned. The great objection to terrorism and rule by force, he warned, was that it was pursued without any regard to the people who suffered from it. And having tried it you had to continue because of the increasing animosity of the people. There was an alternative to terrorism: the people of India could be led to free partnership in the Commonwealth.

'There is a theory abroad on the part of those who have criticized His Majesty's Government upon this issue that an Indian is tolerable so long as he will obey your orders, but if once he joins the educated classes, if once he thinks for himself, if once he takes advantage of the educational facilities which you have provided for him, if once he imbibes the ideas of individual liberty which are dear to the British people, why then you class him as an educated Indian and as an agitator. What a terrible and cynical verdict on the whole!'

The House erupted into shouts of 'Shame', 'No', 'Withdraw' and 'What a terrible speech'.

Montagu eventually managed to proceed and he insisted that if Members wanted to adopt the democratic method of government in India, then Dyer should be condemned.

Before he sat down he made an impassioned appeal. 'I invite this House to choose, and I believe that the choice they make is fundamental to a continuance of the British Empire and vital to the continuation, permanent, I believe it can be, of the connection between this country and India.'

Sir Edward Carson then rose. He said he could not see that Montagu's speech would settle anything. He had told the House that the issue was how India was to be governeed. 'What on earth has that to do with it?' He agreed that the matter under discussion was serious and he regretted that Montagu had not been able to approach it in a calmer way. He would not have taken part in the debate if it was simply a question of how India should be governed, for he did not disagree with him. The question was whether or not Dyer had been fairly treated. Carson, who had been briefed by Sir Michael O'Dwyer, explained that he was solely concerned

229

with justice for a gallant soldier. It was only an hour ago that he had read Dyer's defence of his action, and although it was not up to the House to try him Members had a right to ask: 'Has he ever had a fair trial? And to put this further question before you break him and send him into disgrace: is he going to have a fair trial?'

Fixing his stare on Montagu he said, 'You talk of the great principles of liberty which you have laid down. General Dyer has a right to be brought within those principles of liberty, and has no right to be broken on the *ipse dixit* of any Commission or Committee, however great, unless he has been fairly tried — and he has not been tried.'

To shouts of approval he said that no one but the man on the spot could judge the amount of force to be used. 'It must be remembered that when a rebellion has been started against the Government it is tantamount to a declaration of war, and war cannot be conducted in accordance with the standards of humanity to which we are accustomed in peace.'

He wanted to know what was the error of judgement on Dyer's part. It was admitted he had acted in good faith in the most difficult circumstances and with courage and great decision. While Dyer thought that he should teach a lesson to the Province as a whole, the Committee believed he should have dealt with it solely as a local matter.

'That is the whole difference, and for that an officer who has done his best was to be broken after thirty-four years of honourable service, was to be broken although the authorities had to admit that the action for which he was broken might have saved a most bloody outbreak in that country which might have caused the loss of thousands of lives.'

Carson's speech was repeatedly interrupted by loud cheers and these were particularly marked when he questioned Montagu's claims that he did not know the details until six months later. 'That was really a most extraordinary and unfortunate matter.' (Cheers) 'He never took a single step until the agitation broke out in India, when the situation had been practically saved.' He did not hide his scepticism. 'If there was anything to be investigated and if there was punishment to be meted out, it ought to have been immediate, not only in justice to General Dyer, but in justice to the Indian people. Was there ever a more extraordinary case than that of a man who came forward and told you: I won the approval of my Divisional Commander and the Lieutenant-Governor of the Province. I was given promotion, I was sent to do more and more difficult jobs, and eight months afterwards you tell me I shall never again be employed, because I have disgraced myself by inhumanity and an error of judgement. . .

'For Heaven's sake, when you put a soldier in to these difficult positions, do not visit upon him punishment for attempting to deal to the best of his ability with a situation for which he is not in the slightest degree responsible. If he makes an error of judgement, approach it with the full idea that if he is bona fide and you can see it was impossible for him in the circumstances to have calmly made up his mind in the way you would do, then you may censure him, but do not punish him. Do not break him.'

When Churchill rose to speak he was fully aware that the Government's survival was in jeopardy, for Carson had clearly commanded the support of several of its Members. But he was not prepared to placate them. He believed Dyer had got off too lightly; he certainly had not been punished unfairly. The action taken in India and the decision of the Army Council, he stressed, was based on Dyer's first statement and not what he had said at the Hunter Committee.

'One tremendous fact stands out. I mean the slaughter of nearly four hundred persons and the wounding of probably three or four times that number at the Jallianwala Bagh on 13 April. This is an episode which appears to me to be without precedent or parallel in the modern history of the British Empire. It is an event of entirely different order from any of those tragic occurrences which take place when troops are brought into collision with the civil population. It is an extraordinary event, a monstrous event, an event which stands in singular and sinister isolation.'

Jallianwala Bagh had not saved India. 'Our reign in India or anywhere else has never rested on a basis of physical force alone, and it would be fatal to the British Empire to try to base ourselves only upon it.'

Speaking for himself, Churchill said that Dyer not only deserved loss of employment and censure, but disciplinary action. But as it appeared that his conduct had at the time been condoned the Cabinet decided against further action.

There was a sullen silence from many whose loyalty he had hoped to command. Herbert Asquith, the former Prime Minister, tried to diffuse the atmosphere. Dyer may have been commended at the time but were his superior officer and the Lieutenant-Governor impartial judges? In the hectic circumstances surrounding the incident they might have reached conclusions which subsequent reflection and investigation might not have justified. But purely on the merits of the case he had not heard anything to impugn the correctness of the action taken by the various authorities later. People had been shot down like sheep in a pen. 'There has never been such an incident in the whole annals of Anglo-Indian history, nor, I believe, in the history of our Empire.'

The Labour Party view was put forward by Mr B. G. Spoor, the Member for Bishop Auckland, who said that two weeks previously at the Labour Party Conference a resolution had been passed calling for the recall of the Viceroy, the impeachment of Sir Michael O'Dwyer, and the trial of officers who had been censured and the repeal of repressive legislation. That resolution expressed more clearly the feelings of the people than the exhibition they had witnessed that evening.

'Sir Edward Carson has said, "Let us be fair to the British officers". Yes, but also let them be fair to the hundreds of Indians who lost their lives and to the children who were bombed from the air by British officers. Amritsar was not an isolated event any more than General Dyer was an isolated officer.'

The arguments went over the same ground time and time again. Then Sir William Joynson-Hicks, a well-known solicitor and avowed supporter of Dyer, rose to his feet. He was not, he said forcibly, prepared to abdicate his rights and duties as a Member of the House of Commons simply because of the decision of the Army Council. The House was the last court to which Dyer could appeal against a decision of the Government.

He had just returned from an extended tour of India which included visits to Amritsar and the opinions he was expressing represented eighty per cent of the Indian Civil Service and ninety per cent of the Europeans. Montagu's speech was the most disastrous he had ever heard from a Secretary of State; for some time past he had lost the confidence of the I.C.S. and his speech would have destroyed what shreds of confidence were left in the minds of the British Army in India.

To rousing cheers he said, 'I am prepared to say that General Dyer was right.'

Sir William, from his court-room experience, knew the value of shock tactics and he quoted from a letter from Marcia Sherwood: ' "I am convinced there was real rebellion in the Punjab and that General Dyer saved India." '

Sir William's eloquence had won him much support, but his impartiality was brought into doubt when he admitted that he represented Dyer.

He closed by appealing to the House on behalf of the Englishmen in the Army and the Civil Service in India who upheld the flag in very difficult circumstances, many of whom had their wives and children with them and were living in extremely remote parts. The right thing to do was trust the man on the spot.

He sat down to ringing cheers.

Brigadier-General Surtees, Conservative Unionist for Gateshead, spoke with a bluntness that embarrassed a number of Members. If a plebiscite were held tomorrow as to who should rule India, the result would go against Britain. 'If we do not hold India by moral suasion, we must hold it by force, possibly thinly veiled, but undoubtedly by force.'

Colonel Josiah Wedgwood, Liberal, warned that a shrine would be erected in the Jallianwala Bagh, 'and every year there will be processions of Indians visiting the tomb of the martyrs. . . Whenever we put forward the humanitarian view, we shall have this tale thrown in our teeth.'

The most scathing attack on Mr Montagu came from Mr Rupert Gwynne, who claimed that the former's sympathies were with those who opposed law and order and in pursuit of that had deliberately misled the House by saying he was not aware of the true facts of Dyer's action.

Mr Montagu jumped to his feet in protest: 'Does the honourable Member suggest that I saw the report in August? If he does, it is not true.'

Mr Gwynne stuck to his guns and repeated his allegations. Then, shifting slightly, he said that if, as he claimed, Montagu was not informed of events he was not fit to continue in office.

To roars of support he said that Montagu, under pressure from his agitating friends, had forced the Government of India to reverse their decision.

Again Montagu was on his feet, but Mr Gwynne would not withdraw. 'Their action is amazing if you did not. Why did they suddenly turn round?'

Montagu tried desperately hard to explain his position: 'I deny absolutely that I put any pressure upon the Government of India. They waited to receive the Hunter Report, then made their decision and communicated it to me. The honourable gentleman is making many foul charges against me which are not supported by the facts.'

Gwynne retorted, 'Charges are foul when they are made against civilians, but they are not foul when made against soldiers. General Dyer is disgraced after thirty-four years' service without trial. When the Right Honourable Member is criticized in this House he says the charges are foul. At any rate he is not losing his office. I wish he were.'

When the Labour amendment was put to the vote it was defeated by 247 votes to 37. Many Members did not vote but the Government still had a solid majority of 210.

Sir Edward Carson then rose and, amid loud cheers, moved another amendment to reduce the vote by £100. The amount of money was the same but the reason was vastly different: it was a gesture of protest at the manner in which Dyer had been treated.

When the vote was taken there were sighs of relief on the Government benches. Defeat had been narrowly avoided. Voting for the reduction was 129 and against 230. But a large number of Government supporters had abstained.

The Times next morning had commented that one of the most remarkable aspects of the debate had been the bitterness shown towards Montagu. There had not been personal attacks of such concentrated virulence since party politics ended with the Coalition Government.

Montagu, an extremely sensitive man, was deeply wounded by them and immediately he sent a telegram to Lord Chelmsford detailing the allegations. The Viceroy promptly replied that neither his Government nor the Commander-in-Chief had ever revised their opinion. And he reiterated, 'In no case, and at no time, did he [Dyer] obtain promotion of any sort.' The suggestion that pressure was brought to bear on him and his Council was dismissed as 'a falsity'.

Lord Chelmsford was even prepared to publish their private correspondence, but Montagu was against such a move:

> Public life becomes impossible if, because a minority chooses to believe in the bad faith of a Viceroy or a Secretary of State, correspondence not intended for publication has to be produced. If we are not to be believed we should be dismissed.

18.   The *Morning Post* Fund

'*I am proud to think that so many of my fellow countrymen and women approve of my conduct at Amritsar, and I accept the token of their appreciation in the spirit in which it is offered.*' — *General Dyer*.

The day the House of Commons was due to debate the case of Dyer, the *Morning Post* launched a fund to raise money for 'The Man Who Saved India'. It was instigated by Sir Michael O'Dwyer and Sir Edward Carson and the timing was superb.
  The 'Appeal to Patriots' said:

> While General Dyer saved India, the politicians are saving themselves at his expense. It is a burning reproach to the British nation that such a thing could be possible. But the politicians have the power, and the only appeal is to the generous instincts of the people.

In an attempt to clear his name, Dyer had been put to great expense — 'soldiers do not get the pay of politicians' — and now he was not only broken but crippled financially.
  The appeal was two-fold: not only would it relieve him from financial problems but more importantly it would give him in his hour of bitterness and tribulation an assurance that his fellow countrymen extended their sympathy and confidence and gratitude, 'and dissociated themselves from the mean and cowardly conduct of the politicians and the time-servers'.
  The response was immediate, moving and overwhelming. The amount of money that flowed in was an embarrassment to the editor, Mr H. A. Gwynne, but it was an even bigger embarrassment to the Government for it revealed the depth of feeling that had been aroused by the punishment meted out to Dyer.
  As the lists of subscribers were published it was abundantly

clear that money was pouring in from every class of person and was not confined to Europeans.

An attempt was made to stop it but without success. Major M. Wood, Liberal MP for Aberdeen Central, asked the Secretary of State for War whether it was permissible for an officer to accept a pecuniary solatium as an evidence of sympathy when he had suffered disciplinary action. Winston Churchill replied that his attention had been drawn to Paragraph 443A of King's Regulations which forbade such a presentation, but as Dyer had sent in an application to retire he proposed to take no further action.

It was a wise decision, for nothing would have stopped people sending in their money. The Indian Government had forbidden its officers and servants to contribute; but they did so secretly.

The Countess of Bathurst headed the list, and within 24 hours £1,500 had reached the newspaper's offices. By 16 July it had topped £10,000, and it was proposed to close the fund as far as the British Isles was concerned, but this met with strong protests and the Fund remained open.

In India the response was staggering. Jute workers and railwaymen sent money. Mrs Florence Holland became President of a 13-woman Committee to raise money to present 'The Saviour of the Punjab with a sword of honour and a purse for sparing them untold misery by arresting murder, torture, arson, looting and wholesale anarchy.' They also expressed their sympathy at the unjust sentence passed on him

> as a result of partial and prejudiced evidence and indignation at the dangers of pandering to a small band of disloyal agitators whose noisy mouthings the deluded British public are mistaking for the voice of the loyal millions of India.

Similar organizations were set up throughout the subcontinent. The *Statesman* sent R 20,000, the *Pioneer and Englishman* R 10,000. The *Morning Post Calcutta*, the *Madras Mail*, the *Rangoon Times*, the *Civil and Military Gazette* and many other newspapers sent cheques. The European Association and the Madras Club rallied to Dyer's support. Civil servants and regimental messes sent their contributions under *noms de plumes*. At home and abroad women sold items of jewellery to raise money.

But the sums were not always large. 'Poor and proud' sent an Indian coin. Miss Lillie Faulkner sent a collection of antique coins. 'Two Cornish women' sent an 1823 edition of *Les Confessions de Rousseau*. Two indignant sisters sent four Queen Victoria Jubilee commemoration stamps. Ex-Gurkha Edward Shoesmith sent £5. There were country parsons, high-ranking army officers, admirals, and men from the lower deck. 'A lady who was in Lahore' gave 10s, R. H. Casement, £1. Anon was a frequent subscriber. Five shillings came from Canada. 'A mite for the gallant soldier'. 'An Amritsar Resident', £10. Mr Schuyler Schieffelin of New York, £7. There were many more Americans in the lists that appeared. Letters and money came from all parts of the world.

'One of the women in India who remembers, with thanks in her heart, the name of General Dyer', £10. The Duke of Westminster, £100. The Earl of Harewood, Lady Sumner, the Duke and Duchess of Somerset and many other members of the aristocracy sent money. 'A poor gentlewoman' sent 2/6d, 'a patriotic Englishwoman and one of the new poor' 2/6d. Sir Michael O'Dwyer sent a cheque, as did a 'survivor of the Indian Mutiny'.

Rudyard Kipling, the Poet Laureate of India, subscribed £10. W. B. Gladstone, ten guineas. £10 arrived with a 'Montagu must go' note attached. There were the proceeds from flowers sold in the streets and jumble sales, 'A wife who was there', 10s. A twenty-franc note arrived from 'another victim of the Army Council'. Ten pounds was delivered with a quotation from *Romeo and Juliet*, 'Stop thy unhallowed toil, vile Montagu'.

When the Fund eventually closed the enormous sum of £26,317.4.10 had been raised.

Dyer had been rescued from penury and elevated to the status of a relatively rich man.

19.   Lords and the General

'A Government that allowed its authority to be challenged must go under.' — Lord Sumner during the Lords Debate.

Dyer was understandably depressed after the debate in the House of Commons; he had come so close to victory. His low spirits were further aggravated by the arteriosclerosis that was slowly killing him. But his friends urged him not to despair; the future was not as bleak as it appeared. The Fund had revealed the immense amount of public sympathy his case commanded. Furthermore it was about to be debated afresh in the Lords where the atmosphere would not be bedevilled by personal animosity and political hair-splitting. The Lords also contained many ex-soldiers, judges, and ex-Colonial administrators who would feel more sympathetic to his case.

At 4.15 p.m. on Monday 19 July, Viscount Finlay rose to move: 'That this House deplores the conduct of the case of General Dyer as unjust to that officer, and as establishing a precedent dangerous to the preservation of law and order in the face of rebellion.'

There was, however, very little new that anybody could add to what had already been stressed time and time again in the Commons. The words may have been different but the arguments did not vary: Hunter had been wrong in finding there was no plot to overthrow the Government; Dyer was entitled to look at India as a whole when he took action and not to treat it as a local issue. If he had not fired the rebellion would have acquired irresistible momentum.

At least the debate was conducted with decorum. Lord Sinha, the Under-Secretary for India, himself an Indian, said rather resignedly that he could not throw any fresh light on the

239

controversy which had been discussed until it was threadbare, therefore he could not hope to change or influence the opinion of those who supported General Dyer. The people of India did not, he stressed, want punishment of any individual but simply the vindication of principles. He personally regretted the attacks which had been made on the Indian Members of the Hunter Committee and he hoped he could convince the Chamber that the aspersions were quite unjustified.

The suggestion that the Indian Government had at any time thought Dyer's action was justified was mischievous and almost dangerous. And the suggestion that they altered their views in deference to Montagu was totally unfounded.

The judgement of the Government of India and His Majesty's Government had *not*, he repeated, been based on a single word of the evidence Dyer had given to the Hunter Committee but solely on Dyer's statement to the military authorities long before Hunter sat. As for the often-repeated claim that Dyer had averted a mutiny there was not a single person in authority, Indian or European, who accepted that.

When Lord Birkenhead, the Lord Chancellor, rose he started off on a placatory note by conceding that everyone in the Cabinet agreed that Dyer was an officer who had exhibited discretion, sobriety and resolution before Amritsar and had exercised the same qualities in the months that followed. But at the Jallianwala Bagh he had committed a tragic error of judgement, and it would be disastrous for the Empire if it was thought the act was approved. He had gone there with the deliberate intention of taking life on a large scale, and when the crowd dispersed and tried to escape he had directed his fire where there were the most people. On his own admission if he had been able to get the machine guns into the Bagh the casualties would have been much higher.

'I claim that anyone who stands here and defends the case of General Dyer should be prepared to defend similar conduct in Glasgow or Belfast or Winnipeg.'

Viscount Milner, Secretary of State for the Colonies, who had been a Member of the Cabinet Committee, made an energetic attempt to dispel the belief that Dyer had been the victim of political expediency. He personally had not known anything about the case until he had read Hunter, and if he had approached it with any bias it had been in favour of the soldier.

But the more he studied the report the more convinced he was that there were certain acts committed, especially those of Dyer, which in the long run would not strengthen the maintenance of law and order but undermine it. Nothing could justify the methods Dyer had adopted. 'General Dyer committed a most frightful error of judgement, involving fearful consequences. He made a terrible mistake, but his mistake was nothing like so terrible as would be the mistake of the British Government if for any reason whatsoever it hesitated to condemn the action which he took.'

Lord Sumner, a judge, could not agree: if an injustice had been done it should be righted. In a long and impassioned speech which met with a great deal of approval, he said, 'Are you prepared to lay down a rule that rebels are like dogs, to be allowed to have the first bite? If General Dyer had been tried — tried in any form that you like, such as enabled a man to have it called a trial — he would have been entitled to have a definite charge formulated against him in writing before the Inquiry began so far as it related to him; he would have been entitled to know what the charge was, he would have been entitled to know who was to be called against him; he would have been entitled to cross-examine those persons and to call witnesses to answer them; he would have been entitled to be represented; he would have been entitled to be present at every stage of the hearing, and he would have been entitled if he chose to offer himself as a witness, with the protection of advisers if he gave evidence, not in the capacity of a person charged, but in the capacity of a person who, as an Officer of the Government, was bound to give an account of his doings. He would have been entitled then to be warned that there were certain questions that he need not answer. . . . Of all these things he was — I will not say deprived, because I am not suggesting that there was any trickery here, but by the course of events . . . he was heard without any of these protections.'

Lord Curzon, a former Viceroy, said one of his main criticisms of Dyer was that he had changed his explanation for the 'Crawling Order'. In his statement to the Army Council he said it had been a misunderstanding. It was not intended as an insult or mark of racial inferiority but an Order that would have been well understood by Indians in relation to holy places. 'No one would be more astonished at this description of the attitude of natives of India than those persons themselves. To anyone who knows India and its religious practices, it was obvious that the explanation was an afterthought, if indeed it was not an absurdity. A native of India does not go on all fours to places of special sanctity.'

The argument that Dyer was entitled to take into consideration the effect his action would have in other parts of India was completely wrong. If that doctrine was applied in Ireland, Scotland or England, no government would last forty-eight hours. Curzon said he just did not accept that Dyer saved India.

The House finally divided and when the voting was announced Lord Finlay's motion had been carried by a majority of forty-three.

The Times thought that passions had overriden reason and the vote had gone against the weight of argument.

Although the vote in the Lords could not reverse the Government's decision, it was widely interpreted as a complete vindication of General Dyer. But, as many had predicted, it had an adverse effect on British-Indian relations and gave a new lease of life to the controversy which had shown signs of petering out.

'I realized then, more vividly than I had ever done before, how brutal and immoral imperialism was and how it had eaten into the souls of the British upper classes,' said Mr Nehru.

20. O'Dwyer Renews the Attack

*'I too have received the "praise" of Lord Chelms-
ford's Goverment. But that is no satisfaction to me,
so long as the officers who worked with me are the
victims of injustice.' — Sir Michael O'Dwyer.*

The vote in the Lords was accepted by a great many people as
the end of the affair; General Dyer had been exonerated by the
highest tribunal in the land. Dyer was grateful, as were many of
his loyal supporters. For Sir Michael O'Dwyer it was a clarion
call to further action.

The political unrest that arose in India following the vote
seemed to be conclusive proof that not only had Dyer been
right but so too had the officials and officers who had been
rebuked, and he immediately renewed his campaign to obtain
justice for them and himself. His persistence, however, had
unfortunate repercussions, for, under the relentless pressure,
Montagu was forced to look into their cases and discovered to
his anger that there had virtually been no punishments; those
people censured by the Hunter Committee had been treated
with remarkable leniency. When an irate Montagu took it up
with the Indian Government, Lord Chelmsford said that he
regretted the suggestion that the punishment was considered
inadequate but they had been guided by the Indemnity Bill. If
O'Dwyer had not interfered the leniency would have passed
unnoticed.

When O'Dwyer began bombarding the Secretary of State
with long letters of protest, Montagu had tried to be conciliatory and suggested that no useful purpose would be served
by becoming involved in a lengthy informal correspondence,
as he could not go against the express wishes of the Government. O'Dwyer arrogantly replied that his letters *were* formal
and he wanted justice for those who had served under him.

He had now reached the stage where megalomania and bitterness had clouded his vision. Not getting much change from Montagu, he decided on a direct approach to the Prime Minister, but he received the frosty reply that Lloyd George was in complete agreement with the Secretary of State. It rankled him so much that he called in person at No. 10 Downing Street only to be informed that the Prime Minister was too busy to see him; he was having a meeting with Michael Collins, one of the leaders of the United Ireland movement.

Beside himself with rage, O'Dwyer launched a splenetic campaign that went on and on for years. With the *Morning Post* available as a platform he had a ready-made audience. Other papers and periodicals asked him to contribute, and he was frequently the guest speaker at meetings. The subject seldom varied.

He painted a picture of an India gradually being denuded of officers and civil servants who were sickened by the Government's betrayal of loyal men who had been ruined for doing their duty.

Montagu tried desperately to get O'Dwyer to halt his campaign of vilification and repeatedly reminded him that, while a few officers had been censured, the majority had been praised. Sir Michael's persistence annoyed him on another ground: he ought to be grateful that his own reputation remained untarnished. It had only been on the insistence of the Government of India that he had escaped censure.

After a particularly scathing attack in the *Morning Post*, Montagu urged him in the interests of the Empire not to keep fanning the flames of controversy. Earlier the Duke of Connaught had gone to India for the innauguration of the new legislative council of Madras, Bombay and Bengal, and appealed: 'Do not peer into the troubled waters in the wake of your ship, lengthen the focus of your glasses and look ahead.' Montagu repeated the Duke's exhortation in his letter to O'Dwyer.

Sir Michael replied:

I would gladly follow the appeal in the closing words of your letter, not to peer into the wake of the ship, but to look boldly ahead, were it not that the course now being pursued fills me with alarm as to the future, and that facts like the

above do not indicate that a straight course is likely to be
steered. That feeling is not confined to me. Every Indian
mail brings me letters from tried servants of Government,
who are eager to leave the ship because they have not
confidence in the pilot, and from staunch and loyal Indians
who fear shipwreck unless the present course is altered.

Lloyd George was reluctantly drawn into the conflict and he
appealed to Sir Michael to stop agitating: Lord Chelmsford
had now been replaced by Lord Reading as Viceroy, in whose
hands the rights and prospects of all officers could be safely
left. But O'Dwyer had little time for Reading; one of the first
things he had done was to increase compensation for the
victims of the Jallianwala Bagh.

Lloyd George tried a more placatory approach. Mr P. H.
Kerr, writing on his behalf, said that the interests of India and
the Empire really would best be served by avoiding any future
public discussion. It merely provoked an intemperate reply
asking whether clemency was reserved solely for murderers
and rebels. And he appended a list of the officers, civil and
military whose careers had been ruined: Mr Justice Jones, Mr
Justice Broadway, Lieutenant-Colonel Irvine, T. P. Ellis,
J. P. Thompson, A. J. Kitchin, Miles Irving, Lieutenant-Colonel
O'Brien, S. W. Jacobs, Mr Marsden, Brigadier-General
Campbell, Lieutenant-Colonel MacRae, Major Doveton,
Lieutenant-Colonel Frank Johnson. The first five, he claimed
had been censured by implication and were suffering as a
result. The remainder had been publicly censured under the
orders of the Secretary of State. Kitchin had taken leave pending retirement and the others were contemplating retiring as
soon as possible.

The protest was a travesty of the truth.

Montagu asked for details, and was informed that the two
judges' prospects had not been affected, while Irvine was
eligible for promotion. None had been censured. Ellis was still
in the same job, Thompson was still Chief Secretary. Miles
Irving was still in the same job. Mr Kitchin was not affected.
Lieutenant-Colonel O'Brien had lost six months' seniority.
The same applied to Jacobs. Marsden's prospects had not
suffered. Brigadier-General Campbell had in fact been

demoted. MacRae had been censured. Major Doveton had been promoted.

Montagu was now convinced that the campaign was simply a cloak 'and part of the concerted action of the *Morning Post* party to continue the discussion of the Government treatment of events in the Punjab last year.'

He warned Lloyd George:

> He and his friends do not mean to let the matter drop. He will probably publish the whole correspondence, and I submit that the Prime Minister should not lend himself to the discussion. Sir Michael O'Dwyer seems to shut his eyes to the fact that whilst he is demanding a reversal of decisions come to about officers, Indians are equally ineffectively urging their further punishment.

Three years were to pass before the opportunity came to reopen the controversy. By then Montagu had resigned, hoist with his own petard. He fell a victim to his often repeated pleas to Chelmsford not to publish private correspondence; he published without the Cabinet's consent a telegram from the Government of India urging a more friendly policy towards Turkey. A terse letter from the Prime Minister informed him that they could not usefully co-operate in the same Cabinet. In the General Election that year when the Coalition Government fell, he lost his seat and went into the City and political exile.

21. Dyer Vindicated

*'I want to see that this man who is dying shall have a
fair hearing by a living jury.' — Mr Justice McCardie.*

In March, 1922, Sir Sankaran Nair published, in India, *Gandhi
and Anarchy* which criticized the Indian leader's advocacy of
non-co-operation on the grounds that it was a stumbling block
to political progress. It was an engineered denunciation. Much
of the material had been provided by the Government of India
and Provincial Governments with the intention that Nair
would take some of the steam out of the Mahatma's campaign.
Unaware of the danger, the author sent two courtesy copies to
the India Office, which in effect meant it had been published in
Britain.

Nair, a former judge of the Madras High Court, was the first
Indian to be appointed to the Viceroy's Executive Council, but
he had resigned over the administration of martial law in the
Punjab. He was later appointed to the Council of the Secretary
of State in London.

Ironically his desire to help the Government of India re-
bounded in a way he had never envisaged. A friend in India
informed O'Dwyer that the book was highly critical of him. It
was the moment O'Dwyer had been waiting for. Although the
book met with his general approval he consulted his friend and
solicitor Sir William Joynson-Hicks, and they decided it provided an ideal opportunity to clear Dyer's name.

Nair was asked to withdraw the book, make a public
apology and donate £1,000 to charities of O'Dwyer's choice.
He refused, and an action for libel was instituted.

Considerable pressure was brought to bear on O'Dwyer to
make him drop the action. Official and unofficial sources

advised him that he could not win, or if he did he would not get any money; furthermore, the evidence which Nair might produce would only assist the opponents of British rule. O'Dwyer insisted that his reputation and Dyer's overrode all other considerations.

On the morning of 30 April, Court Number Four in the King's Bench Division was crowded to overflowing. The front rows of the tiered, oak pews were filled with well-groomed barristers in black gowns and pearl-grey wigs. The tables were stacked high with documents tied with pink tape. The seats behind the barristers were crammed tight with members of the public whose social status was readily identifiable by their dress. The gallery above was also filled to capacity.

A few minutes before 10.30 a.m. the protagonists in what was to become an historic legal battle took their seats. O'Dwyer was represented by Mr Ernest Charles, K.C., and Sir Hugh Fraser. Nair was represented by Sir Walter Schwabe, K.C., Mr J. H. Wallington and Mr J. M. Parish. Mr Justice McCardie presided.

When the special jury of nine men and three women was sworn in, no one recognized the small, bespectacled man among them, so none of O'Dwyers's counsel challenged him. It was an expensive oversight. He was Harold Laski, a lecturer at the London School of Economics and Political Science who had worked with George Lansbury on the Labour newspaper *The Daily Herald*. One of the foremost Socialist thinkers in the country, he had met and admired Gandhi. He also had a passion for individual liberty.

When the preambles were over, Mr Charles rose to his feet, tugged at his gown and began outlining the substance of Sir Michael's case. Sir Sankaran Nair, commenting on Lloyd George's policy on the recruitment of Muhammadans, had written, 'The recruitment of non-Mohammadans also went up and both were due to the terrorism of Sir Michael O'Dwyer. Very useful in this instance.' He paused to let the gravity of the remark sink in before he continued.

Nair had then written about the Punjab disturbances:

No one feels more for the Punjab than I do. I doubt if anyone was in a position to know more than I was. Even now, with all the enquiries made by the Hunter Commission and the Congress Sub-Committee, many deplorable incidents as bad as any, worse perhaps than any reported, have not been disclosed. At this distance of time it is best that they should remain so. It is with full knowledge of the facts that I make the following remark.

Mr Charles again paused then read the alleged libel:

Before the Reforms it was in the power of the Lieutenant-Governor, a single individual, to commit the atrocities in the Punjab we know only too well.

That, he declared, was not the end of the libels. He quoted Nair again:

Above all, it will be remembered, it was necessary to pass an Act of Indemnity to save the delinquents from proceedings in Civil and Criminal Courts. Such an Act of Indemnity would scarcely be possible now.

The author had also scoffed at the praise heaped upon Sir Michael:

I realize that the eulogium passed by the English Cabinet on Lord Chelmsford and Sir Michael O'Dwyer was an outrage to public opinion.

Mr Charles looked towards the jury: the eulogy may have offended seditious blackguards but he would prove beyond all doubt that it met with the full approval of all decent people.

'Sir Sankaran, in his particulars of defence, alleged that, notwithstanding his knowledge of the oppressive methods used in recruiting, Sir Michael took no steps to show officials and others that he disapproved of them. The fact is that he disapproved and absolutely forbade the purchase of recruits.'

Mr Charles then referred to the action of Dyer in Amritsar. As he began to give a resumé of events he was halted by the Judge:

'Have we to decide whether General Dyer was right or wrong? If so I shall have to tell the jury that where the safety of the Indian Empire was in question and through that the safety of the British Empire, perhaps it might be necessary to do things which would not be justified in other circumstances.'

Sir Walter interposed:

'We say that what General Dyer did was an atrocity from any point of view of the Punjab then. And we say it was an atrocity which had the consent of Sir Michael O'Dwyer before it was committed, and his practical approval afterwards. One of the questions which will have to be considered is whether the condemnation of General Dyer was right or wrong. Many facts are available now which were not available before.'

Sir Walter had thrown down the gauntlet and chosen the Jallianwala Bagh as the battlefield. A macabre situation had arisen. Not only was the principal character absent but he was so ill that his doctors had deemed it unwise to even inform him of the action. The slightest strain could kill him.

An erie silence settled on the court when Mr Charles quietly announced that it would not be possible to call the General. 'He will not be long with us.'

McCardie: 'Is he ill?'

Mr Charles: 'Oh, very ill — hopelessly.'

The first witness to be called was Sir Michael O'Dwyer and the first day of his evidence was taken up with a long account of conditions in the Punjab. When the witness stated that one of the men who had been convicted and later amnestied was now a Minister of the Punjab, and two others who had been released were again in trouble the Judge said, 'Are they qualifying for ministerial posts?'

When the court rose the audience had heard very little to get excited about. Most of it dealt with the allegations of repressive measures to obtain recruits.

The next morning Sir Walter put to him several cases of alleged beatings to obtain recruits, and O'Dwyer replied that if they had happened it was without his knowledge. It was to be his staple answer to the charge of terrorism.

Sir Walter then read extracts from Dyer's evidence to the Hunter Committee. 'With your present knowledge do you approve of the action taken by General Dyer or not?'

Sir Michael: 'General Dyer's action as stated by him is, I think, indefensible. But I do not think that his explanation is correct. I would have disapproved of it if it had been reported to me in that form.'

'Have you ever said that before?'

'I have never been asked until now.'

'Do you say that firing without warning on a crowd of the

kind that was gathered at Amritsar was right?'

'Yes. Of eight persons who had previously addressed the crowd three were later convicted of murder.'

The Judge then interrupted and said he did not think that Dyer's case had ever been properly put before. He thought that he might be surrounded and cut off, his small force desroyed and the city left in the hands of the rebels. He had not only Amritsar to consider but the entire Punjab Province. When a man with a small force was confronted by twenty thousand men in a city where there had been numerable acts of violence and murders of the most appalling kind he could not be expected to sit back in an armchair and reflect on an infinite variety of circumstances. 'The man must make up his mind and if he thinks he is being surrounded act with iron severity. If we have to go into it I want to see that this man who is dying shall have a fair hearing by a living jury.'

The court then rose for the weekend.

✳   ✳   ✳

But the arguments continued behind the scenes. They centred around the evidence given in camera to the Hunter Committee which had never been disclosed to the public. O'Dwyer had always insisted that his evidence and that of Sir Umar Hayat Khan, Mr Thompson and General Sir Havelock Hudson, together with other unpublished documents, contained material that would totally exonerate him and General Dyer.

Before the court case he had been refused access to much of it on the grounds that it was prejudicial to the national interest. Only after a considerable amount of arguing had he been allowed to see a censored copy. To his astonishment he had noticed that Nair's Counsel had a copy in court which contained the *in camera* evidence. How, he wanted to know, had Nair got hold it. He saw it as part of Montagu's evil machinations and the determination of the India Office to prevent him succeeding in his action. The truth was simpler and less sinister.

When the time came to publish the entire evidence given to the Hunter Committee, the Government of India had suggested that only five volumes should be made available. Volumes VI and VII should be held back on political and military considerations. Montagu, in fact, had not seen any harm in making public most of the evidence, although he did have reservations about General Hudson's.

Chelmsford had also told the Secretary of State that it was important to take a firm stand over *in camera* evidence; it was private and privileged and publication would be a breach of confidence to those who had given it in the belief that it would not be revealed. Not only would it be prejudicial to the interests of the State but 'to some extent it would be dangerous to individuals'. 'The publication of a portion would only stimulate a demand for the publication of the remainder.'

Montagu had reluctantly acquiesced.

In fact, few people ever learned of the existence of Volume VII. Even MPs at the time of the debate believed there was only one volume missing*, VI, which contained the evidence of Thompson, O'Dwyer and Sir Umar Khan. Volume VII contained Hudson's evidence, and the Statements of the Governments of India and the Punjab. A limited number were printed for official use and they were listed as Strictly Secret. (Some of the evidence was in fact included in Volume III which dealt with Amritsar.) The missing volumes were deposited in the National Archives of India and the Public Record Office.

The missing volumes were a red herring. Even if they had not been published their contents had been read and studied by the Hunter Committee. Even so, their existence in court was enough to set the telegraph wires between London and India humming. Lord Olivier, the Secretary of State for India, asked the Viceroy for an explanation.

Lord Reading replied that *both* parties had been supplied with copies in which certain passages had been removed with indelible ink and then covered with white paper. Not that it mattered because it was learned that both parties already had unexpurgated copies. Sir Sankaran had subsequently been

---

*Arthur Swinson in *Six Minutes to Sunset* (1964) wrote of Volume VI: 'Some of this is said to have established Gandhi's implication in the uprising. Montagu, however, succeeded in concealing the existence of this volume well after the debate was over. In fact, few people knew of its existence until 1924, four years later. Even today it is extremely elusive, and this writer has failed completely to run a copy to earth, even with the assistance of the British Museum State Papers section, the Commonwealth Relations Office, and various special libraries. Some experts expressed the opinion that no copy still exists in England. Montagu may have been devious and misguided; but he was certainly thorough.'

asked to send his copy to be censored but he had not done so.
The Government felt he had been guilty of a breach of confidence in giving it to his Counsel.

It turned out to be a storm in a teacup for both sides claimed
that they contained evidence that supported their case.

✼   ✼   ✼

When O'Dwyer resumed his evidence, no mention was
made of the behind-the-scenes row. The questioning on
Dyer's action was resumed. Sir Michael stuck to his guns:
Dyer's action had been justified in the circumstances.

'The highest military authorities in India and at home approved of his action. It is not for me, standing here, to criticize
him.'

Sir Walter Schwabe: 'Has he not been condemned and
punished by the Commander-in-Chief in India and by the
Army Council at home?'

'He was criticized and deprived of his command — not on
merits, I think, but as a matter of political expediency.'

When Schwabe asked Sir Michael, 'Are you entitled to kill
one innocent person to save the life of another?' Mr Justice
McCardie interjected: 'The question should be, "Are you
entitled to kill a few hundred persons to prevent the murder or
death of half a million?"'

Sir Walter disagreed and McCardie retorted, 'If General
Dyer's force had been surrounded and destroyed no one with
the faintest imagination could doubt that Amritsar would have
been delivered over to anarchy. You seem to be ignoring all the
appalling consequences which might have followed if his force
had been destroyed.'

Sir Walter said he was not ignoring that at all, neither was he
challenging whether Dyer was right or not in firing at the time.
'My case is that he would have been right in firing if he had
given the crowd an opportunity of dispersing first.' Sir Walter
and Mr Justice McCardie were never to see eye to eye and their
antagonism mounted as the case continued.

Sir Walter turned again to Sir Michael and asked him if he
approved of firing on a crowd which contained a number of
innocent people in order to produce a moral and widespread
effect.

'If that were the case it was never suggested to me, and I would rather not give an opinion. I consider that General Dyer was responsible for maintaining law and order in his area. The crowd had gathered in defiance of his proclamation and he was entitled to fire.'

Sir Walter kept plugging away in an attempt to show that Dyer had shown a lack of humanity until the Judge again intervened, 'Can a man be said to be guilty of an atrocity who is acting with complete integrity?' and, 'Why should he be guilty of an atrocity if he does what he believes to be his duty?'

Sir Michael gave his own answer: 'If his judgement were so at fault that he killed thousands of people when the situation could have been saved by his killing scores or hundreds, I should be inclined to consider it an atrocity.' When the Judge pointed out that an error of judgement was vastly different to an atrocity, Sir Walter remarked that it was vital that what took place in Amritsar should not be misrepresented.

When the questioning turned to suppression of newspapers, Sir Michael became angry. He resented the implication that the official press communiqués had been deliberately misleading to give the impression that a warning *had* been given.

An open clash was inevitable when the judges suggested that some officers had been punished for reasons of political expediency. Sir Walter: 'I protest against your Lordship saying at this stage with regard to all these people who have been censured by the authorities that they may have been justified in doing what they did.'

On Wednesday, a tired Sir Michael stepped into the box for what was to prove his final day.

Mr Charles rose to re-examine. 'It is said that you had some peculiar power of prescience and knew what was going to happen?'

Sir Michael said that when trouble broke out he had sent Mr Kitchin as he was unable to leave his headquarters. He had no knowledge that Dyer was issuing a proclamation or that the crowd would defy it.

At this juncture the Judge felt compelled to remind the defence that if O'Dwyer was to be accused of atrocity it was necessary to establish that there had been one. Sir Walter reiterated that Dyer's act was just that, and it had been committed on O'Dwyer's general directions to Mr Kitchin.

From the witness box Sir Michael made the important observation that on 12 April he had spoken on the telephone to a representative of the Home Department of the Indian Government who had told him that if the troops were to fire they should make an example. He considered it so important he had jotted it down in his notebook. He did not, however, pass it on to Mr Kitchin.

O'Dwyer was then asked about the evidence he had given to the Hunter Committee.

McCardie: 'Had you any notice of statements adverse to your character before you gave evidence?'

'No.'

'If there were half a dozen allegations against a man, he went into the room without having notice of them?'

'Yes.'

Sir Walter objected: 'That is not so. I know something of the procedure of the Committee.'

McCardie: 'You repeat it so often, that one doubts it. The witness is giving evidence, not you.'

Sir Michael said he was treated as a criminal.

McCardie: 'Your view is that the Hunter Committee was not a judicial committee in the proper sense of that term?'

'It certainly was not, my Lord.'

His evidence, he added, had been taken down so inaccurately that he had spent a day and a half trying to correct it. That applied not only to him but to Dyer and others who were astonished to read what had been put into their mouths.

Sir Walter asked him to point out the passages to which he objected.

McCardie rebuked him: 'You are like the Hunter Committee. You have given him four minutes to look through eighty pages.'

When Sir Michael stepped down, he had given evidence for the best part of six days.

Lord Chelmsford, now First Lord of the Admiralty in Ramsay MacDonald's Labour Government, was called and said that during the recruiting campaign he had never heard Sir Sankaran complain about the methods adopted. When it came to recalling the events in Amritsar, he said that O'Dwyer had so many things to consider at the time that his failure to inform the Government that Amritsar had been handed over to the military was not considered important enough for a rebuke.

But on Sir Michael's responsibilities once martial law had been introduced he was less flexible: he was expected to work in close co-operation with the military. If any case had been brought to his notice that the military would not accept the advice of the Lieutenant-Governor he would have personally intervened.

Sir Walter: 'Did you hear of the telephone message which Sir Michael received from the Home Department that if troops had to fire they should make an example?'

'It is the first that I have heard of it.'

'Would you disapprove of such an order?'

'It has been disapproved of in the despatch by the Government of India on the Hunter Commission's Report.'

Chelmsford agreed that the administration of martial law had been marred by misuse of power, irregularities and injudicious and irresponsible acts and he had signed the Report by the Government of India which accepted that. He also agreed that it was a matter for regret that Satyapal and Kitchlew had not been tried by civil courts.

General Sir William Beynon, giving evidence, proved to be one of Dyer's most unswerving supporters. He had no hesitation in repeating that his action was justified and the more he thought about it the more convinced he was that Dyer had saved the Punjab. Which prompted Sir Walter to ask if he had ever said so before. 'Not in any official statement, because I have never been asked,' said Beynon.

As the Judge clearly agreed with him, Sir Walter dropped that line of inquiry and tried to establish that Dyer had been sent in as the 'iron man', because Major MacDonald had refused to open fire without warning on a funeral procession accompanying the bodies of those killed on 10 April. 'I am afraid I have no recollection of that.'

Had MacDonald managed to disperse it without firing? — again the witness could not remember. Sir Walter's attempt to reveal that the Major had been replaced because he was too lenient drew a blank. He could not agree with Hunter: 'In our opinion there was decided evidence of concerted movement against the Government of India.' He did not think a warning would have made any difference to the crowd; they were all aware of Dyer's proclamation. If they were not they should have been. And he recounted a meeting with Dyer at which he had told him his small force was in danger of being swamped.

'Can you conceive why he did not tell the Hunter Committee that?'

'Because it was not an inquiry from his point of view; it was an inquisition.'

Before Dyer had given evidence he had warned him to be careful in his statements, to tell the truth and not to start talking. 'I told him he was up against three of the cleverest Indian lawyers. He said, "I have no fear." When he came out I said to him, "Why did you say that you went down with the intention of firing?" He said, "I intended to fire if necessary." I said, "That is not the impression which you have given the Committee." '

Beynon added: 'I think General Dyer had been brooding over this matter. I think that he used to talk a lot and I am sorry to say that the evidence he gave is quite different from what he was thinking and doing at that time. You must judge Dyer not by what he said, but by what he did.' Sir Walter asked about Dyer's health and mental condition, but quickly dropped the subject. (Rupert Furneaux suggests that Dyer's action was the result of arteriosclerosis which caused sudden blackouts. He cited the case of *R.* v *Kemp* [1957] in which a man suffering from that disease killed his wife when blood flowed to his brain, became congested and rendered him temporarily unconcious. Mr Justice Devlin ruled that it came within the McNaghten Rules.

Mr Justice McCardie wanted to know whether Indians preferred whipping to imprisonment and the General's reply produced hoots of laughter. 'I believe they would prefer imprisonment, because they do not like physical pain, and the Indian gaols are so well conducted and luxurious that the difficulty is to keep persons out of them.'

As his evidence came towards its end, the Judge asked him why Dyer had been punished by the Army Council. 'I believe it was purely political. I see no other reason.'

He was followed into the witness box by Colonel Johnson (retired), one of the officers criticized by the Committee, who explained: 'I had two objectives in my administration of the law. My first and primary object was to maintain British rule at all costs, even if the streets of Lahore ran red with blood. But my second was, please God, to effect my purpose without shedding one drop of blood.' This he had done.

A whole string of witnesses followed each other into the box to refute suggestions of 'Press Gang' methods of recruitment and to praise Sir Michael's administration. They were familiar names to those who had read the Hunter Report or followed the history of the disturbances.

On 21 May Sir Walter Schwabe opened the case for the defence. Rather surprisingly he began with a bitter attack on the Hunter Committee, but his line of assault was different. The Report, he said, had cast most of the blame on the soldiers and whitewashed the civilians. Even so Sir Michael had not come out of it particularly well. Yet he was coming before the court because a book had been published in India which criticized him. Now he was presenting himself as the saviour of the British Empire. His case was an entirely distorted and exaggerated view of what had occurred in the Punjab.

In April 1919, he said, the policy in India was one of gradual advancement towards self-government. One of the chief opponents of that policy was O'Dwyer, and anyone who was the least like a politician was seized and thrown into prison.

Recruitment in the Punjab was nothing short of terrorism of the worst kind and evidence of the outrages had been supplied by hundreds of people. Sir Michael claimed that he did not know what was going on but he could not escape his responsibilities by claiming he was ignorant of events his subordinates were well aware of.

The jury would also have to decide whether martial law had been necessary and whether it was continued too long. Nair took the view that the Government of India had not been given the true facts when they were asked to authorize it.

Sir Michael's attitude was, 'We will teach these people not to resist the Government. We will spread terror among them. If necessary we will drench the place with blood. We are going to crush all signs of rebellion. We are going to induce proper respect for the British flag and the British Raj.'

When other countries had adopted that policy it had been branded as terrorism for it was not the policy by which Great Britain had won and held her great Empire. That was why Dyer's conduct had met with universal condemnation by the Government. Therefore, Sir Sankaran was entitled to criticize

Dyer's action not only because of what he had done but because of his explanation to the Hunter Committee. The defence's case was that his action was contrary to all the principles on which the military should act when called to assist the civil authority and could properly be called an atrocity. Sir Michael had approved and could not hide behind the skirt of the soldier.

Evidence taken on Commission in India from scores of people was then read out. There were stories of beatings and torture and other repressive measures. Much of it was obtained from people who had assisted the Congress Sub-Committee Inquiry.

There was an almost audible sigh of relief from the jurors when Sir Sankaran Nair was finally called. He explained that whilst he had no personal animosity towards Sir Michael no two people could differ more on the steps that should be taken to give effect to the political aspirations of his countrymen.

One of his tasks had been to assist in the review of decisions made by the Martial Law Tribunals and submit his opinions to the Viceroy. He had found them very unsatisfactory; from the outset they had assumed the existence of a rebellion and he could not agree with their interpretation of sedition. Too much reliance had been placed on the uncorroborated evidence of approvers. In his opinion Sir Michael was largely responsible and he felt it was his duty to say so.

When Mr Justice McCardie began his summing up the case had entered its twenty-fifth day. He soon made it clear to the jury that he preferred the evidence of the Europeans. He singled out Beynon and Johnson: 'When one hears evidence of this kind, one asks oneself this question: are they tried men or not? . . . I do not know what your view is, but I should say that General Beynon was made of steel. . . And no one, I think, could charge Colonel Johnson with being a sentimental man. . . he is apparently a man of iron.' Both said the Punjab was on the brink of a rebellion.

The question of recruitment was swiftly dispensed with. 'In my view the defendant has failed to prove that the plaintiff ever instigated or authorised a single act of terrorism.'

He then dealt with Dyer. 'One cannot help feeling that the time and the method of General Dyer's punishment, if he were wrong, were most unfortunate. It may be said that the full facts were not known to the authorities at home; but after the episode of 13 April it comes out, again and again, from the evidence, that General Dyer was approved by his superior officers; he was given commands; he conducted operations with distinction and ability; he gained the approbation of all; it was a year and three months after Amritsar that he was told that his services would no longer be wanted for the army. He has, one may feel, been punished with a severity that can only be realized by those who are cognisant of the high pride in their service felt by military officers of the Crown.'

It was, however, a matter for the jury to decide. Nevertheless, he felt compelled to give them some very clear guidance.

'Subject to your judgement, speaking with full deliberation and knowing the whole of the evidence given in this case, I express my view that General Dyer, in the grave and exceptional circumstances, acted rightly, and in my opinion upon the evidence, he was wrongly punished by the Secretary of State for India. . .'

There was a subdued ripple of applause which momentarily halted the Judge. But he was still far from finished; there remained the question of Sir Michael's role.

If the jury took the view that Dyer *had* committed an atrocity they still had to decide whether O'Dwyer was also guilty. Before he could be found guilty it had to be remembered that he was not even in Amritsar at the time. Not only did he not authorize the action, he did not know about it until afterwards.

Mr Justice McCardie finished after speaking for seven hours, and at 3.05 p.m. he asked the jury to retire and consider the libels one by one.

Two and three-quarter hours later the jury returned and the foreman announced that they could not agree, and he did not think they ever would.

Mr Justice McCardie then turned to Mr Ernest Charles and Sir Walter Schwabe and asked them if they were prepared to accept a majority verdict. The two lawyers conferred and said they would. Sir Walter said that he and Mr Charles had decided that in the event of that happening they had agreed to the amount of damages.

The foreman then announced that there was a majority of eleven for Sir Michael on all points. (The dissenting voice was

Laski's.)

The agreed damages were £500 but the costs which Sir Sankaran Nair had to pay were estimated at £20,000.

In the corridor outside the court Sir Michael said, 'I am particularly glad for the sake of General Dyer. It was largely to vindicate him that I took the matter up. The case has vindicated not only myself and General Dyer but also British rule in India.'

Later that evening Sir Michael sat down and wrote a long letter to Mrs Dyer informing her of the verdict. Dyer was so ill that all details of the case had been kept from him as any excitement might have a fatal effect. But his doctor had decided he could be told his name had been cleared.

*   *   *

Reaction in India to Mr Justice McCardie's remarks was swift and predictable. The majority of whites welcomed the vindication of General Dyer, the majority of Indians deplored it. But the greatest concern among Indians was that the Judge's comments on martial law suggested that the Labour Government held different views to their predecessor as to how future disturbances were to be dealt with. Condemnation in the Indian press was almost unanimous and was summed up in the reactions of the *Tribune*, Lahore, which said the Judge had been guilty of 'a wanton misuse of judicial authority', and that he had done a great disservice to India and the Empire.

In the Legislative Assembly in Delhi, the Home Rule Leader, Mr C. R. Das, tried to introduce a motion criticizing the summing-up and asking for the costs and damages incurred by Sir Sankaran Nair to be paid from the Indian Exchequer. He was ruled out of order.

On 18 June the Cabinet met to discuss the political row that was brewing as a result of the Judge's observations. Lord Olivier, the Secretary of State for India, said it was essential in the public interest to correct them, especially as George Lansbury intended raising the matter in the Commons and asking the King to remove McCardie from the Bench as he was unfit to carry out judicial duties attaching to his high office.

The Cabinet was told that the Lords would certainly not accept an Address to that effect, and a judge could only be removed by a decision of both Houses. The secretary noted, 'The Cabinet were also reminded that the utmost caution was necessary in criticizing the action of a member of the Judiciary in the exercise of his office.'

Olivier submitted a memorandum in which he stressed that he was not criticizing McCardie for his conduct of the case, or his directions to the jury on matters of law or the evidence submitted. 'What I have to comment on are pronouncements on matters which were not issues in the case, and on which neither judgement nor evidence had been tendered by counsel.'

While the Judge was entitled to express an opinion as to what constituted an atrocity, he was not allowed to make inaccurate statements and assert as sound a principle of civil administration which had been consistently repudiated in this country, the Colonies and India, as to the conditions under which a mob could be fired on or bombed from the air.

Olivier elaborated on two untrue statements:

— Dyer's action received the approval of the military authorities.

— He was wrongly punished by the Secretary of State.

The facts were: After reading the Hunter Report the Viceroy in Council had decided that Dyer had acted beyond the necessities of the case and with a lack of humanity. The Commander-in-Chief had been informed and Dyer was asked to resign before Montagu had received any expression of opinion from India. Dyer's action had *not* been approved by the military authorities.

Oliver suggested that it should be arranged for questions to be asked in either House so that he or the Prime Minister could correct McCardie. After considerable discussion it was agreed that the Prime Minister should deal with it personally.

When Ramsay MacDonald rose in the Commons, he turned to Lansbury and said a discussion about the fitness of the Judge would only add to the harm already done in India. Unfortunate as his words were, they did not amount to a moral delinquency which justified an Address calling for his removal. 'It ought in fairness to be borne in mind that the objectionable passage occurred not in a considered written judgement, but in an oral charge to a jury delivered at the conclusion of a lengthened and somewhat heated trial, and the very form in which it was couched showed that the learned Judge was not informed as to what took place.'

MacDonald was determined that it would not develop into a full-scale debate, so he confined himself to saying that his administration endorsed the policy of the previous Government and the former Secretary of State. Whilst he would always uphold the right of the Judiciary to pass judgement, even on the Executive if it thought fit, it should avoid making pronouncements upon issues which had far-reaching political consequences and which were not being tried.

Lansbury indicated that the answer met his needs and he would not press the matter.

It was left to Lord Olivier to inform the Viceroy that the Government adhered to the principle of minimum force when the army was called in to aid the civil authorities. They did not accept the view that an officer in dispersing an unlawful assembly was entitled to consider the moral effect his action might have elsewhere.

The Government of India published a despatch saying they held the same views.

Unfortunately, Sir Michael O'Dwyer, having accomplished all he had set out to do, would not let the case of General Dyer rest. Three years after the action, which most people accepted as a vindication of Dyer's honour, he was still demanding justice for a dying man and prophesying calamity if Britain continued to rule India with kid gloves.

22. Death of a Hero

'*His death recalls one of the greatest controversies
that ever followed the action of a British officer.*' —
The Daily Telegraph.

The village of Long Ashton on the outskirts of Bristol re-
sembles an exclusive suburban Simla, many of the large houses
and bungalows being perched in tiers on the steep slope that
rises above the road running through it. The windows over-
look gentle, rolling countryside and fertile farmland — an ideal
place for the retirement of the well-to-do. Among its more
elderly inhabitants are some who served in India before
Independence.

It was to Long Ashton that Dyer went shortly before the
libel action to live out his numbered days. Four years earlier he
had been struck down by a stroke while staying on his son's
farm in Cirencester. When he returned to Long Ashton he
lived the life of a semi-recluse, although his frail, stooped
figure, a shadow of the muscular frame that had once supported the full weight of a fallen horse, was occasionally seen
when he ventured out to take a short stroll. The villagers, in
deference to his feelings, passed the time of day but seldom
mentioned Amritsar, but those who did always received the
same reply: he would do exactly the same again.

On the night of 10 July 1927, a violent storm broke out and
Mrs Dyer went to her husband's bedroom to see if he needed
anything. The General was restless, nervous and upset, and she
sat with him until he dozed off. The next morning his
daughter-in-law, Phyllis, kept a vigil by his bedside and some
time during the day he suffered another severe stroke that
partially paralysed him. Phyllis tried to comfort him and assure
him that he would soon be well again.

'Thank you,' he murmured, 'but I don't want to get better. So many people who knew the conditions in Amritsar say I did right. . .but so many others say I did wrong. I only want to die and know from my Maker whether I did right or wrong.' He had a further stroke the next day and lost the power of speech. He died during the evening of Saturday, 23 July, aged sixty-three. His wife and younger son were at his side. His other son was serving with his regiment in Mesopotamia.

In the main the obituaries were gentle and in accordance with the British tradition that if a man did have any faults they should be buried with him. *The Times* retold the whole controversy and reiterated the allegation that the Government of India had first shielded him and then punished him when the full details were revealed. 'The information given under the censorship at the time was so meagre that it attracted little attention in England.' *The Times*, which had never been his greatest champion, had accepted the line that he was unjustly punished.

The *Morning Post* devoted as much space to Dyer as it would have done to the death of a major statesman. In an eloquent and moving tribute the newspaper mourned the passing of a martyr whose name would for ever be linked with Clive and Nicholson. But for his action the Punjab would have run red with blood. He had died a victim of political expediency.

The newspaper recalled the Fund raised in his defence, the unswerving support and loyalty that Sir Michael O'Dwyer had always given, and the libel action that had vindicated him.

Under a large banner headline, 'The Man Who Saved India', Sir Michael contributed a fulsome tribute. 'I had hoped,' he concluded, 'he would be reinstated before his death. Now it is too late.'

The *Daily Telegraph* said that his death had revived one of the greatest controversies that had ever surrounded the action of a British officer. A life-long friend who preferred to remain anonymous wrote:

> He always told me that if he were to re-act the Amritsar case a million times he would always give the same order to fire.

Dyer's body, in a coffin draped with the Union Jack which had flown from his headquarters, was carried from the house and placed on a gun carriage and drawn down the hill through the main street to the 14th-century village church of All Saints, where a short family service was conducted by the vicar, the Rev John Varley. Flowers from Dyer's own garden were laid on and around the coffin and a bugler sounded the Last Post and Reveille.

His body remained in the church throughout the night and next morning it was transported by road to the Guards Chapel in Wellington Barracks. There a large crowd gathered to pay homage. Two women wearing black carried a wreath bearing the words, 'An Englishwoman's gratitude'.

In the afternoon the coffin was carried out of the chapel by a bearer party of eight non-commissioned officers from the Irish Guards, wearing scarlet tunics and black bearskins. It was placed on a gun carriage drawn by three pairs of horses from 'M' Battery, Royal Horse Artillery. Immediately behind the coffin on which rested Dyer's helmet was a detachment of fifty men from the 25th Battalion, London Regiment, who had served with him throughout the disturbances. Two carried a large wreath, 'Deepest respect and admiration'.

A long cortège of cars containing members of the family and many distinguished soldiers followed.

The long procession wound down The Mall where large crowds had gathered to pay their last respects. Men bared their heads as the gun carriage passed. Similar crowds had assembled in Trafalgar Square to witness the arrival at St Martin-in-the-Fields.

Inside the crowded church the service was conducted by the Right Reverend L. H. Gwynne, Bishop of Egypt and Sudan, who was assisted by the Vicar, William McCormick. The wreaths and floral tributes were then laid at the base of the Cenotaph in Whitehall. Among them was one from Rudyard Kipling: 'He did his duty as he saw it'.

After the service the coffin was taken to Golders Green for private cremation.

That day devastating floods swept through a large area of India, threatening hundreds of thousands of lives. There were urgent appeals for relief aid and the response was immediate. At the same time, Norman Bennet, who had served in India as a Garrison Chaplain, wrote to a newspaper proposing that a memorial should be erected in Dyer's honour. The suggestion was taken up by Sir Michael O'Dwyer with the full approval of

Mrs Dyer. By November plans had been drawn up for the endowment of beds or a ward at the Walker Hospital in Simla, which for the first time was now admitting Indian patients.

But even in death Dyer was not allowed to escape controversy. The Viceroy, Lord Irwin, was extremely apprehensive about the scheme: what did it entail and who were the organizers?

He wrote to the India Office:

> If, for instance, it turns out that money was subscribed in effect, as a vindication of action by Dyer which was officially condemned by the Government of India and His Majesty's Government, there would seem to be very strong objections to an institution so largely dependent on Government support and so largely administered by Government officials accepting such money.

Sir Michael O'Dwyer explained that the idea had originated from friends and sympathizers who had suggested to the General's widow that his memory should be perpetuated in some practical form. It would provide beds for wives and families of officers holding the King's Commission.

But the plan was doomed to failure. Mrs Dyer, desperately anxious not to reopen the controversy that had blackened and blighted their lives for such a long time, graciously agreed not to go ahead with the scheme when she was informed that opinion in India and London was that it was too controversial. In any case the Secretary of State for India advised the hospital to decline the offer.

Nothing, however, could deter Sir Michael from continuing to speak about the perils confronting India, or, wherever the opportunity arose, of Dyer and the disturbances in the Punjab. Unfortunately it meant that memories of his own period as Lieutenant-Governor of the Punjab were constantly rekindled. His loyalty and devotion to the soldier were to have tragic and disastrous consequences.

23. A Vow of Revenge

'One day all of you will be astonished to hear this vision of mine turned into a reality of stark truthfulness.' — Udham Singh.

The village of Sunam in the Punjab in the year 1899 was indistinguishable from the many others that dotted the flat, monotonous landscape. It was little more than a collection of ramshackle flat-roofed mud huts and squalid little dwellings. The floors were of mud and there was little furniture apart from the rope-strung charpoys; more often than not the occupants slept on the floor or roof. Round the village peasants tilled the over-worked soil with primitive tools that had not changed for hundreds of years.

Sardar Tehl Singh was just one of many who scraped an existence from a small patch of land. He was married with one son, Sadu Singh, aged two. The year before the turn of the century his wife bore him a second son who was named Udham. Like so many children in a land where life was cheap he was never certain of his exact day of birth.

Unable to exist on what he raised from his patch of land, Tehl Singh took a part-time job as a railway-crossing keeper at Uppali. Then his wife died when their youngest child was three years old. Her widower did not outlive her for long; he died in abject poverty when his sons were aged seven and five. But the orphaned boys fared much better than many of their friends who suffered a similar fate; a band of vagrant gypsies took them under their wing and later a wandering minstrel and preacher, Chandra Singh, came across them and decided they deserved something better than a life of aimless drifting. He took them to the Khalsa Orphanage in Amritsar where they were baptized in the Golden Temple and brought up to be good Sikhs.

Soon afterwards Sadu Singh died and Udham was alone. He was a bright, intelligent boy, anxious to please and quick to learn. He studied carpentry and was taught the rudiments of smithing; ample qualifications to guarantee survival in a city where both trades were much in demand.

It was one of those unpredictable quirks of fate that put him on the path to martyrdom. He heard that a great meeting was to be held in the Jallianwala Bagh on 13 April, 1919, and he offered to act as a water carrier. The slaughter made an indelible impression on his mind and he swore a vow of revenge. By the time he left the orphanage after matriculating he was well on the way to being a dedicated revolutionary. He became a familiar figure in the Hall Bazaar area where he browsed through the bookstalls for any nationalist literature and it did not take long for the hard-line extremists to spot his potential and enrol him in the cause. Within a short time he had worked his passage to America where he immediately became involved with the Ghadrites on the Pacific Coast who used him to pick up immigrants and take them to secret destinations.

While in America he received an urgent message from his hero Bhagat Singh to return to Amritsar with some arms. He would be told why on arrival. Bhagat Singh was one of the leaders of the Hindustan Socialist Republican Association, a revolutionary body aimed at the violent overthrow of the British Raj.

Udham Singh reappeared in Amritsar as suddenly as he had departed, accompanied by a German woman who had helped him smuggle in a supply of guns and ammunition. But at 7 p.m. on 30 August, 1927, a police informant called at the Kotwali with a 'tip off' that a mysterious alien had arrived in the city and was staying in the red light district. The police made a surprise swoop on the home of a prostitute named Nur Jehan who told them the man had just left; she warned them that he carried a pistol. He was quickly picked up by a police patrol but he offered no resistance. In his pocket was a pistol with five bullets in the chamber. Udham Singh made no attempt to conceal his identity and the police report said, 'He has come from America to Amritsar to have the country vacated forthwith from the Englishman.'

After interrogation, he took the the police to a factory where he pointed out a suitcase and handed over the key. Inside was another loaded pistol, an empty Colt and 139 rounds of ammunition.

He was tried before the local magistrate for the illegal possession of firearms and sentenced to five years' rigorous imprisonment. On his release he quickly resumed his political activities.

Bhagat Singh was arrested for a bomb outrage and shooting a European official, and was hanged on 23 March, 1930. He went to the gallows happily prepared to fulfil his wish 'to be married to death'. The composed manner in which he had gone to his death made a lasting impression on Udham Singh; it was an example to all those who were prepared to die for their country. Soon afterwards Udham Singh was seen dancing ecstatically with the miniature portrait of Bhagat Singh clutched to his breast. He repeatedly spoke of the Jallianwala Bagh and when he did he lost his temper and his eyes became red with rage. He talked vaguely of the day of revenge.

His thoughts had now returned to the vow he had taken and the tryst with destiny which had been delayed by his imprisonment and more immediate political involvements at home. He began describing himself as a *desh-bhagat* (Disciple of Bhagat) who had to go to England for a special purpose from which he would not return.

Somehow or other he managed to shake off the police, who were always trying to trace his movements, and slip out of India. His travels took him to Egypt, Russia, France, Ethiopia and Germany, where he established contact with Indian extremists.

Some time in 1933 — the precise date is unknown — he entered Britain on a false passport bearing the name Ram Mohamed Singh Azad. He had obviously been well-briefed, for soon after stepping ashore he was in touch with an I.R.A. cell smuggling guns into the country, and he stayed as a guest of one of their leaders in the Isle of Wight.

After that he adopted an almost nomadic existence, moving through the industrial area of the Midlands under a variety of aliases and gaining the reputation among Indian immigrants as a fiery speaker and a bit of a fanatic.

In 1937 he turned up in London and soon became a familiar figure at the Gurdwara (Sikh Temple) in Sinclair Road,

Shepherd's Bush, a popular meeting place for Indians. But he seemed oddly out of place. He wore smart European suits, was clean-shaven, and spoke, at least to them, extremely good English. Furthermore, his passion for revolutionary songs did not particularly endear him to his countrymen who had left their homeland to start a new life. They were all ambitious, hard-working men and if they had any thoughts about the British Raj they kept them to themselves; they had no wish to be branded as trouble-makers.

One person who was impressed with him was Shiv Singh Johal, an official at the Temple, and to him Udham Singh confided that he was in the country to fulfil a special mission. But he did not elaborate.

Soon afterwards he ceased going to the Temple, and by the beginning of 1940 he had severed all contact with Shiv Singh Johal.

One of his favourite haunts was the Punjab Restaurant owned by Gurbachan Singh in Neal Street, near Covent Garden. Curry houses were a rarity in those days and Indians used to meet there to eat traditional food and talk about old times. They learned little about Udham Singh except that he rode a motor cycle rather recklessly and was not deterred from driving it even after a bad crash. He was also a bit of a womanizer who liked to brag about his escapades. Occasionally he mentioned a place called Thurlestone in Devon where he had worked as a driver-cum-handyman and got to know Sir Michael O'Dwyer. He confided to Gurbachan Singh that they were like father and son. But the name did not seem to strike a familiar chord with anyone.

In the main he bored them and worried them with his incessant talk about the great deed that he planned very shortly. No one paid particular attention to his boastings; he was dismissed as a 'paper tiger'.

'One day,' he stormed, 'you will be astonished to hear this vision of mine turned into a reality of stark truthfulness.' Occasionally he talked about Bhagat Singh and forecast that he too would end up on the gallows.

On Tuesday 12 March, 1940, he surprisingly invited his friends to join him for a traditional Punjabi meal. He seemed high-spirited and happy, almost jubilant, and towards the end he ordered *luddoos*, a sweet made of gram flour, butter and sugar candy which in the Punjab is regarded as a happy augury of success for a proposed venture. Udham Singh said he wanted to fill himself up with them. When the time came for him to leave he turned to his friends and announced that the next day London would witness a marvel: 'The British Empire will be shaken to its foundations.' To Gurbachan Singh he said enigmatically, 'Do not know me.' None of them ever saw him again.

Just before the unexpected farewell party he had been to the India Office where he had seen a poster advertising a joint meeting of the East India Association and the Royal Central Asian Society at Caxton Hall. Listed among the speakers were Sir Michael O'Dwyer, Lord Zetland, Secretary of State for India, Sir Louis Dane, former Under-Secretary to the Governor of the Punjab, and Lord Lamington, former Governor of Bombay.

Revenge on a scale never envisaged in his wildest dreams was within his grasp.

24.   Six Shots

'It was my duty.'— Udham Singh.

The meeting had been a marked success. The 180 people who had packed into the oak-panelled Tudor Room had thoroughly enjoyed a lecture on Afghanistan given by Brigadier-General Sir Percy Sykes. No one had paid any attention to the well-dressed Indian in a blue pin-stripe suit, red tie and rakish trilby who had pushed his way to the front at the start of the meeting and leaned nonchalantly against the wall near the first row of seats.

Seated alongside each other were Sir Michael O'Dwer (75) who had made a rather witty introductory speech, Sir Louis Dane (84) and Lord Lamington (79). Sir Percy was still on the platform with Lord Zetland (63). It was 4.30 in the afternoon.

The audience had risen and were pushing their seats back. Sir Michael was standing shaking hands with the distinguished guests when the Indian moved away from the wall and walked slowly towards the press table at the foot of the platform. Suddenly he drew a pistol from his jacket pocket and fired six shots in rapid succession. The first two, fired from a distance of nine inches, hit Sir Michael in the back and he dropped to the floor. The Marquis of Zetland toppled from his chair, wounded in the ribs. Another bullet shattered the right hand of Lord Lamington; Sir Louis Dane was hit in the arm. Bullets narrowly missed Sir Percy Sykes and Sir Frank Brown, Secretary of the East India Association. Sir Percy, who thought it was a bomb outrage, dropped from the platform and lay on the floor.

There was a stunned silence in the hall which was broken by

a sudden shout of 'Make way', and the man who had fired the shots was seen to be trying to force his way towards the exit. Instantly the audience were galvanized into action. Miss Bertha Herring, a volunteer wartime ambulance driver, called out, 'Get hold of him. Don't let him get away.' As the man tried to thrust his way past she hurled herself at him causing him to stumble. He flung her aside but she managed to grab hold of his lapel and they fell onto some seats. Claude Riches took a flying leap onto the Indian's back and struck down hard on his right wrist forcing him to drop the revolver. Captain Banstead of the Indian Civil Service, an R.A.F. man and several others joined the mêlée and pinned him to the floor. A quick search revealed seventeen rounds of ammunition in a box in his jacket pocket, a razor-sharp linoleum knife, and eight rounds of loose ammunition in his trouser pocket.

Surprisingly there was no panic in the room. Someone shouted, 'Bring doctors and call the police.' Fortunately there was no need to summon the former as there were several doctors in the audience. Doctor Grace Mackinnon, a retired missionary who had spent many years in India, knelt beside Sir Michael and realized he had died immediately. A Muslim friend crouched over the body and whispered a prayer. Colonel D. H. Reinhold, who had retired from the Indian Medical Service, applied a tourniquet to Lord Lamington's injured wrist. Doctor M. R. Lawrence, brother of 'Lawrence of Arabia', also helped with the wounded.

Several people rushed to the public telephones to call the police and ambulances. The reporters who had grudgingly attended the meeting, firmly believing it would make no more than a couple of paragraphs, suddenly found themselves tackling the biggest story since the declaration of war.

Within minutes a large force of policemen arrived and cordoned the building. Close behind was a team of Murder Squad detectives. The Tudor Room was sealed off, all exits locked and no one was allowed to leave or use the telephone. Even office staff and people employed in the kitchen and catering departments were ordered to remain behind.

The murderer meanwhile was sitting quietly in a seat a few feet away from the corpse of Sir Michael O'Dwyer. Next to him sat Inspector William Steven, a Special Constable, who was duty officer for the day.

As order was restored, the 180 members of the audience were taken to various rooms where teams of plain clothes officers took down their statements, a task that took more than three hours. While they were writing, members of the Chase Bank Club arrived in dinner jackets and long dresses for a dance. Incongruously, they began dancing while the murder investigation was still in progress.

A friend of Sir Michael's telephoned his flat in Prince of Wales Terrace, Kensington, but his wife was out and the news was relayed to the maid. In the nine-roomed flat decorated with Indian weapons and mementoes the table was laid for tea. Sir Michael's last words to his wife were, 'I'll be back for tea at five o'clock'.

When Lady O'Dwyer returned home the maid burst into tears and said there had been a bad accident. Lady O'Dwyer telephoned her daughter and then called for a taxi and drove straight to Caxton Hall.

When Detective-Inspector Richard Deighton arrived he immediately took charge of the investigation. He walked over to the Indian sitting a few feet away from the dead Sir Michael and formally cautioned him: 'You will be detained pending further enquiries.' The gunman nodded towards the corpse and said, 'It is no use, it is all over. It is there.'

The Indian, who gave his name as Mahomed Singh Azad, was then taken into a small room adjoining the hall where Deighton placed six cartridge cases on the table. The arrested man said, 'No, no all the lot — six,' and he held up two hands with six fingers extended. Detective-Sergeant Sidney Jones was sitting at the table with a notebook in front of him when the man started making a series of disjointed statements. Then he paused and said quite slowly, 'I did it because I had a grudge against him. He deserved it. I don't belong to any society or anything. Is Zetland dead? He ought to be. I put two into him, right there,' and he held his hand against the left side of his stomach. The sergeant waited, his pencil poised. 'I bought the revolver from a man in a public house in Bournemouth. Only one dead? I thought I could get more. I must have been too slow.'

Sergeant Jones had difficulty getting down the spate of

words that poured out. The man spoke of his early life in India and how he was orphaned when he was four or five. He referred to a property he had sold for £200 in order to get to England and that he had married a young woman who had died.

Then he suddenly added, 'I don't care. I don't mind dying. What's the use of waiting until you get old? That is not good. You want to die when you are young. That is good. That is what I am doing. I am dying for my country.'

The man who was still only known as Mahomed Singh Azad was handcuffed and taken out through a side door where he turned and smiled at the waiting photographers. He was quickly bundled into a Black Maria and driven to Cannon Row Police Station. There he was formally charged and cautioned. In the interview room at Cannon Row he decided to make another statement which was significantly different from what he had already said:

> I took my revolver with me to protest. I did not take it to kill. When the meeting finished I shot like, I think, at the wall. I have seen people starving in India under British Imperialism. I am not sorry for protesting. It was my duty to do so, just for the sake of my country. I don't mind what sentence — 10, 20 or 50 years, or to be hanged. I did not intend to take a person's life; just to protest you know.

In his diary the detectives found an entry: Sir Michael O'Dwyer, Sunnybank, Thurlestone, South Devon.

Lord Zetland had been hit from a distance of six feet and the bullet had scorched his jacket, shirt and vest, but it was found intact in his clothing. Although his ribs were badly bruised it had not penetrated his body. He immediately ordered a telegram be sent to the Viceroy giving brief details of the incident and requesting that nothing should be published until the press reports arrived from England as 'censorship may be operating'. The arrested man Singh Azad, he added, appeared to be a Sikh.

✻   ✻   ✻

The following morning the story of the assassination pushed the war off the front pages of the newspapers. The gunman's name was still given as Mahomed Singh Azad.

The story of the Jallianwala Bagh was recalled but most papers seemed to see a more direct connection between Sir Michael's murder and that of Sir William Curzon Wyllie, political A.D.C. to the Secretary of State for India, who was shot dead in July, 1909, at a reception in the Imperial Institute.

Everyone was united, however, on the apparent senselessness of the crime. The *Daily Mail* said:

> Yesterday's outrage seems to have no connection with present-day politics in India. The situation there is calm, unmarred by violence or terrorism. The differences which exist are being ventilated by peaceful political methods.

Flags flew at half-mast in London and in Lahore. In the House of Commons the Prime Minister extended the sympathy of the nation to the relatives of the dead man. Earl Stanhope made a similar statement in the Lords. Throughout the day and evening hundreds of telegrams, cables and letters were delivered to the home of Lady O'Dwyer, many of them from India. From India, Gandhi condemned the killing unreservedly and said it must have been done in a fit of insanity. In London two hundred leaders of the Indian community gathered at India House to condemn the shooting. The High Commissioner, Sir Firozkhan Noon, announced, 'When one person does a bad thing like that the country he belongs to cannot escape the disgrace brought to its name by one of its misguided children. It is an act of which we Indians feel ashamed.'

Only Germany welcomed the shooting. There the killer was hailed as a 'fighter for freedom', and his act described as 'an expression of the pent-up fury of the downtrodden Indian people'.

That morning Mahomed Singh Azad, described as a 37-year-old engineer of Mornington Terrace, North London, appeared at Bow Street magistrate's court charged with murder. The accused was only in the dock for three minutes before he was formally remanded in custody for a week.

By the time he made his next appearance his true identity was known. The Secretary of State informed the Viceroy on 15 March that he had been in England since 1933 and had been seen in the Southampton area in 1939 after which he kept cropping up in various places including the East End of

London. He continually changed his address and was known to indulge in revolutionary statements.

> The few Indians he met formed the impression that he was not quite normal. Present information seems to suggest isolated crime by mental person. There is no evidence as yet of any general conspiracy.

The picture soon altered. An urgent cable from India identified him as Udham Singh, alias Ude Singh, alias Sher Singh, alias Frank Brazil, alias Frank Barzil, who had been associated with the Ghadr Party. He had been born in the village of Sunam. His convictions for illegal possession of firearms was also mentioned.

When he made a further appearance at Bow Street his real name was given, although Udham Singh insisted that the name he had given in the first place was correct. He was sent for trial at the Central Criminal Court.

✳   ✳   ✳

Like all prisoners awaiting trial for murder, Udham Singh was taken to Brixton Prison and admitted to the hospital where he was placed under constant observation and regularly visited by the senior medical officer and a psychiatrist to see if he suffered from any mental disorder which would justify a plea of insanity or preclude him from standing trial.

He was given the number 1010 and allowed to write letters. He immediately renewed his association with Shiv Singh Johal at the Gurdwara in Shepherd's Bush, although he went out of his way to pretend that they were total strangers; he was aware that his letters would be scrutinized by the authorities. With an obstinacy that his censors found irritating and pointless, he insisted on signing his letters Mahomed Singh Azad and inserting his initials US as inconspicuously as possible at the top of the page. They did not realize that his carefully chosen alias symbolized Hindu-Sikh-Muslim unity.

For security reasons he was not allowed to write in his native tongue and the man who had so impressed his friends with his mastery of the English language revealed himself as a semi-illiterate when it came to writing it. His spelling was to say the least atrocious and unconsciously humorous. But he was discreet enough not to drop the slightest hint that he knew anyone in London; he was determined that none of the people he knew would become the object of police investigation or run the risk of being suspected of taking part in a plot simply by reason of knowing him.

Without his knowledge Shiv Singh Johal and a number of Punjabis in London had launched a fund to raise money for his defence and engaged the services of Bernard Linder & Company of Wembley. When he learned of it, Udham Singh became quite angry:

> I know many of Indians living in this country are against me. But I care Blunt for only one thing I like to tell you I do not know who is doing this all lot for me about Solicitor and the Council. This is very expenses case and I dont want to have there money spent on my case when I am ready to go anywhere whatever it happen to me it is nothing to me, and why then the people are taking trouble for me. I never afraid of dying so soon I will get married with execution.* I am not sorry as I am a soldier of my country since it is 10 years when my best friend has left me behind and I am sure after my death I will see him as he is waiting for me it was 23rd and I hope they will hang me on the same date as he was so if you come to know who those people are helping me please tell them not to do so I will be glad if they spent there money on education instead of helping the murderer.

In the same letter he said he was enjoying himself as 'a Guest of Royal Faimley' and had put on five pounds in weight.

Several religious books were sent to him but the prison authorities withheld them and Udham Singh's mood changed: Brixton Prison was now an 'English Constration' camp where he was maltreated and not allowed to bathe every day according to his religion.

He went on a hunger strike that lasted forty-one days, and he had to be forcibly fed. On 20 May Shiv Singh Johal received a letter in almost copperplate writing asking him to pay a visit before the trial as he might not be allowed to so afterwards. Udham Singh's friend mistakenly believed that he was now so

---

*'To wed the bride called death', an old Punjabi phrase, was used by Bhagat Singh when his father suggested he ought to marry. It was his way of saying he was committed to a cause.

resigned to his fate that there was no longer any need to masquerade as an illiterate. The truth was he was so ill it had to be written for him; all he did was sign it.

The hunger strike, coupled with a decision to change solicitors, delayed his trial and it was not until 4 June that he stood in the dock at the Old Bailey's Number One Court. He looked a pathetic, almost tragic figure; the once smartly fitting blue pin-stripe suit hung shapelessly from his shrunken frame; he had lost five stone in weight and was almost bald. The trial was a foregone conclusion and one of the shortest on record in which a Not Guilty plea had been entered. Although he had the services of three distinguished and able Counsel — Mr St John Hutchinson, K.C., Mr R. E. Seaton, and Mr Krishna Menon — he was not really interested in saving his life. During one of his prison discussions with Krishna Menon he recounted the story of the Jallianwala Bagh and his vow to seek revenge on O'Dwyer whom he saw as the real culprit. But what was more surprising was the revelation that he had worked for Sir Michael and driven his car.

'It was clear from the beginning,' Mr Menon recalled later, 'that our client would be sentenced to death. Udham Singh was surprisingly gentle in talk. He was unhelpful to our attempts at his defence. He, however, stood by the story that was pleaded before the courts. It came as part of instructions from him and on his behalf.'

The court was crowded with many of the people who had been at Caxton Hall, and it was soon obvious that no jury could be expected to accept the story that his arm had been jogged as he was about to fire into the ceiling.

Udham Singh, who had had so many opportunities to murder O'Dwyer, had clearly waited for the moment which would provide him with the maximum publicity. But he was denied the opportunity of stating the real reason for his crime. As early as 2 April the Director of the Intelligence Bureau of India had warned the India Office that Udham Singh intended to pose as a martyr at his trial and play to the gallery by making himself out to be a hero in the cause of Indian freedom. It was imperative, therefore, to see that the trial was reported as unsensationally as possible. Steps were immediately taken to scotch his plans, and a few days later the Secretary of State for India informed the Viceroy:

Arrangements have been made with Reuter's and we will do what may be possible in conjunction with the Censorship Bureau here in regard to messages through other channels. As, however, we can give no guarantee it is presumed that careful censorship will be exercised at your end in relation to messages from correspondents of Indian papers.

The Government's attitude was perfectly understandable. The 'Miracle of Dunkirk' had just been accomplished, the newspapers were still filled with details of the incredible deliverance and everyone was acutely aware that Britain now faced its greatest challenge since it had emerged as a major power and created an Empire, the like of which the world had never known. Europe was firmly under the heel of the Jackboot and invasion was imminent.

Although morale was high, the rest of the world did not rate Britain's chances of survival too highly. It was clearly not the time to allow a doomed man to turn the dock into a political platform. As in the First War, India was providing much-needed men and materials for the forthcoming fight; to turn back the clock and remind Indians of the treatment that had been meted out to them in 1919 would be courting disaster. So it was arranged that there would be a minimum of press coverage.

The prosecuting counsel, Mr G. B. McClure, took only half an hour to open his case. Several people gave evidence of what they had seen at the meeting and various police officers repeated the damning statements the accused had made immediately after the shooting and later at Cannon Row.

The most damaging evidence came from Robert Churchill, the gun expert, who said that if Udham Singh had not been so amateurish the death roll would have been higher. The ammunition he had used was for a .44 Smith and Wesson while the gun he had was a .45 revolver. Lord Zetland had had a miraculous escape from death, 'due to an excess of propelling gases escaping round the bullet in the cartridge'.

When the accused went into the witness box his counsel faced an almost impossible task. Confronted with the eye-witness accounts, the accident theory could not hold water.

Udham Singh did his best to convince the jury that he could

have killed Sir Michael on many occasions, so why choose a crowded hall?

He admitted that he was opposed to British rule in India but his idea was simply to make a protest so that he would be arrested and given the chance of publicly stating his grievances.

Mr Hutchinson: 'Had you murder in your head?'

'Murder? I never could murder a cat — how could I murder anyone?'

In his closing speech Mr Hutchinson asked the jury to consider a verdict of manslaughter. If Udham Singh had wanted to kill O'Dwyer he had had opportunity after opportunity to do it in the blackout.

The jury were out for only an hour and forty minutes before returning with a verdict of Guilty.

When Mr Justice Atkinson asked him if he had anything to say before sentence was passed, Udham Singh held a whispered conversation with one of the warders, then produced a sheaf of papers, put on his spectacles and began to read.

The Judge warned him to confine his remarks as to why he should not be sentenced to death.

'I don't care about the sentence of death,' he shouted from the dock. 'It is not worrying me. I am dying for a purpose.'

Despite the Judge's warning he continued to read aloud in a highly excited voice for some twenty minutes or more. 'I did it,' he shouted, 'because I had a grudge against him. He deserved it. He was the real culprit, he wanted to crush the spirit of my people, so I have crushed him. For full 21 years I have been trying to wreak vengeance. I am happy I have done the job. I am not scared of death — I am dying for my country. I have seen my people starving in India under the British rule. I have protested against this. It was my duty. What greater honour could be bestowed on me than death for the sake of my motherland?'

When Mr Justice Atkinson sentenced him to death and the 'black cap' was solemnly placed on top of his wig, Udham Singh waved one hand in the air and thumped the front of the dock with the other. As warders tried to restrain him he continued to shout defiance and just before he was led to the cells below he turned and spat into the court.

Before the court rose, Mr McClure made an application on behalf of the Director of Public Prosecutions that the statement of Udham Singh should be suppressed under Section 6 of the Emergency Powers (Defence) Act of 1939. Mr Justice Atkinson approved and instructed the Court reporters not to report it.*

An hour later Udham Singh was in the condemned cell at Pentonville Prison playing cribbage with two warders. He was unaware that his defiant speech from the dock had been dismissed as rambling, incoherent and unintelligible.

An Appeal was lodged on his behalf, and shortly afterwards Udham Singh was escorted by four warders into a small gallery above a court in the Royal Courts of Justice where three Appeal Judges heard it. Although Mr St John Hutchinson made a powerful plea on his behalf, the judges found no reason to interfere with the verdict.

Krishna Menon visited him a number of times in prison and urged him to sign a petition to the King begging for mercy, but he was unable to get any response from the condemned man. Several others tried, and it was only during Mr Menon's last visit that Singh signed, but by then it was too late.

✳   ✳   ✳

Udham Singh wrote just one letter from the death cell. He asked the Secretary of the Gurdawara to send him the Sikh Prayer Book.

On 31 July the skies above the English Channel and the Home Counties were latticed with dog-fight vapour trails as Hitler intensified the aerial assault which was to be the fore-runner to Operation Sea Lion — the invasion of England.

That same morning the concealed sliding door in the con-demned cell at Pentonville was pushed back and Udham Singh was hurried into the execution shed. It was all done briskly and efficiently without any delay. Within seconds of passing into the execution shed, his arms were pinioned by the assistant hangman and a hood placed over his head. Two prison officers stood on two planks which bridged the trap door, steadying the condemned man as he stood on a small white square in the centre of the trap door. The lever was jerked and Udham Singh plunged to his death.

Under cover of darkness Udham Singh was buried in an unmarked grave below the prison walls. A request from the

*The extract quoted was published in India many years later.

Sikh Temple for the return of his ashes in order that they could be taken to India for cremation according to the religious rites of the Sikhs was curtly refused.

He seemed to have died in vain, for, apart from a small handful of people, the majority believed the shooting of Sir Michael O'Dwyer had been the senseless act of a demented man.

25.   A Martyr's Return

*'You will have a shrine erected there and every year
there will be processions of Indians visiting the tombs
of the martyrs.' — Colonel Josiah Wedgwood.*

On 13 April, 1961, vast crowds of people began flooding
into Amritsar much as they had done for the Baisakhi festivities in 1919. Again their destination was the Jallianwala
Bagh, the scene of the massacre.

The holy city itself had changed little, but the Jallianwala
Bagh had certainly changed. The dustbowl where people
used to scoop up handfuls of sun-baked earth as souvenirs
was now a beautiful garden. Forty-two years after the
massacre it was to be officially opened as a national
memorial. The Bagh had been purchased from its numerous
owners for 50,000 rupees which had been raised by public
subscription. Pandit Nehru, the Prime Minister, had been
appointed Chairman of the Trust. In 1957 work was begun
to convert it into a place of beauty and tranquillity. For
several years the week of 6-13 April had been proclaimed a
week of mourning, and on every anniversary of the shooting
the Last Post was sounded and a wreath laid.

Many of the people who packed into the Bagh for the
ceremony had survived the massacre, but few now recognized the place. The whole level had been raised several feet
and neat lawns, clipped hedges, flowering shrubs, cypress
trees and flowers now covered the area where hundreds had
bled to death. The raised platform where Dyer had stood
and ordered his men to open fire was a paved patio. The well
in which so many had perished remained untouched, as did
the small samadhi where a handful of people had crouched
to avoid the bullets. The peepul tree remained to mark the

spot where the platform had stood, and parts of the old wall had been retained with white steel rings marking the bullet holes. In the centre, dominating the garden, was a towering red stone pylon symbolizing the Flame of Liberty. It was flanked by four huge lanterns and another fourteen lanterns illuminated a children's swimming pool. The simple inscription in Punjabi, Urdu and English said: 'In memory of martyrs — 13 April 1919.'

Among the guests of honour were Rattan Chand who had spent so many years in the penal settlement in the Andamans — he was now eighty-five years old, white-bearded and frail — and Rattan Devi and Attaur Kaur who had both lost their husbands and spent the night keeping vigil over their corpses.

In the martyrs' gallery adjoining the Bagh were portraits of Satyapal and Kitchlew, Rattan Devi, Attaur Kaur and many others whose names had become indelibly associated with the shooting. At the far end was a magnificent impressionist mural depicting the massacre with falling bodies in the posture of crucified men. In the section containing the portraits of many who had died in the cause of Indian freedom the one that attracted most attention was that of Udham Singh. He was shown bearded and moustached and wearing a turban. A plaque below described him as the man who had avenged the slaughter.

The man whose deed had been condemned at the time by all leading Indians was now a martyr. His portrait also hung in the museum of the Golden Temple where he was hailed as 'The great revolutionary Shahid Udham Singh who shot O'Dwyer the butcher of the Jallianwala Bagh tragedy in England and embraced martyrdom'. Again he was depicted as a traditional Sikh: bearded, turbaned and moustached.

After the official opening the Jallianwala Bagh became a place of pilgrimage for Indians throughout the world.

From time to time requests were made to the British Government for the return of Udham Singh's remains but they were all politely refused.

*   *   *

Thirty-four years were to pass after the shooting before they were returned to his homeland aboard an Air India jet. A crowd of people, of a size that only India can produce, stood in the drizzling rain at Delhi airport to welcome the arrival of the aircraft. As the remains were carried down the landing steps they were formally received by Mr Sharkar Dayal Sharma, President of the ruling Congress Party, Mr Swaran Singh, Foreign Minister, and Mr Zail Singh, Chief Minister to the Punjab.

The wooden casket was solemnly carried into the V.I.P. lounge, draped with the National Flag and decked with flowers, garlands and wreaths. Then it was transported in a decorated bus to Kapurthala House where the Prime Minister, Mrs Indira Gandhi, paid homage: 'We are glad that after a gap of 34 years the remains of Udham Singh who sacrificed his life for the independence of the country have reached Indian soil.'

The man who had been forced to slip out of his country under an assumed name and then condemned by every leading Indian politician was now being accorded a hero's welcome.

Indian newspapers carried large memorial advertisements calling on the people to 'pay homage to the great hero on his last journey'. The story of the massacre was recounted time and time again. Extracts from his letters were published in a special souvenir colour supplement issued by the Punjab Government. There were also passages from the speech he had delivered from the dock at the Old Bailey and which the British Government had suppressed.

After the official ceremony in the capital the remains were taken on an extensive and unprecedented tour of the country. Millions lined the route as the casket was transported from Delhi to the Punjab. Public meetings were held at Chandigarh, Ludhiana, Jullundur and other major cities. There were even night halts to enable people in lesser known places to pay their respects. When the remains reached Amritsar they were taken to the Jallianwala Bagh for a period of lying in state.

The casket was borne along the narrow alley through which General Dyer had marched his small force of men and past a sign bearing the legend:

This ground is hallowed by the mingled blood of about

two thousand innocent Hindus, Sikhs and Mussalmans who were shot by British bullets on 13th April 1919.

Men and women wept unashamedly for Udham Singh who had avenged the dead and wounded with his own blood.

Hour after hour a long queue filed past the casket before it was taken to Sunam for cremation. The ashes were then taken to Anandpur and scattered on the sacred waters of the Ganges and Sutlej. As the current bore them away to be reborn the ritual assumed an almost symbolic significance to the enormous crowds assembled on the banks. It was as if the bitter memories of what had happened in the Jallianwala Bagh nearly fifty years before had finally been washed away.

SOURCES

BOOKS

Allen, Charles, (ed.). *Plain Tales from the Raj*. André Deutsch and BBC, 1975

Anon. *The London Cyclist Battalion*. Forster Groom, London, 1932

'Report of the Commissioners appointed by the Punjab Sub-Committee of the Indian National Congress'.
Deep Publications, New Delhi.

Barrow, Gen. Sir George. *The Life of General Sir Charles Carmichael Monro*. Hutchinson, 1931

Bresler, Fenton. *Lord Goddard*. Harrap, 1977

Callwell, Major-General Sir C. E. *Field Marshal Sir Henry Wilson: his Life and Diaries*. Cassell, 1927

Colvin, Ian. *Life of General Dyer*. William Blackwood, 1929

Datta, V. N. *Jallianwala Bagh*. V. K. Arora, Kurukshetra University Books, Ludhiana, 1969

Amritsar Past and Present. Municipal Committee, Amritsar, 1967

New Light on the Punjab Disturbances 1919. Indian Institute of Advanced Study, Simla

Durga, Das. *India from Curzon to Nehru and After*. Collins, 1969

Edwardes, Michael. *Nehru, A Pictorial Biography*. Thames and Hudson, 1962

— *Bound to Exile*, Sidgwick & Jackson, 1969

Fodor. *Guide to India*. Hodder & Stoughton, 1978

Furneaux, Rupert. *Massacre at Amritsar*. Allen & Unwin, 1963

Gandhi. *An Autobiography*. Jonathan Cape, 1972

Grewal, J. S. and Puri, H. K. *Letters of Udham Singh*. Guru Nanak University, Amritsar

Horniman, B. G. *Amritsar and Our Duty to India*.T. Fisher Unwin, 1920

Malaviya, K. D. *Open Rebellion in the Punjab*. Abhudaya Press Allahabad; 1919

Mohan, Pearay. *An Imaginary Revolution*. Khosla Bros., Lahore, 1920

Montagu, Edwin. *An Indian Diary*. William Heinemann, 1930

Moraes, Frank. *Witness to an Era*. Weidenfeld & Nicolson, 1973

Morris, John. *Eating the Indian Air*. Hamish Hamilton, 1968

Nehru. *An Autobiography*. John Lane The Bodley Head, 1965

O'Dwyer, Michael. *India as I Knew it 1885-1925*. Constable, 1925

Ram, Raja. *The Jallianwala Bagh Massacre — A Premeditated Plan*. Punjab University, Chandigarh

Setalvad, Sir Chimanlal. *Recollections and Reflections*. Padma Publications, Bombay, 1946

Swinson, Arthur. *Six Minutes to Sunset*. Peter Davies, 1964

Wilkinson, Theon. *Two Monsoons*. Gerald Duckworth, 1976

Woodcock, George. *Gandhi*.Collins, 1972

Woodruff, Philip. *The Men Who Ruled India*. Jonathan Cape, 1953

NEWSPAPERS

Associated Press, Simla	2 October 1915
Bombay Chronicle	15 July 1920
Civil & Military Gazette	April 1919
Daily Express	16 December 1919
	20, 21 July 1920
	3 March 1924
	25, 29 July 1927
	14 March 1940
Daily Herald	31 July 1920
	3 April 1920
Daily Mail	4 May 1920
	March/April 1924
	14 March, 2 April, 6 June 1940

Daily News	7 September 1920
Daily Telegraph	9 June 1920
	March/April 1924
	25, 29 July 1927
Morning Echo, Delhi	24 August 1978
Morning Post	July/August 1920
	7 November 1921
	25, 29 July 1927
Pioneer Mail	2 April 1920
Reuter's	18 May 1920
Sunday Express	20 June 1920
The Spokesman Weekly Special Supplement on the 400th Anniversary of the City of Amritsar	
The Times	April 1919
	9 June 1920
	19, 20, 21 July 1920
	5 August 1920
	25, 29 July 1927
	14 March 1940
The Times of India Mail Ed.	17 May 1919
	3 May 1920
The Times Law Reports	March/April 1924
The Times Literary Supplement	19 March 1964
The Tribune	14 April 1961

ARTICLES

Datta, V. N. 'New Light on Jallianwala Bagh'. *The Tribune*, Chandigarh: 22.9.68

Gill, M. S. 'Udham Singh'. *The Illustrated Weekly of India*, 30.1.72

O'Dwyer, Michael. 'Digging our Grave in India'. *Daily Mail*, 4.1.30

'The Peril to the Empire'. *Globe*, 8.1.21

'A Secret of Indian Riots'. *Evening News*, 9.5.29

Unattributable: 'The Man who knows India — special interview with Sir Michael O'Dwyer', 10.2.29

PAMPHLETS

'The Amritsar Incident', Doctor Tom Bowden. *British Army Review*

'*The Golden Temple Amritsar*', published by Bhagat Puran Singh Pingalwara for free distribution

'*Jallianwala Bagh*', Ardh Shatabdi (Government of India publication)

'*Udham Singh*', B. S. Maighowalia

OFFICIAL SOURCES

Amritsar April 1919 — Frank McCullum (Gurkha Museum)

Amritsar Conspiracy Case, Martial Law Commission No. 2

Chelmsford Papers (these include most of the letters and telegrams between Chelmsford and Edwin Montagu. The author read the microfilm copy presented to the Nehru Memorial Library by the Indian Office Library and Records)

Civil & Military Gazette, Text of Mr Justice Broadway's Judgement — 10 July 1919

Command Papers 534, 705, 771 (Dyer's Statement to Army Council)

Debate on the Indemnity Bill, Imperial Legislative Council

Imperial War Museum — Diaries and Memories of the Great War by Ulric Nisbet attached to 3/23rd Sikhs.

— The Truth About Amritsar — by an eye-witness, Lt.-Colonel M. H. Morgan

India Office Library and Records — Privy Council Appeals. P.C.24.1921. Kitchlew and Others — v. — King Emperor L/L Box 244 — 1578A. L/L Box 151 of 1919.

— Report of the Reviewing Judges submitted 24.12.1919 to Secretary of Indian Government Home Department.

— L/PO/361, L/PO 1451, L/PO 362, L/PO 368 L/PO 374, L/PO 343

— Telegrams No. 1827 and 1846 18 April 1940: Secretary of State for India to Viceroy

— Z/L/P&J/712. Telegrams 13, 14 March 1940

National Archives of India, New Delhi — File No. 77.1940 Goverment of India Home Department. (Pol. Secret) relating to desirability of securing the trial of Udham Singh be reported as unsensationally as possible

Government of India Home Department Political A (October 19.421-24)

    Parliamentary Debates Commons 8 July 1920

    Parliamentary Debates Lords 20 July 1920

Proceedings of the Legislative Council of the Punjab 1919. Vol. X.

Public Record Office, Kew

    Cab. 26. 92-93 — Disorders Inquiry Committee

    Cab. 24.93

    Cab. 23/10 War Cabinet Meeting 556

    Cab. 23/21 (19.26.34)

    Cab. 23/22 (Cabinet 39)

    Cab. 24/105 (CP 1240)

    Cab. 24/106 (CP 1306)

    Cab. 27/91-93

    Cab. 23/48 (Cabinet 38)

    Cab. 24/½ 57 (CP 351 and CP 374)

Punjab Government — Home Military Part B January 1920. No. 256.

    Resolution by the Government of India, 14 April 1919

Royal Proclamation. Command 610.

INDEX